Speaking to Teenagers

HOW TO THINK ABOUT, CREATE, & DELIVER EFFECTIVE MESSAGES

Doug FIELDS + Duffy ROBBINS

ZONDERVAN®

ZONDERVAN.com/
AUTHORTRACKER
follow your favorite authors

youth
specialties

 **youth specialties**

Speaking to Teenagers: How to Think About, Create, and Deliver Effective Messages
Copyright 2007 by Doug Fields and Duffy Robbins

Youth Specialties products, 300 S. Pierce St., El Cajon, CA 92020 are published by Zondervan, 5300 Patterson Ave. SE, Grand Rapids, MI 49530.

ISBN-10: 0-310-27376-5
ISBN-13: 978-0-310-27376-9

Web site addresses listed in this book were current at the time of publication. Please contact Youth Specialties via e-mail (YS@YouthSpecialties.com) to report URLs that are no longer operational and replacement URLs if available.

Interior design by Mark Novelli, IMAGO MEDIA

Printed in the United States of America

07 08 09 10 11 12 13 14 15 16 17 • 20 19 18 17 16 15 14 13 12 11 10 9 8 7 6 5 4 3 2

"This book is so packed with practical ideas, riveting illustrations, hard-fought wisdom, and jokes about thinning hair that you'd be crazy to pass it up. Duffy and Doug are the Dream Team of youth ministry communicators, but they have the hearts of two guys who know what it's like to blow it. It's their mix of vigorous thinking about communicating and their rich history of actually doing it well that make this book unique. There's a genuine treasure here—read it, practice it, and you'll make a much bigger impact in your ministry."

—Rick Lawrence, executive editor, GROUP Magazine

"A rapidly changing youth culture requires us to be increasingly deliberate in the preparation and delivery of our messages to the teenage audience. Whether I'm in the audience or sitting across the table, I have learned to listen whenever my friends Doug and Duffy open their mouths. As always, their words in Speaking to Teenagers need to be heard. Listen hard. The principles they communicate in this book will enable you to gain respect and be heard when you speak to kids, so they'll hear the life-changing message you've been called to communicate."

—Walt Mueller, president, Center for Parent/Youth Understanding; author,
Youth Culture 101* and *Engaging the Soul of Youth Culture

"Not a week goes by that I'm not asked by an aspiring young communicator how to become a better speaker to students. Now I can just hand them this incredible book—by two men who know what they're talking about. and have influenced so many—and tell them to leave me alone!"

—Stuart Hall, Dash Inc; coauthor, *Seven Checkpoints for Students* and *Max Q: Developing Students of Influence*

"I presented biblical messages to students for 20 years and taught others to do the same. How I wish we'd all had the wisdom and direction in this book. The vault of experience and insight from decades of communication is opened here. The treasure is there for the taking."

—Dan Webster, founder, Authentic Leadership, Inc.

"Doug and Duffy, two legends of youth ministry, have combined to write what just may be my favorite youth ministry book ever! If you teach once a week, once a year, or simply hope to teach once some day, this book is a must read."

—Kurt Johnston, junior high pastor, Saddleback Church; founder,
www.simplyjuniorhigh.com

"Youth ministry and classic don't often go together, but in the world of youth work, every few years a book stands out as mandatory reading and should be termed a classic. Doug Fields and Duffy Robbins have written just such a book with the very practical, real, and accessible Speaking to Teenagers…"

—Chap Clark, Ph.D., senior editor, *Youthworker Journal*; professor of youth, family, and culture, Fuller Seminary

"Doug Fields and Duffy Robbins are two men who I greatly respect and admire, and they have put together an incredibly practical work that will help anyone who ministers to teenagers. Whether you're a veteran speaker or a new youth worker putting together your first 'talk,' this book is an absolute must read!"

—**Greg Stier, President Dare 2 Share Ministries**

"Simply put, this book is fantastic. The junior highers (and others) who I get a chance to speak to will unquestionably benefit from what I've learned and been reminded of in these pages!"

—**Scott Rubin, junior high pastor, Willow Creek Community Church**

"Finally—a book that is both deep enough to transform the way we talk with students and practical enough to use every week."

—**Kara E. Powell, executive director, Center for Youth and Family Ministry, Fuller Theological Seminary**

"Two veteran communicators have combined to give youth speakers a whole bunch of great guidance for thinking through, preparing, and delivering messages that can effectively speak truth into the lives of teenagers. This one belongs in your library!"

—**Dr. R. Allen Jackson, professor of youth education, New Orleans Baptist Theological Seminary**

"Whenever Doug or Duffy is speaking, I try to listen. They understand the unique dynamics of teaching teenagers like no one else. They are authentic, honest, and a gift to youth workers everywhere. Speaking to Teenagers is more than a book; it's a marvelous contribution to youth ministry that will bless anyone who has ever tried to teach teenagers."

—**Jeanne Stevens, director of training, Youth Specialties**

"This is the best book on Speaking to Teenagers in the world by my two favorite youth speakers. There's no doubt in my mind that after you read and apply the principles in this book, you will be a more effective communicator to students. Don't miss this rare opportunity to learn from the best of the best."

—**Jim Burns, president, HomeWord; author, *Confident Parenting* and *Creating an Intimate Marriage***

"This book, written by two of this generation's most effective communicators, is a 911 call for those of us (full time, part time, or lay leader) serious about the urgent task to use the 30 minutes we have to raise the dead. No more flavors of the month, latest fads, or quick fixes. This is a must-read for those of us who desire crystal-clear communication."

—**Dr. Jay Strack, founder and president, Studentleadership.net**

"I've been waiting for Speaking to Teenagers for some time for a number of reasons. As a professor who teaches a course on communication, I've needed a text that's compelling, academic, and practical. As a 'professional' speaker, I need my skills to be honed and sharpened. As a consultant, I need a first-class resource for speakers of all kinds. Doug and Duffy have put together a humorous, engaging, and profound book guaranteed to be a best-seller in youth ministry venues. They know teenagers and how to speak to them. Doug Fields and Duffy Robbins are excellent communicators, two of the best I have ever known. They have earned the right to write Speaking to Teenagers, you are going to love this book!"

—Dr. David Olshine, director of youth ministries, Columbia International University; cofounder, Youth Ministry Coaches

"Buy this book, read this book, do what it says. It will improve your 'reach' to youth! We need more people who can connect with teenagers with the love and intensity that Doug and Duffy have. I am excited for aspiring speakers to read Speaking to Teenagers. The book is both a great self-help manual and a humorous autobiography of two outstanding speakers who're great at connecting with adolescents. Each of their personalities and styles comes across as though the reader is sitting down, listening to their collaborative discussion. Their guidelines are solid, and their differences of interpretation will speak to a wide range of aspiring, effective communicators. Whether you're speaking to a handful of teenagers or an arena full of them, this book will lead to self-evaluation and improvement."

—Rev. Terry B. Carty, executive director, United Methodist YouthWorker Movement, Nashville, Tennessee

"A central part of every youth ministry is based on effective communication, yet this continues to be one of our most underdeveloped skills! We (okay, I) think we're better communicators than we are. I learned from this book and was reminded of several essential communication principles I rarely put into practice. A big thanks to Doug and Duffy for a nice volume that makes a difference immediately."

—Mark Matlock, author, *What Does God Want from Me*

"Speaking to Teenagers is the most practical, comprehensive, and entertaining resource ever written and available for youth workers, teachers, and other caring adults who desire to speak in a way that invites and compels students to listen. Doug and Duffy have given us a great gift. I will recommend it to every novice and veteran youth worker I know."

—Rich Van Pelt, author, speaker, National Director of Ministry Relationships, Compassion International

"I wonder how many of us over the years have called Doug or Duffy and asked for the chance to 'pick their brains.' Speaking to Teenagers gives all of us that chance at the same time. Profoundly practical, filled with the kind of laugh-out-loud hilarity that years of friendship bring, this book takes the mystery out of preparing talks that hit their mark. I'll take advice from these two any day."

—Mark DeVries, Youth Ministry Architects, www.ymarchitects.com

"God knew the clearest way he could reveal himself to mankind was in the incarnation. God knew we needed to see him with flesh on. The same principle applies today. Most of us grasp Truth best when we see it in the flesh. Even for media-immersed youth, an effective speaker far transcends ones and zeros and virtual identities. That godly, Spirit-empowered speaker doesn't encompass all of God's story in a young life, but he or she is certainly part of that story. Doug and Duffy have written the definitive book on this subject, and it now will show up in every classroom where I teach the next generation of youth leaders."

—Richard Ross, Ph.D., professor of student ministry, Southwestern Seminary

"This book delivers! Doug and Duffy are masters of the craft of handling the serious and practical challenges of communication to teenagers. Homiletics courses everywhere should require this book!"

—Dave Rahn, PhD, vice president & chief ministry officer, YFC/USA Director, Huntington University's MA in Youth Ministry Leadership

"Doug and Duffy have done years of hard work developing their teaching gifts, and now they've provided us with a resource that shares their years of experience and key points of learning. This resource is a true gift to those of us who've been called to speak to this generation. I'm confident this book will help you become a more effective communicator. The stakes are too high for you to not steward the teaching gifts that God has given you."

—Bo Boshers, executive director, student ministries, Willow Creek Association

"Robbins and Fields are two of the most respected youth workers in America. Their combined years of experience speaking to youth, together with excellent research and insightful tips, make this book a valuable resource for those who want their messages to be more effective. Speaking to Teenagers will be required reading for my youth ministry students."

—Dan Lambert, professor of youth ministries, John Brown University

"Doug and Duffy have given us solid help for something we all do as youth workers. I love the combination of 'big picture' perspectives coupled with practical help. Of course their humility and humor make the book a constant delight. This is a must-read for anyone who speaks to teenagers on a regular basis."

—Len Kageler, Ph.D., chair, youth ministry department, Nyack (NY) College

Written in Memory of Mike Yaconelli

Our friend, mentor, and a great communicator who taught us both so much.

Dedicated to Tic Long

In your 30-plus years of creative, thoughtful, and passionate service at Youth Specialties, you've proven yourself a friend to anybody who cares about youth ministry. And for those of us who've known your friendship first-hand, the privilege has been greater still. We love you and respect you. We wouldn't share the type of ministry joys that we've experienced if it weren't for you. You are a gift!

Thanks

From Doug: I wouldn't have anything to write on speaking if it weren't for the three men who've taught me and modeled for me everything I know about speaking since my teenage years to present. I'm blessed to have had Jim Burns, Tim Timmons, and Rick Warren as my mentors and teachers— I'm almost embarrassed to admit that you have been so influential in my life ("Well, no wonder you know what you're talking about—look who you learned from!"). I consider myself most blessed to have been coworkers with you.

There are always close friends around me who don't necessarily write, edit, or contribute to book projects in specific ways, but they're always contributing to my life, and nothing I write is void of their daily influence or inspiration; Matt McGill, Jana Sarti, Josh Griffin, and Andy Brazelton—I'm so blessed to have your friendship.

I'm also very grateful to some friends who read the manuscript and aided and improved it with ideas and questions—thank you Jeff Maguire, Neely McQueen, Jason Petty, and Allison McCroskey.

Thank you Cathy, Torie, Cody, and Cassie Fields for being so wonderful and fun and encouraging—you have all spoken into my life and given me something to say. Thank you for unselfishly sacrificing your husband/dad and for allowing our lives to be an illustration to others.

Finally, I'm so thankful for the all the teenagers at South Coast Community and Saddleback Church who've allowed me the privilege to speak to you about Jesus...what an honor it has been!

From Duffy: One of the great things about speaking on the road is that I get to come home to some dear friends, colleagues, and students at Eastern University! One of those people is our chaplain, and a true pastor, Joe Modica, and our Provost, Chris Hall. You two guys continue to walk with me as brothers, and you never cease to inspire me with your scholarship, your friendship, and your authentic faith. One minute you make me think really deeply, and the next you make me laugh really hard. What a gift! And, of course, there are my trusty coworkers in the Youth Ministry major: Darrell Pearson, Calenthia Dowdy, and Eduardo Ramirez. I love watching you guys use your gifts, and I'm honored to serve alongside you. Thanks for letting me be on your team!

Thanks to Dan Hallock, Larry Renoe, and Casey Prince for reading through this manuscript and giving us your thoughtful feedback.

Thank you, Maggie Robbins, for your continued pursuit of Jesus and your faithful love for your husband. How many miles have we traveled together? (And the adventure continues!) Even when you're not traveling with me, I know you're with me.

And thanks to my girls: Erin and Katie, for loving your dad so well. What a ride we've had! And, now, there's Peter (son-in-law) and Henry and Sadie and....! I didn't think this family could get any better, and then you guys come along! I'm a grateful man.

Henry and Sadie, my personal prayer for this book is that it might in some way wind up in the hands of a youth pastor who will one day be standing up, speaking to you guys in your youth group, and that there will be something in these pages that will help him or her draw you closer to the Savior. What a cool thing that would be!

And finally, I have to thank all the speakers, pastors, and youth pastors from whom I have stolen illustrations over the years. There are way too many of you to mention. That's why I never say your name when I use your stuff. But, thanks! Without you, I truly never would be able to speak to teenagers!

Table of Contents

Cheering You On

Just by holding this book in your hands, you've gained our immediate respect. Regardless of whether you teach weekly, biweekly, monthly, or fill in whenever someone is sick—we understand and respect anyone who tries to teach teenagers God's ways. The task is mighty, the responsibility is high, and the weight that you feel as a communicator is heavy.

Few people are born with the passion, desire, and skills to teach teenagers. Some are, but most of us stumble into this with no training, a little bit of encouragement, and below-average modeling.

Most youth workers learn to speak as they go, and many of them wind up copying the people they've listened to (which can be good or bad). So whether you're a rookie speaker or a professional, we applaud you for wanting to speak to teenagers. And regardless of your youth-working status—volunteer or full-time paid—we want to help you become a more effective speaker.

To do this, we've divided the book into three sections:

1. Thinking about your messages

2. Creating your messages

3. Delivering your messages

This will be a fun journey as you walk through these pages, learn, experiment, evaluate, and set your sights on becoming a more effective communicator. It's a privilege and an honor for us to play the role of guide as you journey and learn.

While both of us speak to teenagers almost weekly, I'm [Duffy] usually speaking to different groups of teenagers at events around the country, and Doug is in the local church teaching the same teenagers each week.

I'd describe Doug as a good-looking, somewhat-fit guy with thinning hair. (Sorry about *somewhat*, Doug.) His look is "Youth Ministry Meets Orange County." Teenagers look at Doug and think, *Hey, this is gonna be good!*

I, on the other hand, look more like somebody's weird Uncle Frank. No facial hair, only a few remaining square inches of scalp hair. *Fit* is not the first word that comes to mind when teenagers see me. My look is more like "Youth Ministry meets McDonalds." When I get in front of teenagers, they usually think, *Is that what I'm going to look like when I grow up?*

We're sharing these author descriptions with you (our photos are on the back cover of this book) because we want to make sure you understand something about this book and the people who wrote it. This book is *not* about two guys who believe they're hotshots who've mastered public speaking. We're just two youth workers who've learned a lot about speaking in the trenches of real-life youth ministry for 25-plus years (Doug—that's why he's a little more fit) and 30-plus years (Duffy—a.k.a., weird Uncle Frank).

We know what it's like to be in the heat of battle, to stand there on the firing line unsure if you're the shooter or the target. We've been there when the talk was a direct hit; we've been there when it bombed (and prayed the bomb would take us away from speaking engagements forever). We know what it's like to be in awe of God's power and the fact that God uses us in teenagers' lives, and we know what it's like to crawl away feeling something between shell shock and post-traumatic stress. Just because we've written this book doesn't mean we have all the answers. But we're hopeful that some of the lessons we've learned will help you become a better communicator.

One quick note about two authors writing one book together: Since we really wrote this book *together*, it's virtually impossible to be clear about where Duffy's words end and Doug's words start. This was not a "you-write-half-of-the-chapters-and-I'll-write-the-other-half" approach. We birthed this baby together! It was quite the delivery—lots of laughs, some deep discussions, a few disagreements, a lot of prayer for the general project, and a lot of prayer specifically for you—the reader/youth worker.

Because this was a writing partnership, sometimes, if you read very carefully, you'll notice that certain sentences seem to be professorial, deep, and thought provoking, while others seem to be more, well...purpose-driven. But for the sake of smooth reading, we've chosen to write as though you're hearing one voice—and not load the book down with obnoxious parentheses or brackets that identify the author for each sentence (like we did a few paragraphs ago). So when you read the word I, you won't know if it's Doug or Duffy writing, unless we think it's a big deal for you to know—and then we'll tell you. But most of the time, we won't.

This one-voice style of writing also helps us protect our reputations because if a certain portion of the book comes under heavy fire as being particularly ridiculous or quoting an invalid source, we can both claim, "Oh, that was written by the *other* guy." Although, most readers familiar with the youth ministry world will certainly know that any theological mistakes came from

Duffy. (See? We don't need to identify who wrote that sentence, we assume you can figure it out.)

Thanks for picking up this book, thanks for committing to grow and learn, and thanks for letting us play a tiny part in supporting your big and difficult role as a youth worker. We value you! We love what you do! We believe you're serving God in life-altering ways. And we're thrilled that God might use us in some small way to make you more effective.

Expectantly,

Doug & Duffy

PS: We understand that you probably already have your office shelves filled with books reminding you as a conscientious youth worker of what you should be doing, what you could be doing or what Jesus would be doing. We're not writing this book to offer you yet another reason why you don't measure up as a youth worker. Bottom Line: We're on this journey together. We hope you'll see this book not so much as ought-to, and must-do, and more along the lines of think-through and how-to. Speaking to teenagers is an adventure that we share together.

Years ago we wrote a book called, Memory Makers and you could read that book while you were standing in the aisle at the bookstore (we think that explains the poor sales). But, this one is different. It's going to require of you a little more work – a little more thought and careful digestion. You'll have to come back to the bookstore several times to read this book the way we hope it might be read because we want you to take some time with this stuff. In fact, here's our suggestion to you: take a chapter of this book, a cup of Starbucks and and give yourself some unhurried time to dream with us about how better communication could impact your ministry. And then, even if it seems difficult, even if it moves you a little out of your comfort zone, even if it requires you to stretch some new ministry muscles, don't back away from that dream. "He who has called you is faithful and He will do it" (1 Thessalonians 5:24).

And, meanwhile, as you sip that latte and turn those pages, remember that we're cheering you on!

Section 1

How to Think about Effective Messages

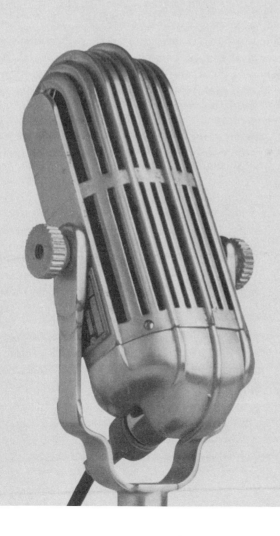

CHAPTER ONE

"The Stakes Have Never Been Higher"

She looked to be in her early thirties. (I'm guessing low 30s, in case she ever reads this.) She was one of 300 youth workers gathered for a weekend of training and encouragement at beautiful Camp Berea on Newfound Lake, New Hampshire. She approached me shyly, reservedly, almost the same way I'd approach someone like Billy Graham, Pope Benedict, Mother Teresa, or Jerry Garcia. And then, grabbing both of my hands, she looked into my face with this wonderful smile and said,

> I heard you speak back in the early nineties, and I remember you spoke about "going the distance." It was an amazing week, and it was the week I accepted Jesus into my heart. Now I have my own youth group, and I'm here learning how to help them grow in Christ. And I just want you to know, it all began with you that week back in Fort Collins, Colorado.

It was a pretty neat moment, at least for me—one of those perks that keeps a lot of us in youth ministry over the long haul. Seeing the fruit grow and mature from something we had the privilege of planting or watering several years ago is an amazing privilege, indeed a gift from God.

But in the midst of that moment of vivid encouragement, two other distinct thoughts immediately came to mind: *First, I knew good and well it didn't all begin with me.* I was just one of many characters in the drama that was this woman's life—one person who walked onto the stage, spoke from his heart, and made his exit. I knew the scene in Fort Collins was only part of a much larger drama being played out under the direction of a sovereign God who'd been at work in that teenage girl's life through countless other relationships, circumstances, and longings, and (probably) lots of other Bible studies, messages, retreats, cabin times, and conversations.

As soon as she said it, I knew it didn't begin with me. And even more than that, I took satisfaction in the fact that, by God's grace, neither did it end with me.

But then came the second thought, just as clear and real as the first: *I was so humbled and grateful to God that the story included me.* I was stunned and amazed that God would use my small loaf of a few messages to encourage someone to eat the Bread of Life.

If you're like me, that's all you ever hoped for when you got into ministry: You knew you weren't going to play the starring role, you just wanted a piece of the action, and you hoped to "do something" for this God who has done everything for you. Thirty years of youth ministry have not dulled that sense of passion and gratitude in my life. If anything, the years have intensified it. Often, when I have conversations like the one above, the person will then step back and say, "Does that make you feel old?" And I say, "No, it makes me feel grateful."

An Improbable Opportunity

This book is written for people who understand that type of gratitude. It's written for those of us who stand up on a regular basis and speak to a room full of teenagers (or maybe it's half full...or one-fourth full...okay, it's really two or three students whose parents made them attend) and share this amazing story of grace and gratitude, bad news and good news, sacrificial giving and joyful giving back.

Each week when we attempt to speak, we don't know exactly how it's going to work. We're not precisely certain how we're going to pull it off. We're not totally confident that we can make the play. But we're so grateful and so stunned that God has simply put us in the game. And we want to give it all we have.

This book is about helping grateful people bear witness to a great God, and doing that through something as mundane and miraculous as the spoken words of broken people. Whether those words appear in Sunday school, a summer camp, a Young Life club, a Friday night outreach, a pregame devotional, a midweek youth group meeting—or whether you're in ministry full time, part time, overtime, as a volunteer or maybe just a draftee who wasn't there the night they voted on who'd "work with the kids"—our intent is to help you carefully craft and speak words more effectively and with greater impact. We never know when that random teaching opportunity might end up being for one teenager the moment when it all begins. And even though we understand it doesn't all begin with us, we want to be faithful stewards of every opportunity God allows us to experience.

Opportunities Missed

In his book, *Telling the Truth: The Gospel as Tragedy, Comedy, and Fairy Tale,* Frederick Buechner describes a scene played out in thousands of churches every Sunday; a scene so commonplace we almost miss its real-life, high-stakes drama.

> So the sermon hymn comes to a close with a somewhat unsteady amen, and the organist gestures the choir to sit down. Fresh from breakfast with his wife and children and a quick run-through of the Sunday papers, the preacher climbs the steps to the pulpit with his sermon in his hand. He hikes his black robe up at the knee so he will not trip over it on the way up. His mouth is a little dry. He has cut himself shaving. He feels as if he has swallowed an anchor. If it weren't for the honor of the thing, he would just as soon be somewhere else.
>
> In the front pews the old ladies turn up their hearing aids, and a young lady slips her six year old a Lifesaver and a Magic Marker. A college sophomore home for vacation, who is there because he was dragged there, slumps forward with his chin in his hand. The vice-president of a bank who twice that week has seriously contemplated suicide places his hymnal in the rack. A pregnant girl feels the life stir inside her. A high-school math teacher, who for twenty years has managed to keep his homosexuality a secret for the most part even from himself, creases his order of service down the center with his thumbnail and tucks it under his knee....
>
> The preacher pulls the little cord that turns on the lectern light and deals out his note cards like a riverboat gambler. The stakes have never been higher. Two minutes from now he may have lost his listeners completely to their own thoughts, but at this minute he has them in the palm of his hand. The silence in the shabby church is deafening because everybody is listening to it.[1]

Obviously, our audience is a lot younger than most of the folks who sit in those pews on Sunday morning, but the reality of their pain and need is just as real. There are hurting kids everywhere dying to know the good news of God's love. That's why there's no question that those of us who teach the Word of God are involved in a serious enterprise. "The stakes have never been higher," and "the silence is deafening."

The bad news: Our attempts to communicate the good news often fall way short of breaking through the silence. So often our speaking opportunities become messed-up and missed opportunities.

The data is pretty discouraging. UC-Irvine psychologist Thomas Crawford, along with his colleagues, visited the homes of people from 12 churches shortly before and after they heard a sermon opposing racial injustice. In the course of the second interview, subjects were asked whether they'd heard or read anything about racial prejudice or discrimination since the previous interview. In other words, let's forget for a moment about whether or not the sermon had any impact on people's attitudes about racial prejudice; let's just see if people remembered hearing it. The response was a little grim, to put it mildly. Only 10 percent spontaneously recalled that the sermon had been preached. When the remaining 90 percent were asked directly whether their preachers "talked about prejudice or discrimination in the last couple of weeks," more than 30 percent said they hadn't.[2]

We'd like to think the results would be different if the study had been done with our youth groups, and maybe they would. But a lot of us have enough experience to doubt that. Giving *a talk* is one thing; being given *a listen* is something else altogether. I remember starting out in youth ministry with my seminary degree in hand. I'd just successfully completed courses in hermeneutics and homiletics, and I thought, *I love Jesus. I love teenagers. How hard can this be?* But within a few months at my first church, I thought, *Gosh, I used to think I had the gift of teaching. Why has God put me with a bunch of kids who don't have the gift of listening?*

Opportunities Blocked

The obstacles to communicating biblical truth are real. In their book *The Human Connection*, social psychologists Martin Bolt and David Myers give us a picture of just what it takes to give a talk or sermon and have it actually stimulate life-change in a teenager (Figure 1-1).

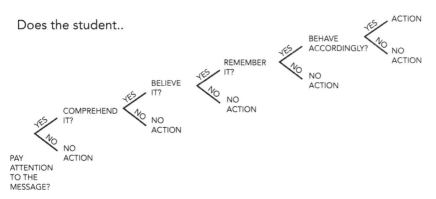

FIGURE 1-1   FROM MOUTH TO EAR TO HEART TO LIFE.
THE OBSTACLES TO COMMUNICATION ARE REAL.

1. First, we have to get them to pay attention to the message. It's a Wednesday night, the crowd breaker and singing are finished, and you begin your message. Some students are intrigued, some are fatigued, some are excited, some are distracted, some appear to be in a totally other place, and some you wish (just a little bit) were actually in another place. How will you gain their attention?

One of the first issues in communication is that *exposure is not the same as attention*. For example, when we're exposed to a print ad, research demonstrates that on the average, only 44 percent of us actually notice it, only 35 percent read enough to identify the brand mentioned, and only 9 percent say we read most of what was written.[3]

And selective attention doesn't just happen with magazine ads. Remember God's words to the prophet Ezekiel: "Son of man, you are living among a rebellious people. They have eyes to see but do not see and ears to hear but do not hear, for they are a rebellious people" (Ezekiel 12:2).

2. And if they hear it, we need to make sure they understand it. It's the last night of camp, and you decide to open up and share your story—all of it—the good, the bad, and the ugly. You openly confess to a pattern of pretty raunchy sexual sin throughout your high school and college years. Students listen intently. Clearly, you have their attention. But while one student walks away from the session with a renewed commitment to the importance of sexual purity, another walks away feeling reassured that sexual sin is a normal part of growing up, that "everybody does it" (even my favorite youth leader), and that the decision for sexual purity can be postponed until he's spent a few more years experimenting and having fun. Moral of the story: What you meant as a painful confession, some teenagers heard as permission. In short, they heard you, but they didn't understand what you were teaching.

3. Then even if they hear it and understand it, that doesn't mean they'll actually believe it. Perhaps they listen to your story, feel moved by it, and even understand the implications of it, but their response at the end of your message is still, "Well, I can understand that it's true for *him*. But that doesn't make it true for me."

4. Even if they believe the message in that moment, there's still the challenge of helping each of them to retain it in their active memory. How many of us have had students who closed out the retreat weekend or the week at camp with what seemed like a genuine prayer of commitment, but by the time the vans unloaded back at church, or the students walked back onto their school campuses or got home among their same groups of friends, that genuine spiritual commitment got stockpiled and stored away with a whole bunch of other wonderful and genuine camp memories or buried under new friendship, calendar, and school commitments?

5. And then, of course, there is the question of obedience. Among those students who remember the challenge of last summer's closing message or last week's youth group talk, there is still the question of whether they intend to fulfill the promises or stick to the commitments they've made.

6. And of the number who retain the message and have some measure of resolve to obey the message, there's finally this question: *Will they actually flesh out the decision by taking action?*[4] If question four points to retention, and question five points to intention, this question points us finally to real-life obedience.

Use the following chart to think about the ministry situation in which you most often teach a message to teenagers. How does this process play out with your students? Which points in the process are most difficult for that venue or setting? At what point in the process do you feel your ministry is strong? It may vary from meeting to meeting or event to event, but this might be a helpful exercise to get started.

1 Communication Challenge	2 What are we doing that might be leading studens to say "Yes"?	3 What are we doing that might be leading students to say "No"?	4 What could we do to create a better "Yes" environment?
EXAMPLE: PAY ATTENTION	• Using media to gain attention; • Incorporating student testimonies to grab interest; • Trying to give attention to what part of the program leads into the message	• Bad seating; some kids can't see very well; • No relationships with students outside the meeting; • All the adult leaders sit together in the back of the room.	
PAY ATTENTION			
UNDERSTAND THE MESSAGE			
BELIEVE THE MESSAGE			
REMEMBER THE MESSAGE			
DECISION TO HEED THE MESSAGE			
TAKE ACTION ON THE DECISION			

FIGURE 1-2   DO A QUICK SURVEY OF YOUR COMMUNICATION ENVIRONMENT.

(Unfortunately, speaking to teenagers is not as simple as "We talk, they listen.")

At this point in your reading, it might feel like a really good time to stop, close the book, and call your buddy about that telemarketing position selling timeshares in Zimbabwe. But that's why this is a good place to be reminded that *it doesn't all begin with you*. Like the apostle Paul, who gave his share of messages and faced his share of critics and discouragement, we can take heart in the fact that this whole communication deal begins with God, is empowered by God, and is sustained by God.

> The god of this age has blinded the minds of unbelievers, so that they cannot see the light of the gospel that displays the glory of Christ, who is the image of God. For what we preach is not ourselves, but Jesus Christ as Lord, and ourselves as your servants for Jesus' sake. For God, who said, "Let light shine out of darkness," made his light shine in our hearts to give us the light of the knowledge of God's glory displayed in the face of Christ. But we have this treasure in jars of clay to show that this all-surpassing power is from God and not from us. We are hard pressed on every side, but not crushed; perplexed, but not in despair; persecuted, but not abandoned; struck down, but not destroyed.... *Therefore we do not lose heart.* (2 Corinthians 4:4–9, 16a; emphasis added)

At the very least this chart (Figure 1-2) reminds us that effective, holistic ministry has to extend far beyond just *speaking* to teenagers. Few of us make this trajectory of discipleship simply because we've heard a really effective youth talk. It just seldom happens. Creating and presenting good messages is only *a piece of the action*. But ministry experience tells us it can be an important and strategic piece of the puzzle that God uses to transform a teenager's heart.

Our goal in this book is to help you look squarely into the face of the challenges of column 1, discover some ways to strengthen what you're already doing in column 2, think about how you might want to work with the issues you face in column 3, and then give you some practical and doable strategies for column 4. We want to help you think about the way you plan, prepare, think about, study for, craft, and deliver your messages to teenagers.

Aristotle, Youth Ministry, and Your Weekly Message

Before there was Peter and Paul, Augustine and Chrysostom, Wesley and Whitefield, Spurgeon and Lloyd-Jones, Graham and Lucado, Penn and Teller, Simon and Garfunkel—before all of those guys, there was a master of communication and philosophy named Aristotle (384–322 BC). His book *Rhetoric*, written around the fourth century BC and subtitled *101 Fun and Wacky Ideas for Philosophers*,[5] was based on his 20 years of study under the tutelage of Plato (c. 427–c. 347 BC) and is still the most influential book on speaking, ever.

Aristotle began attending Plato's academy when he was 17 (imagine having Plato as your youth pastor), and he was heavily influenced by Plato's teaching about rhetoric, which we could summarize with these six statements:

1. Speakers need to know what they're talking about.

2. Speakers need to be able to handle logic.

3. Speakers must pay attention to the order and arrangement of their message.

4. Speakers must know something about human nature and be able to analyze and understand their audience.

5. Speakers should give attention to their style and delivery.

6. Speakers must have a high moral purpose.[6]

While there is still debate and dialogue about how these features play out in the modern and postmodern context, most communication theorists and rhetoricians agree that even some two millennia later, these ideas still have merit.

Aristotle reduced those six basic principles down to three big ideas about rhetoric. He argued that effective communication involved ethos, pathos, and *logos*.[7]

Ethos refers to the speaker. Every time a message is given, there has to be a messenger. *Who* that messenger is, is almost as important as *what* that messenger says. Ethos encompasses everything from the speaker's integrity and trustworthiness to the speaker's subject knowledge and delivery style.

In practical terms, this means our students are asking, *Can I trust you as an adult? As a Christian? You've got it all together, don't you? I'm dying in a pile, and I'm not sure I trust you or your easy answers. Do you really know what you're talking about?* In this book, we'll refer to this as the *ethos* or *ethical* dimension of the message.

Pathos refers to the hearer. Each time a message is given, it's addressed to a particular audience. *Pathos* is an appeal to the passions, needs, tendencies, and hopes of the audience. Who are the students with whom we hope to communicate? This is a student asking as he listens, *Do you really care about me?* We'll call this *pathos* or the *emotional* dimension of the message.

Logos refers to the message itself. Aristotle used this term to refer to the rational dimension of the message. Was it logical? Was it well conceived and constructed? Does the audience understand the message? This is where we give attention to delivery. How was the message "sent"? We'll refer to this as *logos* or the *logical* dimension of the message.

Along with other great philosophers before us, our intention is to hang this book on the hook of these three big ideas. We'll focus, first of all, on the ethical dimension of the message. Second, we'll give some thought to the emotional dimension of the message. What do we need to know about our students to communicate effectively with them? And third, the bulk of this book will give attention to the third element of speaking, the logical dimension of the message. This is the *what* and the *how* of communication—*what* will we say and *how* will we say it?

The woman I met at Camp Berea on Newfound Lake had no idea of the amount of work that went into my journey of learning to create and communicate the messages she'd heard that weekend. And, to be honest, I don't even know what I spoke about. But what I do know is that in that moment of time, God did what God does best—he took my humble efforts and combined them with his sovereign ways. God used the spoken word to illuminate his written Word, and a young woman's life was eternally changed. Wow! Now, years later, she's speaking to kids with the same anticipation, hope, and prayer that I had when God drew her close to him during that weekend two decades ago.

To the rational mind, this speaking thing doesn't make sense—that someone could speak words to a group of people and somehow it could result in changed lives. But to a spiritual mind that understands God routinely turns water into wine, feeds a multitude with minimal food, and raises dead people back to life, impossible feels like the fingerprint of God. The greatest wonder is that we get to be part of the miracle!

We write this book with the confidence that God can do the impossible with the spoken Word. What we want to work on in the pages that follow is the possible part—the part that requires careful reflection, sound research, thoughtful planning, and hard work. We're thrilled that you've allowed us to share this ministry with you. And we're already looking forward to that day 5, 10, or even 20 years from now when someone comes up to us at a conference and says,

> Hey, my youth leader read a book you guys wrote about how
> to speak to teenagers, and frankly, she said there were a lot of
> bad jokes in the book. But she also said it was really helpful,
> and she's convinced it made her a better communicator. Well,
> I just want you to know that I was one of those teenagers she
> spoke to, and through those little talks she used to give to us,
> I heard the voice of God. So, thanks.

If someone does actually say that to us, rest assured it won't make us feel old, and it probably won't make us feel like good writers. What it will make us feel is grateful. Read well. The stakes have never been higher.

CHAPTER TWO

Building Bridges That Connect

Because you can hear doesn't mean that you listen; because you can talk doesn't mean you can communicate. Hearing is an acoustical phenomenon that takes place in our ears. Listening is always an interpersonal experience between people. Talking is a sound we make with our mouths and vocal chords. Communication is a dialogue between people.[8] — KEN OLSON, *CAN YOU WAIT TILL FRIDAY?*

Interstate 75 snakes its way from the tip of south Florida all the way to the upper peninsula of Michigan. Its 2,600-plus miles of concrete and asphalt will probably never be named among America's most scenic highways, but it's a relatively straight line between two distant places. To the frustration of thousands of travelers, until 1988, that relatively straight line was clogged by a drawbridge about two hours north of Detroit, near the little town of Zilwaukee.

When the drawbridge was built in the early '50s by the Michigan Department of Transportation, it probably seemed like a great idea: "A drawbridge on the interstate, why not?" But as traffic patterns changed and automobile volume increased, it became clear that it impeded traffic flow. During peak tourist seasons, the traffic backup could be 20 miles long, with frustrating multi-hour delays. That's when MDOT authorities began to envision a new high-span bridge that would allow ships on the Saginaw River to pass underneath the interstate without any drawbridge delays.

But that plan, begun in 1979, came to an abrupt halt in August 1982, when a monumental construction accident caused a 300-foot-long section of the bridge to sag five feet on one end and rise three-and-a-half feet at the other. It was a debacle that stopped all work on the bridge while engineers and lawyers tried to untangle the mistakes that led to the massive misalignment of the spans. As they sat and waited at the drawbridge through *five more years of slowdowns and backups*, interstate travelers were left to ponder the sight of a massive, multimillion-dollar structure that was high, strong, and impressive but didn't connect anything to anything.[9]

No matter how impressive the structure, or how lengthy the preparation, or how unique the design, Christian communication—whether it's a sermon, a talk, a Bible study, or a devotional—that doesn't help people connect to God is a waste of time, effort, and opportunity. It's a bridge to nowhere, and a bridge to nowhere is no bridge at all.

A Short Course in Communication Theory

Communication is about gaps and bridges.[10] Every time we attempt to communicate to an audience, we're standing on the threshold of a gap. That gap may be created by age, mistrust, apathy, fatigue, a bad sound system, the language we use, or by all kinds of unknown stuff inside the students' heads. To build the kind of bridge that will span those gaps, effective youth workers can use audience appeal, humor, personal testimony, intriguing stories, or a hundred other potential supports.

But as with any good bridge, it has to be properly aligned and well connected at both ends—the end where the message originates ("the communicator") and the end where the message is received and interpreted by another person ("the receptor").

The big idea here is this: Communication is far more complex than "us speaking" and "teenagers listening." Every truth we want to communicate has to be encoded into some channel of communication (it could be a word, a gesture, a facial expression, an image, or some other form of media; it could even be your meeting space). But, as youth workers, we want to make every effort to use the kinds of communication channels that will help our students accurately decode our message on their end of the bridge. In other words, we want them to hear what we really intend to say. If that happens, we connect. (Figure 2-1) If it doesn't happen, we build a bridge to nowhere.

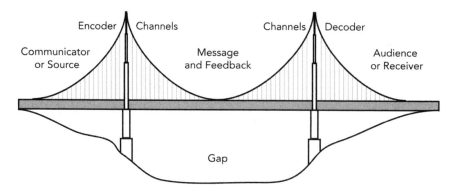

FIGURE 2-1 COMMUNICATION IS ABOUT BRIDGES AND GAPS.

In our attempts at communication, we begin with an idea.[11] It may be a word of encouragement, rebuke, promise, or instruction. It's the "something" in our minds and on our hearts that we desire to communicate.

But that idea can't just travel directly from our hearts to our teenagers' heads like some sort of spiritual wi-fi. We have to encode that message through various channels of communication. We may use spoken words, or drama, or media, or handouts; but in some form or another, we try to make the message clear enough that the listeners on the other end of the bridge can decode what resides in our minds and hearts.

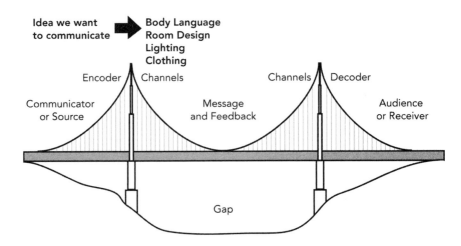

FIGURE 2-2   WE ALWAYS COMMUNICATE THROUGH MULTIPLE CHANNELS.

Notice we use the term *channels* (plural) because we always communicate through more than one channel (figure 2-2). *Channels* can be both verbal and nonverbal—facial expressions, gestures, posture, seating arrangement, room design, and even our clothing (e.g., clerical collar, coat and tie, casual dress, immodest dress, nerdy dress—wearing your pants too high—and so on). One of the keys to effective communication is to deliver the same coherent, unified message through the various channels so the decoding process isn't confusing.

For example, if my mouth says *yes* but my body language says *no*, then it makes it tough for the audience to crack the code of what I really mean. Or if my message is about "joy" and my face and tone communicate "death," I confuse my audience. My goal as a speaker is to communicate through the various channels in such a way that my audience can properly decode the idea I've encoded in word, gesture, or media.

Think about, for example, all of the various channels of communication during the typical Sunday morning sermon. Consider the impact those channels have on the message being communicated. Beginning with architecture, lighting, seating, and continuing all the way through to spoken words, body language, inflection, gestures, and even dress (what the speaker wears, or what members of the audience feel *they* are expected to wear),in what ways do these channels of communication help, confuse, distract, or distort the congregation's ability to decode the real intent of the communicator?

For example, sometime back I spoke to about 5,000 teenagers at a well-known denominational summer camp in Oklahoma. One of the rules of the camp was that no students were allowed to wear shorts in the worship services, even though the temperatures that week soared into the high 90s and we were meeting in an open-air pavilion. Of course everybody was miserable in the sessions, with several kids passing out due to the heat. I even tried faking it once myself, thinking it would offer a way out of the misery, but I was reminded that I had to speak.

No matter how bad it got though, the rule remained unchanged: God wanted us to wear long pants during worship no matter how oppressive the heat and discomfort. (It made me wonder why I'd never seen pictures of Jesus wearing Levis or dress slacks.) Now I'm certain the pastors and folks in charge of the event felt they were communicating reverence for God by this rule. But I don't think the teenagers passing out from the heat decoded their message that way. And it was a perfect example of how even the way teenagers in the audience were expected to dress could impact my efforts to accurately communicate a biblical message. Paying attention to these channels of communication is one of the most important-yet-overlooked elements of effective communication.

The important fact about bridges is that they allow movement in two directions. Cars can go both ways across that span, and that's good news because that two-way movement lets us know if our bridge is connected on the far end, or if it's misaligned. Are we really communicating what we plan to communicate?

Our teenage audience takes their cues (and their clues) from the various channels of communication and then begins to *decode* our message. Hopefully, they're hearing what we think we're saying. That's the goal! But as every communicator to teenagers has experienced, that's not always the case. Teenagers often communicate back to us (through the bridge) laughter, bad behavior, eye contact (or lack thereof), nodding heads (meaning "I agree"), nodding heads and closed eyes (meaning "I find your message very restful"), and any number of other responses. (Figure 2-3)

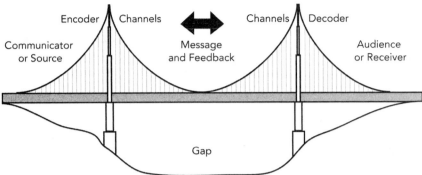

FIGURE 2-3   THE COMMUNICATION BRIDGE ALLOWS TRAFFIC
FROM BOTH DIRECTIONS.

When communicators receive those various messages of *feedback*, we go through our own decoding process to determine what our audiences are communicating to us about how our messages are coming across:

- "Why didn't they laugh at that? I thought it was funny."

- "There's a lot of extra talking, I'd better... (*choose one:* cut to the video, ask a question, raise my voice, close in prayer, set my eyebrows on fire)."

- "Wow! Every eye is focused; this must be connecting."

- "It just got really quiet in here; are they still with me?"

- "Oh gosh, Cassie's sleeping through the sermon again. I've got to tell her it's embarrassing when she sleeps through Daddy's messages."

Based on that decoding process, we may need to call an audible and either fine-tune or change channels in an attempt to help teenagers decode our messages more accurately.

Distortion and Disregard

The decoding process happens constantly during the course of a message, and it vividly shows us the two biggest dangers for communicators: *Distortion* on the source side and *disregard* on the receptor side. Let's unpack this for a moment.

1. Distortion on the source side. We want our teenage audience to receive the message. We desperately want them to hear us and to like us. So we often end up changing the message, dumbing down the Word of God, dulling the blade of his two-edged sword to make it more appealing and palatable. Of course, we do this with the heart of caring for teenagers and desperately wanting them to "get" the intent of the message. But when we approach speaking this way, it treats the students as customers or consumers and the speakers as salespeople (see 2 Corinthians 2:17–3:6). The apostle Paul referred to this as "peddling the word of God" (v. 17).

Our responsibility is to faithfully retell God's story "as though God were making his appeal through us" (2 Corinthians 5:20), even if popular cultural wisdom doesn't like it or buy it. Distortion of the message happens when we put *retail* (sales) above *retell* (Scripture).

2. Disregard for the receptor side. An equal error, but on the opposite end of the bridge, is to be so focused on the message and so intent on maintaining faithfulness to the Word that we forget those who desperately need to receive the message. We're so determined to say what we have to say that we completely disregard the understanding and comprehension of our listeners.

For example, we may naively quote Isaiah 55:11 where God promises, "My word...will not return to me empty," and then approach our audience as if we're throwing spiritual hand grenades—as long as one lands near them, there's bound to be some impact.

One of the classic examples of this sort of error was Campus Crusade for Christ's massive "Here's Life, America" campaign back in 1976 and 1977.[12] Motivated by a genuine passion to reach the world for Christ, Campus Crusade undertook an ambitious effort to mobilize churches and employ all forms of media to saturate some 250 U.S. metropolitan areas with the claims of Christ. One of the principal strategies was to utilize billboards, buttons, and bumper stickers to display the message, "I found it." It was an impressive evangelistic bridge-building project, but did it connect?

Here's what we know:

- Crusade announced that 175 million people were exposed to the claims of the gospel through the outreach,[13] and by virtue of media saturation, that could well be true.

- Researchers at Wheaton Graduate School discovered that in one survey sample of Upper Arlington, Ohio (an upscale suburb of Columbus), about 80 percent of the town's residents were aware of the "I found it" theme. But that same survey found that *only 40 percent of those who heard it actually understood the message.* And at least half of that 40 percent were already Christians or

Christian-oriented. The vast majority of nonbelievers never comprehended what had been "lost" or what had been "found."

- More than a half-million people indicated they'd received Christ as a result of the campaign, but *fewer than three percent of those people ever joined a local church.*[14]

In no way is this meant to indict the folks at Crusade. At least they tried. And we do know from other studies that the "Here's Life, America" campaign motivated many congregations and individual Christians to be more aware of opportunities to share their faith. But that wasn't Crusade's goal. They fell short because although they were faithful to the message, they didn't give enough attention to the audience.

This communication bridge is filled with heavy (and significant) two-way traffic, so understanding this process and being able to decode it is essential for effective communication. That's why we talk about *communication that connects.* A bridge that doesn't connect at both ends is a bridge to nowhere.

God: The Master Bridge-Builder

Missiologist Charles Kraft reminds us that the first communicator/bridge-builder was God himself.[15] From the beginning of time, God sought us out, God revealed himself to us, and God spoke to us. (See Genesis 3:9; Psalm 19:1–4; Hebrews 1:1–2.) And it was God who came to this planet as a human being to heal the tragic and cosmic misalignment between God and ourselves. (See John 1:1–14; Philippians 2:5–7.) All of our human efforts to bridge the gap between earth and heaven—regardless of how noble, impressive, or sincere—are fruitless projects, the tragic result of a massive fall, and little more than bridges to nowhere. So it makes sense that, as bridge-builders, we'd give at least some thought to how God chose to do communication.

When we speak to teenagers, we're addressing a number of gaps not only between them and God, but also between them and—

- Their parents

- Their friends

- Authority figures (teacher, employer, youth worker)

- People of other ethnicities

- Their peers in various school or youth group clusters—middle school and high school, guys and girls, skaters and geeks, jocks and home-schoolers

We also address the gaps between those who know Jesus and those who don't (Figure 2-4).

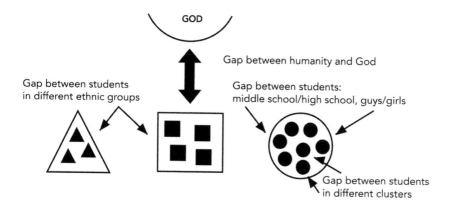

FIGURE 2-4 COMMUNICATING WITH TEENAGERS IS ABOUT BRIDGING GAPS.

And then, of course, there's the gap between those of us who speak and those who listen. These are the gaps we seek to bridge every week when we attempt communication to teenagers. Yikes! No wonder it often feels as if we're in the middle of a never-ending building project, stuck somewhere between here and Zilwaukee. How do we do it?

Well, we'll begin in the next chapter by thinking about how God did it.

CHAPTER THREE

God: The Bridge-Builder

If communication is about bridging gaps, then we communicators have our work cut out for us because we live and do ministry among students whose lives are marked by profound disconnection. In some ways, it's a remarkable irony since this generation has more connecting devices and options than any previous one. But all the digital gadgets on the planet can't heal the profound sense of lost-ness and abandonment felt by so many of our teenagers.

God Builds Bridges

The good news is that God is the Great Bridge-Builder, the Great Bringer-Together, the Master Architect. Before you journey through this chapter, take a minute to read through Ephesians 2:13–22. As you do, underline every phrase in the passage that points to God as the Great Bridge-Builder.

> But now in Christ Jesus you who once were far away have been brought near by the blood of Christ. For he himself is our peace, who has made the two one and has destroyed the barrier, the dividing wall of hostility…His purpose was to create in himself one new humanity out of the two, thus making peace, and in one body to reconcile both of them to God through the cross, by which he put to death their hostility. He came and preached peace to you who were far away and peace to those who were near. For through him we both have access to the Father by one Spirit. Consequently, you are no longer foreigners and strangers, but fellow citizens with God's people and also members of his household, built on the foundation of the apostles and prophets, with Christ Jesus himself as the chief cornerstone. In him the whole building is joined together and rises to become a holy temple in the

Lord. And in him you too are being built together to become a dwelling in which God lives by his Spirit.

As we think about building bridges of effective communication, it only makes sense that we'd look to God to see what we can learn about bridging the gaps.

We Can Build Bridges

There are four basic communication lessons[16] we can learn from the One who has been the Word from the very beginning (John 1:1). We aren't claiming these are new ideas; we're saying these are really important old ideas that undergird all that we say in this book.

Make Them Understand

To communicate as God has communicated requires that we take radical, potentially inconvenient measures to make sure teenagers understand God's Word and its power to transform—even in the twenty-first century.

What do the following items have in common?

- A burning bush

- A talking donkey

- An illustration with a mustard seed

- A potter working his wheel

- A fig tree that met an early death

- A distant star

- A story about a man and his pet lamb

- Strange graffiti on the banquet room wall

- Swarms of frogs and locusts

- Countless dreams and visions

- Stunning miracles

- The Word become flesh

- A prophet commanded to marry a prostitute named Gomer

They all remind us of the amazing lengths God will go to in order to make himself known.[17] God understands that building a bridge between him and humanity means the work has to begin from his side. God also understands that the bridge can't reach us if he doesn't fully understand what life is like on our side (Hebrews 4:15).

All of God's communication was geared toward the contours and contexts of life on our end of the bridge. God started high and stooped low because God is *receptor-oriented* (Philippians 2:6–7). He's determined to do whatever it takes to communicate to specific people in specific places and specific times. It's not always easy or convenient, but it's important that he make himself known.

When I first started teaching as a rookie youth pastor, I taught my teenagers using the same kinds of talks I enjoyed listening to. I loved the expository preaching of John Stott, R.C. Sproul, and Eugene Peterson. So naturally that became my preaching style—thorough exposition, clear outlines, lots of notes, and meaty teaching. I always thought that if I'd been sitting under my own teaching, I probably would have really liked it and been more Christlike. And more humble.

But after a few months, it became painfully clear that my students and I did not see eye to eye about what made good preaching. By the time I'd whittled the group down to a few diehard kids (whose parents must have bribed them to come), it dawned on me that John Stott probably wasn't speaking at very many middle school events, and there was probably a good reason for that.

If I were going to continue to speak to teenagers, I'd have to adjust my methods accordingly. I still wanted to present sound, solid, biblical teaching, but I realized how much more effective it would be if there were actually students in the room to hear it! So I needed to offer it in ways that teenagers could receive it. That's what it means to be *receptor-oriented*.

There are elements of life on our end of the bridge that are quite different from life on a teenager's end of the bridge. If we want to take seriously the lessons God teaches us about communication, then we'll need to take the initiative and make the effort to bridge the gap. The apostle Paul put it this way:

> Though I am free and belong to no one, I have made myself a slave to everyone, to win as many as possible. To the Jews I became like a Jew, to win the Jews. To those under the law I became like one under the law (though I myself am not under the law), so as to win those under the law. To those not having the law I became like one not having the law (though I am not free from God's law but am under Christ's law), so as to win those not having the law. To the weak I became weak, to win the weak. I have become all things to all people so that by all possible means I might save some. (1 Corinthians 9:19-22)

Don't Communicate from a Distance

To communicate as God has communicated is to remember that the most important place to speak is not from the front of the room.

For me, one of the scariest parts of fatherhood was trying to instruct my older daughter how to operate a motor vehicle. Teaching her to drive our manual-transmission car was an exercise in faith. She's an extremely bright young woman, but she never seemed to grasp the delicate dialogue that takes place between clutch and accelerator—that when one increases, the other decreases. Consequently, whenever the car lurched into forward motion, we were jarred by a sequence of quick jolts and jerks: dashboard—headrest—dashboard—headrest.

I can still remember how she'd occasionally look over at me with her beautiful eyes opened wide and say, "Daddy, how come when I'm driving you can't control your saliva?"

And I'd have to explain, "Sweetheart, Daddy's being whip-lashed into oblivion."

Day after day, week after week, these driving lessons were tough. It was intense. There was anger. There were tears. There was pain. There was yelling. There was pouting. And then, of course, my daughter would get emotional too.

But no matter what happened during the lesson, when we got back to the house, it was always the same thing: My wife would meet us at the front door (with an ice pack for my neck); then she'd look into my bloodshot eyes and say, "Don't forget why you're doing this. *Don't* forget *why* you're doing this!"

She was reminding me of what all of us know intuitively: *There are certain truths that we simply cannot communicate from a distance.* My daughter wasn't going to fully comprehend the principles of driver safety by reading our state's driver education handbook or the latest edition of *Driving for Dummies: An Operator's Manual to Minimize Concussions.* She wasn't going to completely embrace those truths simply because she heard them cited in a driver's ed class. She wasn't going to be impacted by those ideas just because she watched scary movies about defensive driving and teenagers being burned and buried in their cars.

The only way she was going to really learn those truths was if I got in the car *with* her and drove on the road *with* her—in good times and bad times, uphill and downhill, sore neck, sore back, concussion, and so on. I needed to be right beside her. That's the only way it works because some truths simply cannot be communicated from a distance.

Clearly, God understood that if human beings were ever going to comprehend his love for us, it would have to be done in a way that was up close and personal. It couldn't just be the Word becoming words. It would have to be the Word becoming flesh, God incarnate. Jesus said, *"Come* to me," not just *"Listen* to me" (Matthew 11:28).

One of the pivotal elements of Christian communication is that it must be more than informational; it must also be highly relational. We don't just read teenagers the operator's manual for life, we join them on their journeys—in good times and bad times, uphill and downhill. Our students are much more likely to remember what we've said while we're walking beside them than while we're standing in front of them. Plus, if we spend time walking beside teenagers, then it's more likely that they'll be interested in what we have to say when we *are* speaking to them. Is it any wonder that in the three years of Jesus' public ministry, he spent only a fraction of his time preaching to large crowds and the bulk of his time in the company of individuals and small groups of disciples?

One of my mentors drove this principle home for me with these words: "If you want to make a big *impression,* speak to a crowd; but if you want to make a big *impact,* speak to a person."

The Methods Shape the Message
To communicate as God has communicated is to take seriously both the method and message, form and content.

I used to believe that God doesn't care about our methods—only our message. "It's *what* we say, not *how* we say it that really defines faithful communication." The first time I said something like that, it was probably in defense of some kid who was in trouble for bringing a guitar into the sanctuary.

But when we read, for example, through the hundreds of verses in Exodus in which God gives attention to minute details of tabernacle design, or when we note the care with which Jesus and his disciples observed the Passover on what he knew would be their last night together, it becomes quite clear that the neat and clean boundaries we draw between form and content, method and message, and *how* and *what* aren't so neat and clean.

In Marshall McLuhan's groundbreaking text *Understanding Media: The Extensions of Man,* he makes his famous observation, "The medium is the message."[18] In simplest terms, it's the notion that a message doesn't stand alone—that the medium through which we communicate a message is itself a part of the message. The medium isn't neutral. The medium actually shapes the message.

- If we worship in a room that is largely dark except for the lights on the stage, what does that say about the focal point of our worship? And what does speaking in that dark room—in which reading from one's own Bible is difficult, if not impossible—teach our students about corporate study of God's Word?

- If I speak to my students using sarcasm or crude humor, what is my unintended message to them?

- If it's essential for me to be funny when I speak, how does that limit the range of topics I can talk about? And in what kinds of situations would that approach limit my effectiveness?

- If I limit my communication to only creative and engaging stories, it might win me a wide audience, but what's the implicit message to my students when I shy away from taking them into the text of Scripture?

- Probably one of the tougher issues: Suppose I encourage my students to be discerning about what they watch and what they listen to, but then I find a strong illustration in a video clip from a raunchy movie. Do I use it, and what's the message of that medium?

What this means in practical terms is this: The means by which I communicate to my students—the way I use media, the language I use, the way I approach Scripture, the way I talk about the church or authority figures in the church, the way I use humor—*all of it*—all of those methods shape and become part of the message I communicate to my students.

A speaker who chooses to communicate by means of smoke signals is, by default, limiting the kinds of topics she can talk about and the depth with which she can have dialogue with her audience. The medium impacts the message.[19] Maybe this is why God married form and content, word and flesh—he understood that, to some extent, *how we speak determines what we say.*

Speak to Transform

To communicate as God communicated we need to speak not just to inform but also to transform.

Locked up and serving a life sentence, the Prince of Granada found himself in solitary confinement, imprisoned by order of the Spanish Crown in Madrid's ancient dungeon—the Place of Skulls. As an heir to the Spanish throne, the fear was that he might aspire to be king. So he sat alone for 33 years, locked away from all but the most minimal human contact.

In an act of cynical kindness, his captors gave him one book to read in his cell, one book with which he'd be locked away in isolation for the whole of his imprisonment. That book was *Memory Makers* by Doug Fields and Duffy Robbins. (Just kidding. A more appropriate book might have been Duffy and Maggie Robbins' *Enjoy the Silence.*) The book they actually gave him was the Bible.

We know the Prince of Granada studied the Bible meticulously during his years in jail because he used a nail to scratch out his notes on the soft stone of his cell walls. What was remarkable were the kinds of notes he made. Through years of solitary confinement with the Bible—a book that even its enemies would probably agree is the zenith of all written documents—the Prince of Granada came up with observations like these:[20]

- In the Bible, the word *Lord* is found 1,583 times.

- The word *Jehovah*, 6,855 times, and the word *Reverend* but once, and that in the ninth verse of the CXIth Psalm.

- The eighth verse of the CXVIIth Psalm is the middle verse of the Bible.

- The ninth verse of the VIIIth chapter of Esther is the longest verse; the thirty-fifth verse, XIth chapter of St. John is the shortest.

- In the CVIIth Psalm, four verses are alike, the eighth, fifteenth, twenty-first, and thirty-first.

- Each verse of the CXXXVIth Psalm ends alike.

- No word or name of more than six syllables can be found in the Bible.

- The XXXVIIth chapter of Isaiah and XIXth chapter of 2 Kings are alike.

- The word *Girl* appears but once in the Bible, and that in the third verse of the IIIrd chapter of Joel.

- There are found in both books of the Bible 3,538,483 letters; 773,693 words; 31,373 verses; 1,189 chapters; and 66 books.

First of all, you've got to give the guy credit; he really had a grasp of Roman numerals. But what's really stunning is that someone with such intense and prolonged exposure to the Word of God, the Book of all books, could come away with little more than trivia.

More stunning still is the fact that this kind of trivial communication probably happens every week in youth groups, Sunday schools, and Young Life clubs around the country. Students are exposed to biblical teaching week after week, month after month, and they're graduating from their youth ministries with little more than disconnected Bible stories and random factoids. Clearly, this isn't what God intends from his Word.

If we can observe anything about God's approach to communication, it's that God speaks not to inform, but to transform (1 Samuel 15:22; Romans 12:1–2; James 1:22). When we speak to teenagers, our first priority is never just providing information. Paul doesn't mince any words about this: "Since, then, we know what it is to fear the Lord, we try to persuade people" (2 Corinthians 5:11).

There is a prominent school of communication theory that all communication is some form of persuasion.[21] It's not our purpose here to make a strong argument one way or the other. But what is clear in Christian communication is that people do not simply need more information about God;[22] they need to be persuaded to act on the information they already know. Any serious reading of Romans 1 leads us to conclude that humanity suffers not because we lack knowledge of God, but because we refuse to acknowledge God (Romans 1:18–32).

This isn't to say that Bible knowledge is bad. It's definitely good! Teenagers can't obey a God they don't know, and they can't obey teaching they haven't heard. But with Christian communication, it always comes back to obedience. If we read Jesus' words, it's obvious that he was intent on hearing *and* doing:

- "Now that you know these things, you will be blessed *if you do them*" (John 13:17, emphasis added).

- "Jesus told him, 'Go and *do likewise*'" (Luke 10:37, emphasis added).

- "But everyone who *hears these words* of mine and *does not put them into practice* is like a foolish man who built his house on sand" (Matthew 7:26, emphasis added).

- "For whoever *does the will* of my Father in heaven is my brother and sister and mother" (Matthew 12:50, emphasis added).

- "Not everyone who says to me, 'Lord, Lord,' will enter the kingdom of heaven, but only those who *do the will* of my Father who is in heaven" (Matthew 7:21, emphasis added).

- "Anyone who loves me will *obey* my teaching" (John 14:23–24, emphasis added).

- "Blessed rather are those who hear the word of God and *obey it*" (Luke 11:28, emphasis added).

Truth from God's Word isn't just for ordering thoughts; it's for ordering lives. We're not trying to just make it across the bridge; we're trying to bring others back from the other side. "The Son of Man came to seek *and* to save what was lost" (Luke 19:10, emphasis added). As Christ-followers who also communicate, we seek to persuade.

The Anatomy of Persuasion

Before we close out this chapter, there are three mission-critical questions that must be asked.

Question 1: What Does Authentic Persuasion Look Like?

There are two essential tests of genuine persuasion.

1. Are we able to observe authentic change in a student's inner attitude? Attitude is the sum of three variables: (a) what a student *thinks*, (b) what a student *feels*, and (c) what that student *intends* to do with what he knows.[23] One is an issue of the *mind*, one is an issue of the *heart*, and one is an issue of the *will*. Like a three-legged stool, persuasion sits on the balanced footing of all three.

If you speak to only address the mind, your message is dismissed and ignored by the heart. Likewise, truth that only grabs the heart will lose its grip on the mind in the passion of temptation. A heart and mind that "accept Jesus" but don't intend to follow through with action will grow callous, more cynical, and tougher to reach the next time—like an inoculation that builds up immunity after a series of shots. Students can be entertained, blown away, offended, shocked, impressed, moved, and intrigued, but none of those reactions is the same as being persuaded. Authentic persuasion impacts *beliefs*, *feelings*, and *intentions*.

2. Is that change of inner attitude manifest in a student's outward behavior? (Romans 12:1–2; Matthew 7:18–21)[24] We have to be careful how we frame this. Ultimately, only the Spirit knows how a truth needs to be applied in our students' lives. We want to be cautious about boxing the will of God into something as small as our limited imaginations. But at the same time, Jesus was quite clear that we could discern the root (inner attitudes) by observing the fruit (outward behavior). If impressive bridges and great talks don't help people move forward in their spiritual journeys, then they're a wasted effort and a bridge to nowhere.

Question 2: What Is the Primary Challenge of Persuasion?

One of the most telling passages in C.S. Lewis' *Chronicles of Narnia* comes midway through *The Magician's Nephew* when we hear Aslan's voice for the first time—and he's *singing*. In the midst of the mystery and delight of Aslan awakening plants and animals with his song, there's one who's disinterested and hiding at a distance:

> Ever since the animals had first appeared, Uncle Andrew had been shrinking further and further back into the thicket. He watched them very hard of course; but he wasn't really inter-

ested in seeing what they were doing, only in seeing whether they were going to make a rush at him. Like the Witch, he was dreadfully practical. He simply didn't notice that Aslan was choosing one pair out of every kind of beasts. All he saw, or thought he saw, was a lot of dangerous wild animals walking vaguely about. And he kept on wondering why the other animals didn't run away from the big Lion.

When the great moment came and the Beasts spoke, he missed the whole point; for a rather interesting reason. When the Lion had first begun singing, long ago when it was still quite dark, he had realized that the noise was a song. And he had disliked the song very much. It made him think and feel things he did not want to think and feel.[25]

The great challenge in bridging the gap toward effective communication is that some of our students simply don't want to hear what we have to say. Sometimes it's because we make them "think and feel things [they do] not want to think and feel." Sometimes it's because they come to a message with preconceived notions about God. Sometimes it's because they have preconceived notions about those of us who talk about God. As C.S. Lewis points out, "What you see and hear depends a good deal on where you are standing: it also depends on what sort of person you are."[26] The primary task of persuasive communication is to break through the listener's unwillingness to hear.

Using the metaphor of a craftsman forging wax into a candle, communication theorist Em Griffin boils down this persuasion process into three simple actions: to melt, to mold, and to make hard.[27]

Communication specialists refer to this unwillingness to hear as *psychological reactance*. It's the natural tendency to resist persuasion: "Don't tell me what I need," or "My mind's made up; don't confuse me with facts!" We see this vividly in the attitude of Uncle Andrew:

And the longer and more beautifully the Lion sang, the harder Uncle Andrew tried to make himself believe that he could hear nothing but roaring. Now the trouble about trying to make yourself stupider than you really are is that you very often succeed. Uncle Andrew did. He soon did hear nothing but roaring in Aslan's song. Soon he couldn't have heard anything else even if he had wanted to. And when at last the Lion spoke and said, "Narnia awake," he didn't hear any words: he heard only a snarl.

Our initial job as speakers is to help teenagers overcome that *reactance*—to get them to the point where they can hear the song instead of the snarl. It doesn't matter what we say if we can't get them to listen.

Question 3: What Are the Keys to Effective Persuasion?

Charles Kraft, in his book *Communication Theory for Christian Witness*,[28] offers the following practical suggestions. Let's think about them in the context of youth ministry:

1. Principle of Acceptability. Given where my students are (on their side of the bridge), how open are they going to be to what I have to say in this message? If they're closed to what I have to say, how can I adjust the *code*, the *channels*, the *content*, and the *circumstances* to reduce any unnecessary *reactance* and make it more acceptable?

2. Principle of Relevance. Why should my students be interested in what I have to say in this message? How does it relate to their lives? When we speak, our students are constantly asking several types of questions: *Why should I listen to you? (ethos); Do you really care about me when you're speaking? (pathos); Why should I listen to this information?* and *What does this have to do with my life anyway? (logos);*[29] *When are you going to stop speaking so we can get some snacks? (Fritos); Now that you're done speaking, your breath is nasty (Mentos);* and finally, *Why aren't you interesting like the guy who spoke last week? (wise-os).*

I remember being at a midwinter Bible conference in Florida where I was, by far, the youngest person there. Most of the other people were in their eighties, but the title of the preacher's message was "Why Premarital Sex Is Unbiblical." I leaned over to my wife (okay, I was the second youngest person there), and I said, "The topic for this crowd should be, 'Why Premarital Sex Is Impossible.'" Effective persuasion begins when we scratch where people itch.

3. Principle of Specificity. Our students aren't primarily concerned about concepts. We certainly wish they were; and to some extent, they probably ought to be. But wishing won't make it so. They're far more interested in concrete application: *How does this truth look in real life? How does this biblical principle play out in my school? Yeah, neat idea, but what about...?* In our speaking, we must constantly move from general to specific, from the Word to their world.

4. Principle of Surprise. Our students sit in front of us each week with expectations—some of them good, and some of them bad. Communication research reveals that one of the ways to increase impact and enhance persuasion is to breach those expectations.

Have you ever had a new student walk up to you at the end of the meeting and say, "That was a great message, you sure don't sound much like a preacher"? (Yeah, that's never happened to me either.) But that kind of rewiring of teenagers' expectations opens them to hear what they might not have been willing to hear. Or have you ever noticed how, when some dignitary is speaking, even the slightest use of humor draws strong audience response? And why? Because the humor doesn't fit the expectations the audience had for the speaker.

That doesn't mean doing things or saying things for shock value. But it does mean anticipating what an audience expects and trying to catch them off guard by being, saying, or doing otherwise.

5. Principle of Discovery. Our students are much more likely to embrace a truth they discover for themselves than one we shove down their throats. The Church has always been quick to jump in and say, "Jesus is the answer." But persuasion research suggests we might be more effective by asking some well-formed, real-life questions. It's no wonder that some of Jesus' favorite teaching devices were questions, parables, and stories. He understood the *Principle of Discovery*. There are two ways to get people to admire a rose: One is to shove it in front of their nostrils; the other is to let them follow the scent to its source.

As we move through the remaining chapters of this book, our goal is to take these principles of communication and see how they play out in the way you plan, craft and deliver your messages. We hope this material will help you not only think about communication but also challenge you to build bridges that connect your teenagers to the One who loves them most. Why? Because it's all about persuasion.

CHAPTER FOUR

Who You Are Speaks Louder Than What You Say

I remember it vividly. It was the last of our four premarital counseling sessions, and the minister of my (now) wife's home church was wrapping it all up. He said things like, "Well, it won't be long until the big day...," "You're a very, very fortunate young man to be marrying someone so out of your league...," and then, "Oh, yeah, I wanted to tell you this myself—I'm going to tell the church board tonight—my wife and I have decided to get a divorce."

Now obviously that doesn't mean everything the pastor had told us about marriage was wrong. After all, everyone who knows both my wife and me clearly agrees that I married out of my league. And there were other helpful insights as well. But unfortunately, what he told us about his own impending divorce really drained the impact of almost all that he'd said about marriage in our previous three sessions. It wasn't that his content was unsound; it's that what he said with his own life drowned out the sound of his teaching.

In chapter one we looked at Aristotle's use of *ethos, pathos,* and *logos. Ethos* is the ethical dimension of the message—the element that begins with the speaker. It's that element of speaking that has spawned the famous aphorism: **Who you are** *is more important than what you say.* That statement, in a nutshell, summarizes the ethical dimension of communication.

Consider "The Way of a Man with a Maiden"

The writer of Proverbs speaks of his amazement at "the way of a man with a maiden" (Proverbs 30:18–19). In my mind, these words evoke a soft pastoral image of a grassy knoll overlooking a lazy river. Sitting and basking in the warm glow of the afternoon sun is a strikingly handsome bald man who's deeply in love and trying to woo a young woman who has yet to decide if he's worthy of her affections.[30]

But if we can see beyond the romance, it just might be that this passage will offer us a fitting picture of the ethical dimension of speaking. It probably wouldn't be the kind of imagery you'd want to use at the next parents' meeting (i.e., "Y'know, Mom and Dad, whenever I speak to your kids, I like to think of myself as sort of…like…seducing them"). But it was precisely this imagery that Plato used when he wrote about rhetoric and effective communication,[31] and it's a good place to begin our look at why your life matters more than your message.

Em Griffin[32] makes use of this same passage from Proverbs to help us see some of the unethical roles we can fall into as Christian communicators:

1. The Non-Lover: Like a postman delivering flowers, the *non-lover* is faithful to get the message through, but there's no apparent passion attached to the delivery or to those who will receive the bouquet. "Here's the gospel, kids. If you believe it, great! If you don't believe it, that's fine, too. I don't really care. Basically, I've got a commission to fill, and I don't have time for all of your problems."

2. The Flirt: Not so much in love with students as with the idea of *speaking to* students, *the flirt* winks, smiles, whispers sweet nothings, tries to be a flashy speaker, and then moves on.

3. Seducer: The speaker who will do or say anything if it moves students to respond. Crude humor? "Hey, it works." Dishonest illustrations? "What they don't know won't hurt them." Watering down the meaning of God's Word? "Look, we've got to change the message as the times change." The *seducer* does whatever it takes to score points with his audience.

4. The Rapist: This is the communicator who doesn't allow students the freedom to question, think through, doubt, or reject. He uses coercion, threat, and manipulation to get an audience to respond. It's the speaking equivalent to the Crusaders who marched out in the eleventh, twelfth, and thirteenth centuries with a desire to reclaim Jerusalem and the Holy Land for God. It was evangelism by force—sometimes brutal. Our call as communicators is to be persuaders, not crusaders (2 Corinthians 5:11).

The True Lover: Motivated by Love and Truth

"For Christ's love compels us, because we are convinced" (2 Corinthians 5:14, emphasis added).

When we speak to teenagers, there are two biblical motivations: One is love; the other is truth. We speak because we're compelled by the *love* of Christ, and we're compelled by the love of Christ because we're convinced of the *truth* that "one died for all." Both love and truth are important. Truth without love is unattractive and coercive. Love without truth is sloppy agape.

Paul's ministry was clearly a combination of both. Take a minute to read through the following passage:

> **For the appeal we make does not spring from error or impure motives, nor are we trying to trick you. On the contrary, we speak as those approved by God to be entrusted with the gospel. We are not trying to please people but God, who tests our hearts. You know we never used flattery, nor did we put on a mask to cover up greed—God is our witness.** We were not looking for praise from any human being, not from you or anyone else, even though as apostles of Christ we could have asserted our prerogatives. Instead, we were like young children among you.

> Just as a nursing mother cares for her children, so we cared for you. Because we loved you so much, we were delighted to share with you not only the gospel of God but our lives as well. Surely you remember, brothers and sisters, our toil and hardship; we worked night and day in order not to be a burden to anyone while we preached the gospel of God to you.

> You are witnesses, and so is God, of how holy, righteous and blameless we were among you who believed. For you know that we dealt with each of you as a father deals with his own children, encouraging, comforting and urging you to live lives worthy of God, who calls you into his kingdom and glory. (1 Thessalonians 2:3–12)

Note that Paul characterizes his preaching and his ministry with two different metaphors: (a) *"Just as a nursing mother cares for her children"* is a picture of love. And (b) *"We dealt with each of you as a father...encouraging, comforting and urging you to lead lives worthy of God"* is a picture of truth.

Go back to the passage and underline these two verses. Then read verses three through five again (the ones in bold font) and circle the phrases that you believe point to the motives of *seduction, rape, flirtation,* and *non-love.*

Okay, *now* reread the whole passage one last time to really understand that the power of Paul's ministry was not that he said, "Listen to me," but that he could say, "Imitate me" (1 Corinthians 11:1). That's the ethical dimension of the message.

Essentials of *Ethos*

On the blank page inside the back cover of this book, write the names of three speakers you really admire. Underneath each name, write down the qualities that, in your opinion, make each speaker especially effective.[33]

Now go back over the list. If you've listed "premature hair loss" or "deep receding hairline" under the names of at least two speakers, give yourself a perfect score. If, perhaps, you've listed other qualities as well, then circle those that could fall under one of these three categories:

1. Passionate (she cared about the audience, cared about the message)

2. Knowledgeable (the speaker seemed to know what she was talking about)

3. Trustworthy (she seemed genuine, authentic, honest)

Almost all of the research in oral communication and public speaking suggests that the main criteria by which an audience evaluates the credibility of a speaker essentially boils down to these three factors: *passion, knowledge,* and *trustworthiness.*[34]

And why?

Passion connects to caring. As your students listen to you, they're constantly asking questions like these (probably unconsciously): *Does he care about me and my life?* (That's the first question every teenager asks about every encounter with every person!) *Am I safe opening up to her? Do I like him? Does she really care about this subject, this passage, this idea? What's her angle?*

Knowledge connects to competence. Your teenagers are asking, *Does he really know what he's talking about? Does she really understand my life and my issues? Has he really given this some thought about how it will impact my life? Does her teaching make sense?*

Trustworthiness connects to character. Like any other audience, teenagers want to know: *Do you practice what you preach? Can I really trust you?*

The ethical dimension of an effective message is all about *caring, competence,* and *character.* Let's look at each of these in more detail.

Caring

In John Wesley's journal, he describes a mob scene outside the house where he's staying. It was so violent and so raucous that it looked as if it might erupt into a full-blown riot. Wesley was watching from an upstairs room as people threw rocks through the windows. Then he heard crashing sounds and angry voices as the mob stormed inside the house and began attacking some of Wesley's traveling companions.

Then he writes this:

> Believing the time was now come, I walked down into the thickest of them. They had now filled all the rooms below. I called for a chair. The winds were hushed, and all was calm and still. My heart was filled with love, my eyes with tears, and my mouth with arguments. They were amazed; they were ashamed; they were melted down; they devoured every word.

It's really quite stunning—an angry mob, hungry for blood, captivated by an English vicar who has as his only arsenal a heart filled with love, eyes filled with tears, and a mouth filled with arguments. Of course, it was God who intervened in the room that day. But the scene also shows us a powerful drama of *ethos* in action within Wesley's life. Even with the most unwilling audience, there's something compelling about a person who seems to really, genuinely care.

Communication research is unanimous in its verdict that one of the major factors by which an audience judges a speaker is with this simple question: *Do I like this person?* Avery and Gobbel, in a study published in the *Review of Religious Research*,[35] cite two surveys of listening attitudes among Lutheran congregations in south central Pennsylvania in which the findings were clear:

- 83 percent judged warmth, friendliness, and likeability just as important or more important than theological expertise or intellectual soundness.

- The survey went on to demonstrate that when the audience perceives the speaker to be kind, likeable, and understanding, the listeners will seriously consider the preacher's interpretation of the gospel—even if it varies widely from their own.

Most of us have learned from experience that these are not just the tendencies of Lutherans in south central Pennsylvania. Teenagers are far more likely to evaluate a spoken message on the basis of the speaker's personality than on her persuasive arguments. So if this is true, then how do you communicate warmth and likeability to a roomful of teenagers in the middle of a talk?

- *Use their names.* In illustrations, in referencing common memories—any way you can. Their names are their greatest possessions.

- *Use humor.* We never joke with our enemies. You'll never see Darth Vader stride menacingly onto the bridge of an enemy's spacecraft and say, "Okay, stop me if you've heard this one—an android and a wookie walk into a bar..." In communication, humor, *if it's really humorous,* is the great global warmer.

- *Avoid profanity and vulgar language.* Despite the growing use of mindless, crude humor that we're exposed to every day, research has shown that "people who casually use profanities and vulgarities to pepper their speech are often perceived as abrasive and lacking character, maturity, intelligence, manners and emotional control."[36]

- *Try to draw references to what you have in common with your audience.*

- *As often as possible, when you're using rebuke, correction, warning, or accusatory type language, speak in the first person plural.* Instead of saying, "A lot of *you guys* have been dealing with..." say, "Some of *us* in this very room are dealing with...."

- *Stand as close as possible to the group,* and if it's feasible, speak from the same level as your students.

- *Be conversational.* Teenagers are much more responsive to someone who's *talking to them* than they are to someone who's *giving a talk at them.*

Too many of us approach speaking as if communication hinges on a mouth filled with compelling, logical arguments. Naturally, in matters of persuasion, truthful teaching is a good thing.[37] It's part of the whole competence piece, which we'll discuss in the next section. But a mouth filled with arguments that's not compelled by a heart filled with love will seldom engage and persuade teenagers. Audiences want to know that you care about them—and that you care about what you're telling them. What they want to sense is your passion for them.

Competence

In my opinion, over the last three decades few speakers have been as compelling as Tony Campolo. When Tony speaks, he does so with such authority, such passion, such force, and such saliva, that people simply accept what he has to say. And why not? After all, Tony graduated from an Ivy League school, he studied with Einstein, he has an earned doctorate, he travels all over the world, and he speaks about 500 days a year. He's also written enough books to fill a small library.

During his delivery, Tony never reveals any doubt in his content. He cites the works of obscure sociological writers whose names the average human can't even pronounce, let alone read their writings. And he yells a lot. Everything about Tony Campolo's delivery says, "Pay attention! I know what I'm talking about! I'm smart...very smart."

And people do pay attention—even people who strongly object to his premises—because Tony Campolo exudes *competence.*

But what about the rest of us? I'm from North Carolina. We don't talk fast and spit into the audience; we talk slowly and spit tobacco. I didn't go to an Ivy League school; I went to the University of North Carolina. (Our basketball team can out-dunk your honor student.)[38] I didn't study with Einstein—I thought he made bagels. And I don't quote many sociologists. I usually reference folks like Grisham, Clancy, Rowling, and Fields.

It's tough to portray competence when you don't feel competent: *I didn't do this. I don't have that.* You know the drill. But competence is an important element if your students are going to listen to you. So the question is—*How do you portray an authentic competence to your audience?* Here are some practical suggestions.

1. Know Your Stuff!

Study and prepare. (We'll talk more specifically about this in chapter 8.) When I was a high school student, I went to a seminar where a guy was going to talk to us about the subtle, hidden, evil messages of rock 'n' roll music. But I loved rock 'n' roll. I played drums in a rock 'n' roll band. So I'd already decided this guy didn't know what he was talking about before he even opened his anti-rock 'n' roll mouth.

But then about halfway through the seminar, he was discussing a song by a group called the Byrds (circa late 1960s) and how it was laced with vague references to drug use. Now I might have found all of this intriguing if he hadn't then cited the name of the song as "Nine Miles High," but the actual name of the song is "Eight Miles High." Of course, a reasonable person might think, *What's a mile between friends?* But this guy wasn't my friend, and when it came to *my* music, I wasn't reasonable. If this guy had any hope of gaining my attention, he needed to prove he knew what he was talking about. Instead, he was a mile off and a planet away from reaching me. He could have been correct with his premise, but he lost me because he hadn't done his homework. The moral to this story: Know your stuff.

- Know how to pronounce the names you'll need to pronounce (biblical locations, names, terms, and people who are part of the pop-culture lexicon).

- Know something about the movie or book you want to talk about.

- Go back and make sure you have your facts right about the sports story, the incident at the high school, what happened on the TV show you're referencing—especially if you lack firsthand knowledge. Why not run that kind of stuff by teenagers before you give the talk? Let them be your fact checkers.

- Conduct sound biblical exegesis so you can speak with confidence about what the Word is teaching (see chapter 8). Be sure you've considered some of the tough questions that might be raised by a text and possibly mention the questions you know they may have (e.g., "Some of you might be thinking..."). That statement will increase your credibility. It says, "I know what you're thinking, and I'm not afraid to deal with it."

2. Be Organized

If the students really know you, they might be patient with a few botched lines, an uncertain start, or the butchered name of their favorite music icon. But don't expect the audience to always play fair[39]—especially an audience of teenagers. The average listener might hear you say very standard things like:

- "Oh man, I forgot the exact passage..."

- "And, ummm..."

- "Oh, I've lost my train of thought..."

- "I don't know how to say what I want to say..."

- "Whoops, my media screwed up."

- "Oh, this *isn't* the scrapbooking banquet?"

But they'll quickly conclude that you lack competence. Maybe it shouldn't be that way, but it's often on the basis of that kind of stuff that an audience forms an impression of you.

Some suggestions:

- If you use media, check it in advance. Make sure it works properly and that your words are spelled correctly. And then double-check it. Your third point—GOD GIVES US HELP—isn't nearly as poignant when, thanks to a typo, the *p* in *help* is replaced with an l.

- If you plan to use teaching notes, make sure they're in order. Most of us know what it's like during those scary moments when you're hunting down page numbers and collating your talk *after* you've already started to deliver it.

3. Dress

Perhaps it shouldn't make a difference, but communication research shows that audiences do judge a speaker on the basis of physical appearance.[40] Just typing that sentence reminds me of the time when I was speaking at a conference to a few thousand teenagers, and I gave the entire talk with my shirt buttons misaligned. My dress said, "Now listen, guys, you can trust me to help you make serious, life-shaping decisions. Never mind that I don't have the necessary hand-eye skills to button my shirt properly."

Obviously this is not an exhortation for you to pimp your wardrobe, go gangsta, wear your boxers in a revealing manner, or get your old Rolling Stones tattoos updated. The key here is awareness. We all know how quick teenagers are to judge one another on the basis of appearance. Should we expect them to suspend those kinds of judgments when we stand up to speak? Fair or not, people will draw conclusions about you and about what you do based on how you look.

4. Fluent Delivery

The pace of your delivery communicates to an audience that you've given thought to your message. Teenagers can tell if the first time you've ever actually heard your talk is when you're delivering it to them. If you're a really good speaker, then maybe you can wing it on occasion; and maybe, on rare occasions, you'll need to. But audiences are funny—generally they want to believe you've thought about what you're going to say *before* you actually say it.

"But What If I'm Afraid?"

Of course, one of the biggest reasons some of us have trouble projecting competence is that we lack confidence. To some degree, it comes down to just plain old fear. Several years ago, a team of market researchers asked 3,000 Americans, "What are you most afraid of?"[41] Of course, lots of folks named more than one great fear, and we can probably assume that feelings have shifted a bit over the years. But this chart (Figure 4-1) gives a pretty clear picture of how most people feel about speaking.

Biggest Fear	Citing as Greatest Fear
Speaking before a group	41%
Heights	32%
Insects and Bugs	22%
Financial Problems	22%
Deep Water	22%
Sickness	19%
Death	19%
Flying	18%
Loneliness	14%
Dogs	11%
Driving/Riding in a car	10%
Riding in a car driven by dogs	9%
Darkness	8%
Elevators	8%
Escalators	5%

FIGURE 4.1

Speaking is kind of like skydiving: It's a lot of fun—and downright awe-inspiring if you're successful. But if you're unsuccessful, the consequences can be very unpleasant. For most of us, that's where the fear comes in.[42] Let's think about how to deal with fear.

1. Some Level of Fear Is Common and Completely Normal

Even with all of the years and all of the events and all of the talks, there is seldom an occasion when I stand up to speak to teenagers without feeling some level of apprehension. Call it fear, call it nervousness, call it a holy responsibility. But whatever it is, I wouldn't call it abnormal. In fact, I'd probably call it healthy to have some degree of fear. To proclaim the Word of God with clarity and accuracy is a holy and grave responsibility.

Of all the words penned by C.S. Lewis, the following have impacted me the most:

> The load, or weight, or burden of my neighbor's glory should be laid daily on my back, a load so heavy that only humility can carry it, and the backs of the proud will be broken. It is a serious thing to live in a society of possible gods and goddesses, to remember that the dullest and most uninteresting person you talk to may one day be a creature which, if

you saw it now, you would be strongly tempted to worship, or else a horror and a corruption such as you now meet, if at all, only in a nightmare. All day long we are, in some degree, helping each other to one or other of these destinations. It is in the light of these overwhelming possibilities, it is with the awe and circumspection proper to them, that we should conduct all our dealings with one another, all friendships, all loves, all play, all politics. There are no ordinary people. You have never talked to a mere mortal. Nations, cultures, arts, civilization—these are mortal, and their life is to ours as the life of a gnat. But it is immortals whom we joke with, work with, marry, snub, and exploit—immortal horrors or everlasting splendors. This does not mean that we are to be perpetually solemn. We must play. But our merriment must be of that kind (and it is, in fact, the merriest kind) which exists between people who have, from the outset, taken each other seriously—no flippancy, no superiority, no presumption. And our charity must be a real and costly love, with deep feeling for the sins in spite of which we love the sinner—no mere tolerance or indulgence which parodies love as flippancy parodies merriment. Next to the Blessed Sacrament itself, your neighbor is the holiest object presented to your senses.[43]

If you believe C.S. Lewis' words, there will always be—every time you speak—a certain degree of healthy fear when approaching the front of the room. Surely this is what Paul is talking about in 2 Timothy 2:15, "Do your best to present yourself to God as one approved, a worker who does not need to be ashamed and who correctly handles the word of truth." For most people who speak on a regular basis, the question is not whether they ever face fear or nervousness; the question is *How do I respond to fear?*

Here are some ideas to consider:

- Harness that negative energy to motivate you for better preparation (2 Timothy 2:15). One communication trainer put it this way: "It's not possible to remove your butterflies entirely; it is possible to get them to fly in formation."[44]

- Translate your fear into a passionate delivery.

- Let fear be your call to fervent, specific prayer. Pray for the audience—for open ears, open hearts, and open minds. Pray for yourself. Pray for the sound system (and if there isn't one, pray that you might get one). Pray for the parents in the back of the room who look angry because they want to get home. Pray that the band will stop repeating the same phrase over and over so you can get up to speak before the junior highers graduate to the college group.

2. Analyze What You Fear May Happen

Make a list and write down precisely what your fears are so you can address them. When you do this, don't settle for generalities:

- "I'm afraid it won't go well."

- "I'm afraid I'll humiliate my family."

- "I'm afraid of unemployment."

Generalities can't be remedied. Be specific about your fears. Chances are you'll discover that some of your fears are *irrational*.

- "If this talk doesn't go well tonight, it could wipe out our fall semester."

- "But what if I get my notes mixed up, and I totally freeze?"

- "I'm afraid the kids will take me hostage and begin using explosive gels to vandalize the youth room."

- "I'm worried that I'll make some minor exegetical error, and 10 years from now, I'll hear one of my kids being interviewed by James Dobson about how he became a serial killer, and the kid will point back to tonight's message as the time when he walked away from God."

These are the kinds of thoughts that come straight from the Enemy, and the only way to address them is to take them captive (2 Corinthians 10:5). Strangle them before they have a chance to breed.[45]

You'll also realize that some of your fears are *preventable*.

- One of my personal fears is that I'll be using a wireless mic and the battery will go dead—right in the middle of the talk. So now I've made it a habit to use a fresh battery or a wired microphone. Fear eliminated.

- I also have a concern about tripping over cables, either from the sound system or from my computer. So now I use wire wraps to make sure everything is secure and taped down before I start speaking. It takes a little extra set-up time, but it's one less thing I have to worry about. Another fear smacked down.

- I also have a fear of not having my shirt buttoned properly, so I have my wife dress me before I speak.

You'll see that some of your fears are practical.

- Maybe you're worried that your hands will shake or that your voice will crack. Common enough. Defeat that fear by practicing your message in front of a mirror. Do it several times until you feel more comfortable with what your body is doing. This is why athletes practice long hours. They want to train their bodies to perform without having to think about their performance.

- Maybe you're concerned that the wording isn't right, or the amazing illustration won't work, or the funny story is funny only to you. That's probably reason enough to take the practical step of asking someone who'll tell you the truth. Don't be afraid to ask a trusted friend, "What about this? Does it work? Does it make sense? Do you get it?" I'll occasionally be working on an idea, and I'll ask my wife, "There are two ways I can say this; which do you think is funnier?" Then I'll try them out, and she'll say something like, "Maybe you want to look for a third way...." Okay, not what I wanted to hear, but still helpful. Fear is born of uncertainty, and she's made any uncertainty about that particular story an impossibility.

Occasionally, I'll ask a small group of students to be part of my message preparation team and serve as my sounding board by simply listening to me talk through my message prior to giving it. I don't do this as often as I'd like, but when I do, it's always beneficial. They give me current illustrations; I receive direct feedback on what makes sense; and after I make their suggested changes, I gain a greater sense of confidence that what I've prepared will work.

If you choose to do this, use no more than a few students. (Number one, you don't want most of the students to hear your message ahead of time; and number two, you don't want it to become a pre-youth-group youth group.) Also, make sure you ask different students each time and be careful to use a diverse sampling—the skater guy, the one who wears nothing but black, the hip-hopper, the home-schooled kid, the home-schooled hip-hopper, and (especially) the student who thinks you're the most engaging speaker since Billy Graham.

3. You Probably Feel More Nervous Than You Seem

If you're uneasy about speaking, then your audience may feel uneasy about listening. To that extent, worrying that you won't connect with the audience can be a self-fulfilling prophecy. But that doesn't mean all of these things must come to pass.

- First of all, never let them see you sweat. Research has demonstrated that audiences rarely detect the anxiety the speaker says is present.[46] They won't know if you don't tell them. Remember the proverbial duck who looks calm and serene above the surface of the water, but underneath he's paddling furiously. Now, you might think, *That sounds like acting.* No, it's making the extra effort of laying aside your own natural feelings to put your audience at ease. If that's acting, then it's an act of care and concern.

- Since they won't know if you don't tell them, don't tell them. Stay away from tip-off statements like: "Wow, I can't believe how many (or how few) of you are out there," "Man, I just want you guys to know I'm really scared up here," "Gee, kids, I'm sweating in parts of my body they don't make sweat bands for." Just keep those comments to yourself.

- Focus on slow rhythmic breathing. When you slow down your breathing with deeper, more rhythmic breaths, that's your body saying to your brain, *Hey, relax. Just chill.*

- Always have a glass of water nearby. One of the physical manifestations of fear is a dry mouth; and when the mouth gets dry, the tongue can't interact with your teeth, your lips, and the roof of your mouth the way it needs to.[47] Then if you stumble over your words, your anxiety will be heightened. (Just a side note: I prefer to use a cup of water rather than a bottle because I can drink it more quickly and a little more subtly.)

Character

If caring opens the door, and competence gains you entry, then character allows you to stay engaged over time. I'm always encouraged by Paul's words in 1 Corinthians 2:1–5:

> When I came to you, I did not come with eloquence or human wisdom as I proclaimed to you the testimony about God. For I resolved to know nothing while I was with you except Jesus Christ and him crucified. I came to you in weakness with great fear and trembling. My message and my preaching were not with wise and persuasive words, but with a demonstration of the Spirit's power, so that your faith might not rest on human wisdom, but on God's power.

I read Paul's words, and I think, *No eloquence, no superior wisdom, no wise and persuasive words, but just weakness, great fear, and much trembling. Hey, I can do that!* I don't have to be Super Speaker to communicate effectively. I just need to faithfully live out the Jesus-life. Paul's ministry clearly reminds us that a demonstration is always more convincing than an explanation.

Obviously, when we look at Paul's preaching in the book of Acts, he was a competent, learned communicator. He knew his stuff. But he never banked his ministry on wise and persuasive words. He spoke them, but even more convincing was the way he lived them.

Early in my ministry, I spoke at a large outreach weekend at a church. They also brought in a big-name Christian rock band. All the guys in the band were from southern Mississippi, and they sounded like it. I'm from the South, so I speak *southern*; but these guys made the Dukes of Hazzard sound scholarly. In fact, there were twin brothers in the group. I don't remember their names—maybe Wilbert and Gilbert. And when they referred to each other on stage, they were like cartoon characters. They wouldn't say, "Wil" or "Gil." It was always, "Ma bruther, Geeelbert" and "Ma bruther, Weeelbert." That probably would have been okay, but they also gushed. Whenever they spoke from the stage about their relationship with Jesus, it was always this kind of a mushy, gushy, "Ain't he wonderful, young people?" or "Don'cha luv him, young folks?"

I probably wouldn't have thought that much about their speech, but having already spoken to these students three times prior to the concert, I'd come to think of them as a pretty snooty bunch. The church was affluent, cool was the order of the day, and their vibe was, "I dare you to bless me." So when the band performed, I was worried for them. Sure, they had really heavy accents, but they were brothers in Christ—and I was afraid these sophisticated teenagers would just eat them alive. During the entire concert, I kept praying, *Lord, don't let these guys be humiliated. Don't let these kids get turned off by* The Beverly Hillbillies Go to the Holy Land. *Please, Lord, these are sincere guys; don't let them be embarrassed.*

Finally, it was the end of the concert, and the band gave an invitation for the teenagers to respond to the love of Jesus. I looked up, and I saw students literally pushing chairs out of the way to get to the altar. Kids were crying, hugging each other, bowed down praying. I was shocked! Then I prayed, *Lord, pleez help me lern howta tawlk like those bruthers.*

The guys in the band weren't cool, but they loved Jesus. And there was something very real about their faith that God used to reach out and grab that group of students in a wonderful way. It definitely wasn't their wise and persuasive words. It was the way they demonstrated the Spirit's power.

Ultimately, judgments about who you are as a communicator aren't made by you, but by the teenagers seated in front of you. Depending on the venue and circumstances, even before you get up to speak that audience is asking questions and forming opinions about you. A wise speaker is aware of those questions and thinks about them long before her first words are spoken.

Consider These Questions

Just before this chapter closes, read through the following questions. They represent more or less an inventory of the kinds of questions you'll want to consider before you speak to your students.

Perceived Motivation to Speak

- *Am I flirting, seducing, raping, or just going through the motions because it's my job?*

- *Is my message born of compulsion and conviction or obligation (2 Corinthians 5:14)?*

- *Am I grinding an axe or am I mad at my audience?*

- *Is this a roundabout way of expressing my* (choose one: *political, musical, congregational, denominational, doctrinal*) *opinions to an impressionable audience?*

- *Am I speaking to the whole group about a matter that really concerns only one or two teenagers? Am I using this talk to avoid a difficult conversation?*

- *Do my students perceive this?*

Perceived Commonality

- *What do I have in common with these students?* Youth workers are almost always speaking to a younger audience. In some cases, quite a bit younger! We intuitively understand that the age difference puts us at a disadvantage because teenagers automatically suspect that our agenda isn't necessarily their agenda. They don't typically place the same amount of value on hearing a message as you do on speaking it. You can almost see it in their eyes. They're thinking: *Of course you're interested in God. You're old. You're going to die soon. Dude, when I get to be your age, I'll probably be interested in the afterlife, too. But for now, all I really care about is the location of the food.* So what are your connecting points? What do you have in common with them—memories, sports teams, movies, camps, failures, and so on?

- *Do teenagers see that we have these same points in common?*

Perceived Concern

- *Do I have a sincere love for these students?*

- *Why am I interested in the lives of these teenagers?*

- *Do they sense that I really care about them?*

Perceived Knowledge of the Subject

- *What qualifies me to give this talk?*

- *What do I know that they need to hear?*

- *Do my students perceive me as credible when I talk about this topic? Why or why not?*

Perceived Trustworthiness

- *Have I been true to my word in my personal encounters with my students?*

- *Do I have a hidden agenda?* For example: My message is on "evangelism," but what I'm really concerned about is low attendance for winter camp and we need more students to invite their friends. (NOTE: There's nothing wrong with wanting students to invite their friends to the winter camp as long as we're honest and up front about that. It becomes wrong when we use one topic as a decoy while we shoot at another.)

- *Am I honest with my audience?* (For my illustrations and stories, have I really read what I say, "I've read..."? Have I really studied what I say, "I've studied..."?)

- *Am I using pretense to impress?*

- *What*—and this is the real issue—*is my students' perception of my answer to the previous four questions?* It's not enough that you know you're trustworthy...your audience needs to know that as well.

CHAPTER FIVE

Listening to the Audience

One of the staple bits from late night comedy shows is highlighting crazy headlines and news stories, usually consisting of words that are misspelled or so poorly chosen that they change the intent of the message. Consider these gems:

- From a police blotter: "Sent city police out at 11:38 A.M. to kick kids off the roof of a downtown furniture store"

- "Shortly after 8:30 A.M., Wednesday, Feb. 22, a Sikorsky S76A Helicopter made an unscheduled crash a few yards off Rt. 19 at the Mansfield Rd. intersection"

- "One-legged man competent to stand trial"

- "Man says body is his wife, but she tells police it isn't"

- "Overnight, second-day mail will be delivered a day later"

- "Three ambulances carry blast victim to hospital"

We smile at these bloopers, but those of us in the church have also become fairly proficient at unclear communication:

- "The Hampton United Methodist Church will sponsor a Harvest Supper on Saturday, October 1...The menu for the evening will be *a traditional New England boiled sinner*, rolls, homemade apple pie, coffee, tea, and cider."

- "Hibben United Methodist Church will sponsor a chicken dinner on Saturday, March 2...Adults $4.50, children 12 and under, $2.50, *children under five free if eaten in the dining room.*"[48]

- "Thursday at 5 P.M. there will be a meeting of the Little Mother's Club. All wishing to become little mothers please meet with the pastor in his study."

- "This being Easter Sunday, we will ask Mrs. White to come forward and lay an egg on the altar."

- "For those of you who have children, and don't know it, we have a nursery downstairs."

- "On Sunday a special collection will be taken to defray the expense of the new carpet. All those wishing to do something on the carpet will please come forward during the offering."

These are mildly amusing (keyword: *mildly*). But in fact, these headlines and bloopers help illustrate one of the most basic truths of youth ministry communication: It's not about what we say; it's about what teenagers hear. It's not about what comes out of our mouths; *it's about what goes into their brains.*

It's a principle illustrated in a favorite Gary Larson cartoon. In frame one, titled "What we say to dogs," a guy yells at his dog, "Okay, Ginger, I've had it! You stay out of the garbage! Understand Ginger? Stay out of the garbage or else!" The second frame is titled "What dogs hear" and the bemused little pooch stares up at her master and hears, "Blah, blah, Ginger, blah, blah, blah, blah, blah, Ginger, blah, blah, blah..."[49]

Anything like that ever happen in your ministry? If it has, then you know *it's not about what we say to teenagers; it's about what they hear.* It all boils down to how the message is received and translated by those who hear it.

Of course we need to get the headlines right, but we also need to get into the heads of those who are going to hear the lines.[50] That's *pathos,* the emotional element of a message.

Or think of it this way: Every time you speak to teenagers, they're asking questions such as:

- *Does he really understand me?*

- *Does she care about me?*

- *Does he even like me?*

- *I wonder when he started losing his hair?*

Basic Premises That Shape Communication

Before we ask who the audience is, it's probably important to briefly consider why it matters. *Why* is the "who" important? It boils down to five basic premises that shape the way we think about communication.[52]

Premise #1: Tap into Their Needs and You Can Talk into Their Hearts

One of the most fundamental principles of communication is that "the audience is always sovereign" (1 Corinthians 9:19-23).[53] You gain permission to cross the communication bridge if, and only if, the students allow you access to their side of the bridge. In that sense, every time you speak to teenagers there is an immediate and unspoken negotiation between you and your audience. They agree to listen to you because they believe (a) that you understand their needs, (b) that you care about their needs, and (c) that you will address those needs.

Because they're humans who also happen to be teenagers, their perspective on needs can be a little...well, let's say, *skewed*. There are pseudo-needs they feel keenly, and very real needs they don't feel at all. But the bottom line is this: *Whatever those students perceive as their needs, that's the reality with which you must begin the communication process.* If you knock on that door, you'll usually be allowed inside.

Premise #2: Speak to the Big Questions and You'll Speak to Their Souls

A lot of youth workers get intimidated by the notion that "kids are so different today." And then, to heighten the inadequacy, we're told that all of these "different" kids are also drastically different from one another—that you have to communicate one way to one type of teenager (jock, computer geek, emo, goth, party animal, Calvinist), but then you have to communicate a completely different way to another type of teenager (surfer, headbanger, gangsta, spelling-bee freak, polka lover). And, to be sure, in some respects that's true. (If you don't believe us, try using your "God is the coach" athletic metaphors on the goth kid who despises sports.)

But maybe the big story is not how *different* all of our students are, but how *similar* they are. For example, anthropologists have noted that if we dig down deep enough (no pun intended) we can begin to see how human beings across the ages and around the world have been amazingly similar in their basic hopes and longings—young and old, North and South, East and West, black and white, yellow and brown, guys and girls, skaters and geeks, Red Sox fans and Yankees fans. Why? Because we're all created in the image of God.

It was Eugene Nida, one of the deans of missionary anthropology, who reduced all of these basic longings to four big questions[54]—questions that are still remarkably vivid in the life of every teenager—both *inside and outside* of your ministry.

1. "Am I loveable?" The quest for *community*. At the core, our students, like the rest of us, long to be loveable and love-able. Every statistic you read about teenagers and sexual promiscuity, every story you hear about broken families and scarred lives, every teenage clique and cluster in your ministry—*all of it*—is rooted in a deep, God-given desire to know and be known.

2. "Who am I?" The quest for *character*. This is the marriage of *identity* and *integrity*—the uniquely human desire to integrate who we are on the inside with who we are on the outside. One of the main realities of teenage life is the struggle to forge some sense of identity, to figure out who they are.[55]

3. "Why am I here?" The quest for *calling*. Standing beside the grave of his mother, Forrest Gump said longingly, "I don't know if we each have a destiny, or if we're all just floating around accident-like on the breeze."[56] With those simple words, he struck a chord that resonated deeply with those of us who've asked, in one way or another, "Does my life really matter?"

Author John Eldredge describes it like this:

"Our problem is that most of us live our lives like we've arrived 20 minutes late for the movie. The action is well under way, and we haven't a clue what's happening. Who are these people? Who are the good guys, and who are the bad guys? Why are they doing that? What's going on? We sense that something really important, perhaps even glorious, is taking place, and yet it all seems so random."[57]

Deep in the soul of every teenager is a desire for a calling, a part to play, a role in the story of life. At the end of the day, they want to feel that it will matter that they were here. They try to construct these narratives out of recognition, accomplishment, beauty, wealth, and popularity, and do so by shrinking big dreams to fit into small stories. But all they're left with is a hunger for a life that means something.

4. "Is there really a God?" The quest for *communion*. The most basic of all human longings is a longing for God. As Augustine puts it, "The thought of you [God] stirs mankind so deeply that he cannot be content unless he praises you, because you made us for yourself and *our hearts find no peace until they rest in you*" (emphasis added).[58] The myriad expressions of this longing are everywhere. Whether it be in the latest Hollywood blockbuster about life after death or the seminar that promises "spirituality coaching" or the Oprah author whose book promises that "faith can make a difference" or the crystal dangling from the rearview mirror or the mask-and-magic ritual of a tribal ceremony, human beings are inherently seekers.[59] Our students don't know what to call it, and they may not even know how to describe it, but they all start out with God-shaped holes in their souls.

Just consider how many songs, movies, magazine ads, television shows, and Internet sites speak to one of these four quests or questions. Why? Because this is where our teenagers live. Their hearts beat with these yearnings (Figure 5-1).

UNIVERSAL HUMAN QUESTS		
Longing to know and be known Psalm 139; 1 Corinthians 13:1-7a	"How can I love and be loved? How do I relate to other people?"	**Community**
Longing to know who I am Jeremiah 1:4-10, 1 Timothy 4:12	"Who am I and who do I want to be?"	**Character**
Longing to know why I am here Ecclesiastes 1:2-10	"What will I do with my life: do I want my life to count for something?"	**Calling**
Longing to know God Psalm 42:1-11	Is there is a God, and does God care about me?"	**Communion**

FIGURE 5-1   THE FOUR UNIVERSAL HUMAN QUESTS

What an amazing privilege to speak God's good news to those needs! You can do it in a hundred different ways. You can use texts and topics, stories and illustrations, media and music—you name it. You can put it in the unique language of the jock, the skater, the hip-hopper, or the Mac user. But if you don't know anything else about the teenagers you're speaking to, you can know for certain that when you speak to these four questions, you'll always be speaking to deep needs and hungry souls.

Premise #3: Speak to the Whole Life and Teenagers Are More Likely to Listen

All teenagers are on a journey in progress. Every time you speak to an audience, you're walking into a movie that's already begun. Whatever words you say are being spoken into a plot that is already unfolding—dramas you don't know about, dialogue of which you're unaware, subplots that are numerous and complex. Even the students themselves aren't fully aware of all the backstories, subplots, and characters on the stage. As social researcher Hugh Mackay says, "People are a pulsating bundle of attitudes, values, prejudices, experience, feelings, thoughts, sensations and aspirations."[60]

To put it simply, there aren't any kids in any youth meeting anywhere who walk into those settings as blank slates on which you simply write your message. They have lives, and those lives aren't lived in vacuums. When you speak to teenagers, you're speaking into a network of relationships, commitments, responsibilities, and circumstances. And when even one fiber of that web is touched, the vibrations impact every corner of life.

For example, when you speak to a ninth-grade guy whose friends are skaters, or a tenth-grade girl who's a cheerleader, or a 17-year-old guy who's part of a gang, or a 13-year-old girl who has an overbearing father, they aren't just listening to what *you* have to say. They're listening through the filter of what *their friends, their fellow cheerleaders, the guys in the gang, or their family members* might have to say about what *you* have to say.

Communication theorists call these clusters of relationships *reference groups*. They remind us that because we're human, we're interconnected through a matrix of relationships. Every time we listen to a message, we're asking, *How will my response to this message affect those relationships?* These reference groups may be made up of family members, good friends, kids on the team, the folks at an after-school job, members of a gang or club, even members of a youth group.

What we've learned from research on group conduct is that if the behavior change is trivial, groups normally grant their members lots of leeway in the choices they make. But if you've spent much time around teenagers, you've probably observed that the "rules" are pretty strict—there isn't much that's trivial to teenagers. The way you dress, the way you talk, the music you listen to, and the activities you're involved in can all have some real bearing in terms of your connection to a reference group.

Therefore, as a speaker I have to understand that my students aren't listening to me from a position of passionless, isolated logic. They're listening through the filters of their reference groups. They're not just asking themselves, *What do I think about this?* but they're also asking, *What will they think about how I think about this?*

Premise #4: Take Their Commitments Seriously if You Want Them to Take Commitment Seriously

Our job as youth workers is not to get kids committed; they're already committed. In fact, many of them are overcommitted. They may or may not be self-aware enough to name those commitments, but the commitments are real just the same. Unless we're preaching in never-never land, then every time we ask our teenagers to say yes we're also calling them to say *no* to an existing commitment.

To speak to students as if their current commitments aren't genuine is to be either very naive (*about* our audience) or very dishonest (*with* our audience). Whenever you speak, you've got to ask yourself, *What are the commitments already embraced by this group of teenagers?* and *What will persuade them to exchange a current commitment for a new or a renewed commitment to Christ?*

Premise #5: They're Not Just Hearing Your Message; They're Creating Your Message

Any experienced speaker knows what it's like to search the room during the message, hoping for any signs of connection, recognition, or consciousness, no matter how remote—but instead see mostly expressionless faces, eyes half-closed (actually *half*-closed is a good sign!), and body language that asks, *Uh...can we go now?* The perfect picture of "boredom on downers."

But don't think for a minute those students aren't involved in your message. They're always actively and critically involved in your talks in at least two ways. First of all, *they grant to you (or withhold from you) permission to speak into their lives*; and second, *they actively interpret what you say when you do speak.*

Let's look at each of these in a little more depth. *They grant to us (or withhold from us) permission to speak into their lives.* One of those youth ministry proverbs that will stand the test of time is—"You've got to earn the right to be heard." Kids won't donate their attention spans. Practically speaking, that means we want the audience to buy into the idea of paying attention to what we have to say. Wise youth workers will always shape their programming and their messages with the notion that *the first task is not to speak to the kids; the first task is to get them to listen.*

One helpful way to think about teenagers' willingness to listen is to understand it in terms of *the action continuum* (Figure 5-2).

HOSTILITY [permission not granted]	NEUTRALITY [permission, but no promises]	ACCEPTANCE [permission granted]
Defiant	Curious	Hungry to Hear
Disruptive	Willing to Listen, but Noncommittal	Eager to Learn
Unwilling to Listen		Teachable
Forced to Attend	Came for the Food, Willing to Listen to the Talk	

FIGURE 5-2   STUDENTS MAY GRANT US (OR WITHHOLD FROM US) PERMISSION TO SPEAK INTO THEIR LIVES.

Here's how it works: Let's pretend it's February, and for your midweek Bible study you've decided to conduct a four-week series on sexuality and issues of sexual purity. For the most part, the students in a youth group setting know you. From that standpoint, they might be a little more receptive to what you have to say about sexuality and sexual purity. And it seems fair to say there will be some curiosity about this topic. That also helps you gain their attention. (It sure beats your three-week series on supralapsarianism.)

On the other hand, sexual purity is a topic that will probably make some of your students uncomfortable. There may even be some outright opposition to purity. After all, some of the biblical notions about chastity and modesty are fairly countercultural. So we might expect the audience response to be mixed and skewed toward an unwillingness to listen. Were it a different topic and a different group, we'd likely see a completely different range of responses; but realistically, this could be a tough sell.

They're actively interpreting what we say. A brilliant TV commercial[61] from the French film industry promotes the notion that people need to see movies in the theater to fully understand them. (To really get the point of the commercial, you have to understand that the documentary film *March of the Penguins* was originally released in France as *March of the Emperors.*) In the 30-second ad, a guy is talking to a girl about this wonderfully powerful film he's seen. But as he describes the movie and it's depiction of the migration and mating habits of Emperor penguins, she thinks he's describing a documentary about French kings.

For example, when he describes the migratory march of the penguins, she imagines a long line of Napoleon-like rulers walking across the frozen tundra. When he describes the danger penguins face from attacking seals, she envisions a monstrous seal rising out of the water and terrorizing the marching line of kings. But when he communicates the wonder and beauty of the Emperors mating with each other and then transferring their eggs, she just looks at him with disgust.

It's a basic fact of communication: There's the message that we speak and the message that they hear. We create the first one, and they create the second one. Jesus' own ministry shows us that even a Master Communicator isn't going to change that reality (John 7:12-43). In practical terms, that means we're always alert for that one word, that one phrase, that one line or illustration that will establish and frame the picture—that will somehow put the scene in its proper context so our students will accurately hear what we're saying. We have to do that because they aren't just hearing the message; they're also creating the message.

Hostile, Neutral, Willing to Act: Three Different Audiences

How would it shape your message if you knew in advance the way students would respond? Suppose you knew that in a given speaking situation, the students' responses were likely to fall somewhere between cool and frigid. Would you:

> a. Plunge ahead and give 'em the gospel with both barrels?
>
> b. Arrange to have laryngitis that day?
>
> c. Use this as a strategic opportunity to give other team members a chance to step up and exercise their gift of teaching?
>
> d. Present the gospel, but adjust the message to fit the audience?

If you chose *b*, you're a wimp. If you chose *c*, you're a wimp who reads too many leadership development books. If you chose *a*, there might be a job for you in Christian television.

If Scripture is any kind of guide, the answer you should have chosen is *d*. *Different types of audiences require different types of approaches.* (Figure 5-3)

ACTION CONTINUUM

HOSTILE	BELIEVE AGAINST: DON'T BUY IT BUT NOT HOSTILE	NEUTRAL	BELIEVE FOR: BELIEVE IT BUT DON'T BEHAVE IT	WILLING TO ACT: BELIEVE & BEHAVE
Entertain	Inform	Change Belief	Convince	Move to Action

MAIN EFFORT IS PERSUASION

FIGURE 5-3   IF WE UNDERSTAND WHERE STUDENTS ARE ON THE ACTION CONTINUUM, IT HELPS US SHAPE THE BEST COMMUNICATION APPROACH.

Let's flesh out the action continuum a bit more by looking at a hostile audience, a skeptical audience, and an open audience.

Hostile Audience

As a result of our hypothetical series on sexuality, one of your students persuaded her high school health teacher to invite you to speak in her sex education class (a secular setting). You're excited because it's a good opportunity to be light in the midst of darkness, but it's also a pretty different venue. The students don't know you, they don't hold a biblical worldview, nor do they have a biblical understanding of sexuality. Plus, your message is radically different from the one they've been hearing from a teacher they do know and who is very much admired (by some students at least). This is apt to be a fairly hostile audience, and they may make that point perfectly clear by their comments, their questions, their disinterest, and perhaps even their desire to disrupt your presentation.

For the most part, your best approach is to merely *entertain*. Now, don't assume that means stand-up comedy, because it doesn't. For one thing, there's nothing less entertaining than someone who isn't funny trying really hard to be funny. (Since you've read to this point in the book, you probably already know how true that is.)

Entertain, in the sense that we mean it here, is what happens when someone is invited to your house for the first time. You *entertain* them. You're trying to make them feel comfortable. You're trying to build a bridge so that, later on, maybe the bridge can lead to a connection.

Think, for example, of the decision to confront your neighbor about his pit bull because the cute little guy (the dog, not the neighbor) keeps chewing the bumper off your Hummer. You and the neighbor both know what this conversation is about. You both know it could be uncomfortable. You're concerned that he could just storm out of the house and never even listen to you. And you're a little concerned he might bring along the dog in question (which is why your children have been locked in a bathroom upstairs). It makes little sense to approach this meeting and come out with both guns blazing, complaints spewing, and threats flying. Your neighbor simply isn't going to hear it.

As we all need to be reminded, the goal of good communication is not to win an argument; it's winning a person (that's persuasion). What's the point of providing really great content to an audience that isn't even going to hear it? (See Matthew 7:6.) From our earlier discussions of *psychological reactance*, we know that the harder an audience feels pushed, the more likely they are to push back.[62] So you *entertain*. It doesn't mean you say nothing; it means you realize that you don't need to say *everything* on the first visit.

Surely this is why some made the accusation that Jesus entertained drunkards, tax collectors, and sinners (Matthew 9:11; 11:19; Luke 5:30; 15:2; 19:1–10). It wasn't a question of Jesus having nothing to say to them or being afraid to say it. He just knew it was useless to say much until they were willing to listen.

Skeptical Audience

These are the students in the room who've already formed strong opinions against what you're teaching. Unlike those who are hostile, skeptics are willing to listen, but they aren't neutral (Figure 5-4). They'll have to be convinced that there is merit to what you're saying. They need to be *informed*.

HOSTILE	BELIEVE AGAINST: DON'T BUY IT BUT NOT HOSTILE	NEUTRAL	BELIEVE FOR: BELIEVE IT BUT DON'T BEHAVE IT	WILLING TO ACT: BELIEVE & BEHAVE
Entertain	Inform	Change Belief	Convince	Move to Action

MAIN EFFORT IS PERSUASION

FIGURE 5-4

This isn't simply a matter of presenting evidence. Communication specialists tell us there are several steps[63] in this dance from being a closed mind to being a mind willing to embrace. And what's most significant is that *"the primary ingredient in each step is an emotional response rather than an increase of knowledge."*[64] In other words, ultimately it won't just be the evidence that demands a verdict.[65] Emotion gets to vote. The door that inches open is hung on two hinges: head *and* heart. That's one reason why the Holy Spirit's ministry is so critical. The Spirit moves the message beyond our words, convicting of sin and convincing of truth, penetrating to where bone and spirit meet (Hebrews 4:12).

Open Audience (Anything from Neutral to Willing to Act)

Typically, persuasion of this audience comes in small steps. Communication researchers call this the *foot-in-the-door* syndrome.[66] Essentially it's based on the observation that people who respond positively to a small "ask" are more likely to respond to a bigger "ask" later on (Figure 5-5).

HOSTILE	BELIEVE AGAINST: DON'T BUY IT BUT NOT HOSTILE	NEUTRAL	BELIEVE FOR: BELIEVE IT BUT DON'T BEHAVE IT	WILLING TO ACT: BELIEVE & BEHAVE
Entertain	Inform	Change Belief	Convince	Move to Action

MAIN EFFORT IS PERSUASION

FIGURE 5-5

Remember the adult volunteer who was willing to help behind the scenes but had "no intention of teaching or leading a small group of adolescent delinquents"? And remember how you said, "Oh, of course we don't need you to teach; we just need you to help with refreshments." And then, one ask led to another ask, and that ask led to another ask, and now that volunteer is Billy Graham! Okay, just kidding. But you get the idea. Leading kids through the latter part of the action continuum is a step-by-step process—a progression from small ask to big ask that appeals to the head *and* the heart.

So understanding the action continuum can help you to target your communication more effectively. That's important. But it can also help you think about how to increase your students' willingness to listen.

Opening Up the Audience

As a communicator, you want to do everything possible to open the audience to what you have to say. If communication is a bridge, you want to try to make that bridge as short and wide and inviting as possible. From a practical standpoint, there are several strategies you can use to help your audience be more open to your message.

Creating Openness: The Flow of the Program

To some extent, the speaking part of your ministry hinges on every other facet of your youth ministry program. For example, think about the way this principle plays out on the average weekend retreat. Kids begin forming their opinions about the credibility of the spoken messages from the moment they arrive at the church parking lot. Do the adults interact with kids? Is any effort made to help newcomers feel welcome? Is the music during the van ride congruent with the other messages of the weekend? What are the attitudes of the adults and other people in authority? And, of course, those impressions continue to be formed throughout the retreat event, from the ride up in the van to the quality of the accommodations and the food on site. (Sorry about the last two—accommodations and food. You may now be thinking, *Oh, we're in trouble.*)

This is all "programming" that impacts the receptivity of the message prior to its delivery. By the time you get up to speak, any one of those elements can sabotage or strengthen the talk before you utter the first word. One of the most basic principles of youth ministry is that a student must feel environmentally comfortable before he can become theologically aware.

I remember speaking at a denominational weekend event, when literally, the first words to come out of the emcee's mouth at the very first meeting on Friday night were, "Okay, look. Last year at this event we had somebody urinate on the wall of the men's room, and we're not going to have that this year!"

You could see it on the kids' faces: They were looking at each other and thinking, *Gee, this is going to be fun!* Unfortunately, the second phrase out of this guy's mouth was, "Now, here's our speaker, Duffy Robbins." I was so taken aback, all I could think to say was, "I promise—it wasn't me...I wasn't even here last year!" All of a sudden, I'm no longer starting at square one. Because of the "don't urinate on the wall" comment every teenager in the room is on the defensive. Now I'm not starting at square one, I'm starting at about square negative-ten.

The program and message content are shaped by the notion that we have to earn the right to be heard.

This chart[67] (Figure 5-6) shows how the programming at a weekend event might be constructed to make the students environmentally comfortable so they can be made theologically aware. If an event were structured along the lines suggested by this chart, we'd expect the Friday night session to have a relatively short message with more emphasis on creating an atmosphere conducive to communication. That might be reflected in the types of music used, the amount of media, skits, fun, and so on, as well as the pacing of the session. The idea is for that first session on Friday night to set the stage (or in the language of Matthew 13, "prepare the soil") for the seed to be planted in the remaining three sessions. The intent in the first session isn't to get students to *cross* the bridge; it's to get students to step *onto* the bridge—to help them be open to the possibility that there might be something worthwhile on the other end.

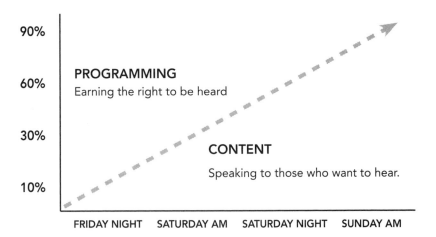

FIGURE 5-6   PROGRAMMING FLOW CAN HAVE AN IMPACT ON HOW RECEPTIVE TEEN-AGERS ARE TO A MESSAGE.

Then perhaps on Saturday morning, and surely by Saturday night, there's a shift in the balance. The Saturday night message would be more intentional. Programming and pacing would still be important, but there would be more of an emphasis on saying what you came to say. By Sunday morning, it's not that programming and pacing are unimportant, but the agenda would be shaped less by earning the right to be heard and more by galvanizing the decisions and forward progress of those who chose to listen.

This is only one example, of course. But it demonstrates how your message and the program that surrounds that message must be cohesive. It's not about isolated tiles of programming. It's about a total mosaic that hopefully helps your teenagers to see the big picture clearly.

Creating Openness: Your Credibility as a Speaker

Depending on the audience, this may be a factor of relational connection, physical appearance, title, credentials, sense of humor, or competence in some specialized field—like athletics. (See the section about *ethos* in chapter 4.)

Creating Openness: The Spiritual Maturity of the Students

The apostle Paul's direct words to the Church at Corinth remind us that not every message is appropriate for every believer: "Brothers and sisters, I could not address you as spiritual but as worldly—mere infants in Christ. I gave you milk, not solid food, for you were not yet ready for it. Indeed, you are still not ready" (1 Corinthians 3:1–2; Hebrews 5:12). Clearly, Paul wasn't watering down the message, but he was trying to serve it up in a way that his audience could digest.

Within every youth ministry setting, the students involved will be at varied levels of commitment and spiritual maturity. Ideally, they would all be eager disciples, ready to grow, thirsty for Bible study, and asking if they could please borrow your Bible dictionary and concordance for the weekend. But realistically, there will be some students who are truly committed, some who are moderately committed, some who are neutral in their commitment, some who are moderately *un*committed, some who are *radically* uncommitted, and some who just need to be committed before they harm someone (more on this in chapter 9).[68]

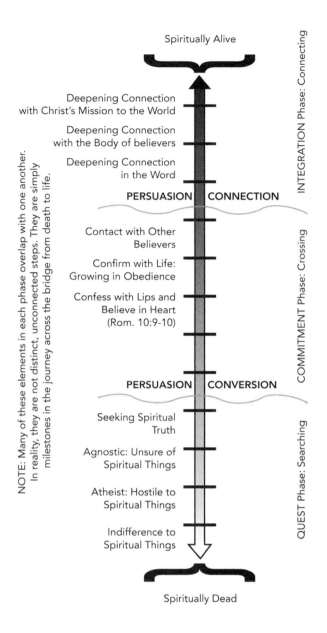

Spiritually Alive

INTEGRATION Phase: Connecting

Deepening Connection
with Christ's Mission to the World

Deepening Connection
with the Body of believers

Deepening Connection
in the Word

PERSUASION | **CONNECTION**

Contact with Other
Believers

Confirm with Life:
Growing in Obedience

Confess with Lips and
Believe in Heart
(Rom. 10:9-10)

COMMITMENT Phase: Crossing

PERSUASION | **CONVERSION**

Seeking Spiritual
Truth

Agnostic: Unsure of
Spiritual Things

Atheist: Hostile to
Spiritual Things

Indifference to
Spiritual Things

QUEST Phase: Searching

Spiritually Dead

NOTE: Many of these elements in each phase overlap with one another. In reality, they are not distinct, unconnected steps. They are simply milestones in the journey across the bridge from death to life.

FIGURE 5-7. *PEACE'S THREE PHASES OF SPIRITUAL RESPONSE HELP US TO EVALUATE THE SPIRITUAL MATURITY OF OUR STUDENTS SO WE CAN MEET THEM AT THEIR POINT OF NEED.*

Tailoring our message to the appropriate level of spiritual commitment can reduce resistance to the truths we want to communicate. Missiologist Richard Peace has offered us a way of thinking about this by dividing the spiritual pilgrimage into three phases (Figure 5-7): The *Quest Phase*, the *Commitment Phase*, and the *Integration Phase*. [69]

A message tailored to meet the students in the Quest Phase is going to be very different in content and length from a message designed to meet teenagers in the Integration Phase. Bottom line: Make sure the message you give fits the commitment level of the students in the room, not the students you wish were there or hoped would be there or parents believe *are* there, but the ones who are there.

Creating Openness: Students' Openness to New Ideas

In this age of postmodernism, where there is a suspicion of absolutes and certainty, we have to recognize the influence of culture on our teenagers. That doesn't mean we need to censor the Word of God. What it does mean is that we need to be sensitive about how we express it.

In his book *Preaching to a Postmodern World*, Graham Johnston offers these suggestions:

1. Choose carefully and strategically what to say. Not every point should carry the same weight as in, "I'll go to the Cross for this." Be mindful not to allow salvation by faith to take an equal footing with the prohibition to attend R-rated movies. Know what's critical for the moment, and what's secondary.

2. Learn to speak in a positive manner about what the Christian faith is, and not what it's not. If people perceive a "preacher" taking a cheap shot at other people, other denominations, or even other religions, their faith becomes suspect as petty and mean-spirited. Learn to affirm the truth without resorting to an attacking style that may appear vindictive and create a sympathy backlash against your message.

3. Openly acknowledge that amid the categories of right and wrong, Christians do face a world of gray, where not all of life's answers are simple and cut and dry. Oversimplifying life's issues will only increase the postmodern skepticism.

4. Admit to your own struggles and allow your listeners to see that you know you haven't arrived yet. Even in preaching, we're all traveling the same road, the journey of faith in Christ. Your teenagers know you're farther down the road than they are, but they need to know that you don't think you've "arrived" yet.

5. Don't go looking for a fight. When you argue a minor point, people will lose sight of the main point you wish to convey. Ravi Zacharias declares: "In addressing skeptics, the biggest trap is getting sidetracked into symptomatic issues. The most volatile of these, of course, are sexuality and abortion."[70]

Creating Openness: The Potential Threat of the Message

Students are asking, *What are the potential costs if I respond to this message?* (John 6:60, "This is a hard teaching. Who can accept it?")

Creating Openness: The Language You Use

Missionary Cam Townsend founded the Wycliffe Bible Translators because a Guatemalan Indian posed to him the question, "Why doesn't your God speak my language?" It's still one of the great, fundamental questions that teenagers ask about our teaching. This question doesn't mean we should speak like teenagers ("Ohmigosh that would be, like, *so* lame if we did!"), but we surely need to craft our messages based on how teenagers speak.

Creating Openness: The Time and Place of the Message

We've all had conversations in which someone has said, "Can we talk about this later? Now is not a good time." The ambiance of time and place makes a difference in what we hear and the way we hear it. A group that is open and receptive in a late-night lock-in setting might not be so interested the following morning. The message that seemed powerful and inspiring when you gave it around the campfire somehow seems cold and sterile during the Wednesday night Bible study. Time and place matter. That's why wedding proposals are made in romantic, softly lit bistros and not in the drive-through line at Taco Bell.

Creating Openness: The Moods of the Students

Sometimes a crisis at school or a national news story provides a unique window of opportunity to address a topic with our students when that topic might otherwise be very tough to talk about.

Creating Openness: Crowding

Yeah, believe it or not, there is substantial evidence that having students crowd together in a room makes them more susceptible to persuasion than would be the same number of kids sitting in a larger room.[71] Moral to the story: Always use a room—or at least try to arrange the room you're using—so the students feel crowded.

Creating Openness: Humor

Communication research has confirmed what most youth workers have learned through experience: Humor makes an audience more open to persuasion. Numerous studies have shown that "appropriate humor relaxes an audience making them feel more at ease and breaks down barriers to increase receptivity to a speaker's ideas."[72] Again, that doesn't mean you need to be Rev. David Letterman. If you're naturally funny, that's great. But for the humor-impaired, there are wonderful resources for visual humor (still pictures, funny movies, outtakes, clever television commercials, YouTube clips) and humorous stories on the Internet. One of the keys to being funny is not creating humor but learning to see it in everyday life.

Creating Openness: The Perceived Relevance of the Message

This may be the most important gateway factor. Are we speaking to their felt needs? One of the ways that we can get at this kind of question is by asking of every biblical text, before we speak on it, four simple questions:

1. What would my students find hard to embrace in this text? What would my students doubt to be true?

2. What do my students need to know or re-hear in this text?

3. With which inner feelings, longings, hopes, and hurts does this passage connect in their lives? How will they *feel* this truth?

4. If this text is true, what does it say about the world in which my students live? What might they need to rethink or reevaluate if they accept the truth of this message?[73]

Jesus understood that even the disciples had limits to what they might hear. And whether it was due to their lack of maturity or their circumstances at the time, Jesus was wise enough not to push matters beyond their limits, "I have much more to say to you, more than you can now bear" (John 16:12). Understanding the action continuum helps us temper our messages to the teenagers who will hear them.

Listen Before You Speak

The whole thrust of this chapter has been to help us think about the emotional dimension of the message so before we decide *what* we plan to say (*logos*), we'll give careful attention to *whom* we hope to say it (*pathos*). Now in the remaining pages of this book, we'll move to the talk itself (*logos*): Planning, creating, and delivering a talk that touches the hearts and the heads of our teenage audience.

CHAPTER SIX

A Good Message Starts with Thoughtful Planning and Careful Preparation

Chris Bender, 22 years old, was by all accounts one of the most conscientious workers in the Hamilton Standard Maintenance Facility at Rock Hill, South Carolina. His skill in doing the "taper bore work" on the aircraft propellers manufactured and inspected by Hamilton Standard earned him the respect of his coworkers and supervisors. Meticulous and thoughtful, Bender often arrived early in the day so he could do his most exacting work before afternoon fatigue set in. He was described as a mechanic who "followed instructions to the letter." What a great trait to have... unless he was following instructions that turned out to be wrong.

In fact, it was National Transportation Safety Board (NTSB) inspectors who determined that it was precisely this factor that led to the deterioration of the blade on the left propeller assembly of Atlantic Southeast Airline flight #590 as it was in mid-flight, on a short trip from Atlanta, Georgia, to Gulfport, Mississippi. Only a few minutes after departure, the 26 passengers, along with a crew of three, realized something was wrong. They heard a loud bang and then saw through the passenger windows on the left side of the aircraft the spectacle of a mangled propeller assembly that had chewed up most of the left wing. It would be a horrifying nine minutes and 20 seconds before the Embraer ENB 120 fell several thousand feet and crashed into Paul Butler's cornfield near Carrollton, Georgia. In the fiery wreckage, 10 people lost their lives, and almost everyone who survived received serious burns. The blade that caused the accident—serial number 861398, style 14RF9—had been inspected, prepped, and approved for flight by none other than conscientious worker, Chris Bender.

In the massive yearlong investigation that followed, the NTSB determined that the fault for the crash should be laid at the feet of the Hamilton Standard Maintenance Facility. The NTSB board concluded their finding with this observation, "Although the sanding repair *was inappropriate* and *had camouflaged a deeper crack in the propeller blade* from being detected in the later inspection, *Chris Bender had done essentially as he was instructed*"[74] (emphasis added).

It was that short sentence that told a sad story—the story of a conscientious young man[75] who performed as he was trained to perform,[76] but who had in fact been incorrectly trained. It wasn't a failure of effort or technique; it was a failure of objective. The crash of Flight 529 was a classic and tragic example of how doing the *right* things is more important than doing *things* right.

Most of us in youth ministry are temperamentally predisposed to action. We don't like to think so much about *why* or *what*; instead, we prefer to buy books that tell us *how*. We desperately want to know how to make it work "in the trenches" because it's in the trenches that we feel the desperation. And that's not such a good thing!

Unfortunately, our approach to warfare in the trenches is often, "Ready… Fire…Aim!" We expend a lot of unprofitable time and energy on "how to" because we don't often give enough serious thought to "how come?" If Chris Bender's story teaches us anything, it's that doing the wrong things—even if done with great care, creativity, intention, passion, love, and skill—can still lead to ministries and ministers who crash and burn.

What and Why?

Before we jump into the next section of this book on *how* to prepare your message, we want to help you think about *why* you're giving a particular message and how to plan *what* your message might be. The remaining half of the book talks about technique, but before we get there, let's spend a little time and focus on the right objectives:

- What will you talk about?

- Why are you giving that specific talk, and how does it tie in with what's happening in your overall program?

- What will be the primary objective of your message: evangelism, nurture, leadership development, or something else altogether?

- Will it be a topical or textual message?

- Who will you unashamedly plagiarize?

What Will You Talk About?

The vast majority of youth workers are convinced that Bible study should be a main component of their ministry's program. But the confusion I often hear voiced by both volunteers and professionals generally revolves around two questions: *What do I teach?* and *How do I teach it?* Hopefully this book has already helped you to think about the latter question. So let's focus a bit on the first question.

Somewhere around the 10-year point in my own youth ministry experience, I began to realize that I was teaching some of the same topics over and over again and that I didn't really have a plan. I was improving my speaking skills, but that could just mean I was getting better at saying stuff my students didn't need to hear. I went back over three years' worth of messages and discovered that (a) we spent almost six times as much time in the New Testament as we did in the Old Testament; (b) we spent more time studying general topics than we spent studying specific biblical texts; and (c) our teaching curriculum was more a reflection of my training and biases than it was a reflection of the whole counsel of God.

I decided to get together with my volunteers and talk with them about this situation. I also discussed my observations with our pastor and some godly members of our Youth Advisory Team. As a result, we developed a curriculum plan of topics and texts that we wanted our teenagers to be exposed to prior to graduation. We began with the basic assumption that we might have a student in youth ministry for three years. We were in a highly mobile, middle- to upper-middle-class community, and we weren't naive about the fact that there would be students who were exposed to our group less than three years. However, a three-year stay seemed a reasonable assumption for the majority of the group. We also figured we could repeat this three-year cycle and essentially cover grades 7 through 12. We then discussed what kinds of topics and themes we wanted our students to be exposed to by the time they graduated from high school. That process helped us develop the curriculum you see below (Figure 6-1).[77]

7TH/10TH GRADE	8TH/11TH GRADE	9TH/12TH GRADE
BIBLE		
Gospels	Letters of John	Book of Acts
Who Is Jesus?	Romans	The Holy Spirit
What is a Christian?	Who is God?	Study of Nehemiah
Genesis	Study of Jeremiah	Study of Jonah
Study of David	Study of Exodus	1 Timothy, 2 Timothy
Study of Paul	Study of James	1 Thes., 2 Thes.
How to Study the Bible	Prayer	Parables of Jesus

7TH/10TH GRADE	8TH/11TH GRADE	9TH/12TH GRADE
LIFE		
Peer Pressure	Making Wise Choices	Knowing God's Will
Dealing with Temptation	Stewardship/Money	Sex/Dating
	Drugs/Alcohol	Lifestyle Evangelism
Friendships	Family	Christian View of Marriage
Self-Image		
BODY		
What is the Church?	Worship	Spiritual Gifts
Body Life	Caring for Others	Mission
Call to Service	Church Membership	Relationships within the Body; confrontation, encouragement, etc

FIGURE 6-1.   LONG-RANGE CURRICULUM PLAN

Obviously, each local youth ministry is going to have different texts and topics they'll emphasize based on the unique and different needs of their teenagers. But this can serve as an example to get you thinking this way so you can develop your own chart and long-term plan. It should be noted here that we made up a similar plan with some of the same topics for our midweek Bible study. That meant that students who came to our Sunday night youth group and our smaller Wednesday night Bible study might hear some topics or texts more than once, but we didn't identify that as a dangerous problem. Also, we intentionally covered some topics (sex and dating) more than once in a three-year period. But whenever we repeated a topic, we used different curricula or came at the topic from a different angle. We kept in mind that good communication and solid biblical education require some repetition.

We broke all the topics and texts into three broad categories that represented a healthy balance—Bible, Life, and Body:

1. Bible—topics anchored in and suggested by the biblical texts

2. Life—essentially lifestyle issues, a topical way of addressing how to apply what we'd heard and studied in the Word

3. Body—some of the core issues that related to "being the body of Christ" and living out kingdom values as a Christian community, both locally and globally

Obviously, we understood that the whole counsel of God is not so easily separated into these three tidy categories. But this approach helped us think strategically about what we wanted our teenagers to know and live out. Once we identified the messages, we could plan for them and around them—this became an important foundation as we tried to build a healthy youth ministry.

If you choose to develop a potential curriculum like this, you might want to get input from a wide range of sources: students, parents, leadership overseeing your ministry, coworkers (paid or volunteer), peers in youth ministry, and others who've walked with God for many years and might have some additional wisdom. But when you gather multiple opinions, don't feel pressured to cover every topic suggested (or you'll wind up doing a five-week series on the biblical benefit of a clean room and the importance of obeying authority figures).

Still, it's wise to let people know their ideas are heard and appreciated. And, of course, if you ignore the felt needs of the students and only teach them what you think they should know about the Bible, doctrine, and theology (i.e., "We're going to keep talking about premillennialism until they all agree with me."), you'll find yourself teaching an empty room. (On a positive note, this makes your prep and planning a lot easier.)

The advantage of this kind of long-range approach to topic planning is that it helps us avoid three common mistakes in speaking:

1. Teaching our pet topics repeatedly

2. Teaching some topic just because we have a cool new media resource

3. Trying to determine your message from week to week

A plan like this (even if it's held "loosely") helps us make sure our teaching is guided by long-term objectives and not just short-term whims, current trends, or a regurgitation of the last devotion you read.

Why This Specific Talk? How Does It Tie In?

No individual youth meeting stands alone. Every meeting you plan, every talk you give, and every event you do is part of the larger mosaic of your youth ministry program. In one sense, what that means is that every tile of the mosaic has to fit with the overall big picture. A lot of us are guilty of just piecing together a bunch of neat little tiles of "youth stuff" without really considering how it all fits together. When this happens, we end up with something less than a work of art. To maximize the impact of each individual message, you'll want to give thought to how your talk on a given night ties in with another message you gave the week before—and how those two talks might tie in with what's happening with other facets of your youth ministry.

There are lots of different ways of doing this, and the best one is the one that works best for *your* ministry. But if this feels like a new concept for you, here's a simple way to think "big picture" about your ministry. Let's say, for the sake of simplicity, that there are three broad pieces to a balanced youth ministry environment: *outreach, nurture,* and *leadership development.* Your talks at various times will reflect each of these three emphases.

- *Outreach:* Your speaking is targeted to unchurched students.

- *Nurture:* Your speaking is targeted to students who've made an initial commitment to follow Jesus and now need motivation and training for their spiritual growth.

- *Leadership Development:* Your speaking is aimed at students who are willing to take an additional step in their faith, discover their ministry area, and possibly own some piece of the leadership for the youth ministry.

Thinking in these three broad ways can help you maintain balance as you plan messages for a given three-to-six-month period. One way to conceptualize it is to think of the year in terms of youth ministry "seasons." Try to recognize that certain times of the year lend themselves to certain types of ministry emphases, and therefore to certain types of topics and themes when you speak.

This idea could vary by region of the country and even by the events and emphases within a certain community. But, as an example, Fall often feels like a natural time to emphasize outreach/evangelism. In the Fall you have the potential to reach new teenagers who've never attended youth group before. Teenagers have new energy and motivation to develop relationships at the beginning of the school year. They've just moved up to a new grade, they may have relocated into the area,

There are several ways to say the same thing, and Duffy and I are definitely like-minded, but we've chosen to use different terms over the years. When I teach Purpose Driven Youth Ministry (PDYM), I simply slice things a little more specifically. Instead of *Outreach, Nurture, and Leadership Development,* I've used the terms *Evangelism, Fellowship, Discipleship, Ministry,* and *Worship.* But for the sake of clear communication, we decided to go with Duffy's terms. (Plus, my mother taught me to respect my elders.)

I'd view *Outreach* as similar to *Evangelism. Nurture* would encompass the biblical purposes of *Discipleship* and *Fellowship.* And I view Duffy's definition of *Leadership* as being similar to how I challenge teenagers to get involved in serving God through their *Ministry.* Finally, I view all of these—regardless of the terms—as an act of *Worship.*

For more information on building a youth ministry that reflects the biblical purposes of evangelism, fellowship, discipleship, ministry, and worship, you might want to check out Purpose Driven Youth Ministry or www.PDYMcommunity.com. —Doug they're joining new organizations and new teams—basically the Fall is a season where teenagers are open to change and hoping to be invited to something. Because of this, an emphasis on outreach/evangelism might be translated into every facet of your ministry—the topics you choose for small groups, the direction of your leadership training, the way you organize and shape a Fall retreat, the manner in which you motivate your key or "regular" students to reach out and invite their friends, how you teach your message, and how you communicate to parents. Basically, this emphasis can impact everything (especially your teaching). Each piece of the mosaic is part of a larger picture.

And then, let's say, by November, when the main thrust of the beginning-of-the-new-school-year emphasis begins to level off, that would be a reasonable time to then shift gears and teach on topics and themes more related to nurture or discipleship. However, when you transition to another emphasis, you'd still have outreach/evangelism on your mind and ministry radar—it's not finished until next Fall. It's just not emphasized as strongly.

For example, if a new teenager comes to one of your nurture events and says, "I'd like to know more about making a commitment to Christ," you're not going to say, "Uh...well, I'm sorry but that usually happens in the early Fall. Right now we're into discipling, but we'll be sure to get back to you during our next outreach emphasis."

Your shift in emphasis can be woven through every facet of the program so that what's happening in small groups, or in Sunday school, or in midweek Young Life Club serves as a complement to support the message you're presenting in any given week. By using the natural tides of your ministry, the school seasons, and the calendar year, you can best choose when to teach the texts and topics you've planned.

But adequate planning is only one of the keys to effective communication. Once you've determined what to say, you need to plan carefully how to say it.

Careful Preparation

When Duffy and I travel together, we almost always eat at a steak-type restaurant. And there is usually one driving motivator to our dining decisions—Duffy.

Duffy is a great friend, but he's definitely a little odd when it comes to food. He doesn't eat any food that ends in a pronounced vowel. I'm not making this up! Cake—yes. Spaghetti—no. Barbecue—yes. Lasagna—oh no. Cookie—yes, but it has to be more than one. Having known him now for almost 20 years, I'm aware of four exceptions to this policy: banana, tomato, mahi (fish), and Chick-fil-A (for which he gladly waives all vowel rules and, if tempted, might disavow his own children). He even says *no* to the ultimate youth ministry cuisine—pizza.

At home, I frequent Taco Bell. I like it, and it's cheap. Of course, when Duffy and I are on the road together, he routinely dismisses Taco Bell because it specializes in foods that end with pronounced vowels. And Duffy is just a steak-and-potatoes kind of guy. (Although, he won't eat just one potato, since it ends in a pronounced vowel.) Therefore, he always guides our restaurant selections toward a great steak house—lots of beef, many potatoes, and not a vowel in sight. It gets expensive eating out with him; so fortunately, we live on opposite sides of the continent.

Still, we've eaten in some great restaurants over the years. And, nothing against Taco Bell, but you know what? It's really easy to tell the difference between a well-cooked meal and fast food. In a fine-dining restaurant, the food tastes better, the preparation looks better, the environment feels better, and the dining experience is more rewarding overall.

Well Cooked Versus Fast Food

This principle is also true when it comes to communication. When I bypass the temptation of "fast-food" message preparation and take the time to prepare a "finely cooked" message, it serves everyone better. Think about it: What do you want your students to experience every time they hear you teach? Do you want to offer them a fast-food diet of quickie messages and freeze-dried talks, or do you want to take the time to nourish their souls with well-cooked meals? Then again, you could use Duffy's approach—he takes a lot of time to prepare his messages but refuses to preach on topics that end in a pronounced vowel: Jesus—yes; parousia—no; grace—yes; glossolalia—oh no.

Anyone who wants to deliver well thought-out messages will need to work at their preparation. You can't "wing it" every week and end up with convicting and challenging messages that have good content. Effective preparation will require intention and discipline that doesn't just happen—you've got to work at them. There are easy-does-it books that teach a simpler approach to effective message preparation—sort of Dr. Seuss Gives His Testimony—but that approach isn't worthy of the apostle Paul's mandate to present ourselves "to God as one approved, a worker who does not need to be ashamed and who correctly handles the word of truth" (2 Timothy 2:15).

Great Messages Require More Than Great Delivery

Most youth communicators you know and respect work hard on their preparation and delivery. If it appears they don't struggle because they seem so natural, just remember that they have to work hard on that too! They do struggle, pray, doubt, and take time to become more effective—just like you're doing now.

While delivery is important, and it certainly deserves our attention (see chapters 13–15), the actual message preparation is essential. Bad food served well is still bad food, and careful preparation is the easiest part to overlook and undercook! The speaking part is fun: You start, you finish, and you get the immediate feedback of an audience. That's invigorating! After all, being out there feeding and eating with our students—that's why we got into youth ministry. It's that hard work that goes on back in the heat of the kitchen while we're getting the message prepared that makes speaking such a tough course.

It becomes very obvious to me, to my students, and to anyone who listens when I've skimmed on the hard work of my preparation. At times, I've gone into the message thinking, *Oh, I speak all the time, this will be a breeze,* and then I walked away thinking, *You should have put more effort into preparation. That "breeze" was nothing more than hot air.*

But the opposite is true, too. I've been there when the message was right on target, connected with the students, and was faithful to the Word of God. It was amazing! I've thought, *Why can't I preach like that guy?* But seriously, when we've adequately prepared, it's obvious—to us, to our students, and to the only Audience that matters: The One who calls us to be workers unashamed.

Great Messages Require a Strategy

There are several basic strategies for message preparation. If you've been speaking to teenagers for very long, one of the following will probably sound familiar. Let's assume you're preparing a youth group message for Sunday night:

Strategy #1

Step One (Monday): Develop theme

Step Two (Tuesday–Wednesday): Worry about theme

Step Three (Sunday, 5 P.M.): Panic

Step Four (Sunday, 5:15 P.M.): Abandon theme

Step Five (Sunday, 7 P.M.): Give message you used two years ago

Strategy #2

Step One (Monday–Saturday): Do nothing

Step Two (Sunday, 5 P.M.): Develop theme

Step Three (Sunday, 5:30 P.M.): Go online to find finished message that fits theme

Step Four (Sunday, 7 P.M.): Steal message and deliver

Strategy #3

Step One (Monday): Develop theme

Step Two (Tuesday): Find video that teaches on this theme

Step Three (Tuesday P.M.): Cease any additional preparation work

Strategy #4

Step One (Monday): Develop theme

Step Two (Tuesday–Thursday): Worry about theme

Step Three (Friday): Go online to find finished message on planned theme

Step Four (Saturday): Pray for a miracle because you couldn't find one

Step Five (Sunday, 5 P.M.): Panic

Step Six (Sunday, 7 P.M.): Explain to students, "Tonight will be a little different than most Sunday nights. I feel the Lord is leading us to have small groups instead of a message."

If you've used any of these preparation strategies before (and most of us have), or if you're hoping there might be a Strategy #5 outlined somewhere else in this book, we want to finish this chapter by introducing you to another way of approaching your message preparation process that may be more helpful than what you're currently using. This is a synthesis of ideas we've begged, borrowed, and stolen from other communicators who were gracious enough to share their message preparation "techniques" with us over the years. These aren't entirely new ideas, but maybe they'll help you think about message preparation in a new way.

S.T.I.C.K.

The easiest way to remember this strategy is to simply remember the acronym—S.T.I.C.K. No youth worker wants to speak to a group of teenagers only to have them forget what they've heard before they leave the church parking lot. The hope is that if you carefully and prayerfully prepare your messages with attention to these five steps, the messages will have a better chance to S.T.I.C.K. in the minds and hearts of your students.

The five steps are—

Study

Think

Illustrate

Construct

Keep Focused

They're easy enough to understand, but they can be difficult to combine into a weekly preparation routine. In time, of course, they can become second nature. (Now I can't imagine doing anything else). But at first, it seems pretty intimidating and time consuming. Even as you read through that list of steps, you may be thinking, *Wait a minute! If you guys think I have time in my schedule as a youth worker to do all five of those actions on a weekly basis, you're S.T.U.P.I.D.* —

Stoned

Totally Naive

Unrealistic

Purpose Driven

Impractical

Delusional

How can I do all of that on a weekly basis? How much time will this type of preparation take?

First of all, if that describes what you're thinking, you're not alone. I remember the first time I heard about the benefit of planning my messages 12 months in advance. I was so discouraged that I mentally checked out of the guy's seminar. I wasn't planning one week in advance, let alone 52! In fact, when I first started out in ministry, I was still planning my message conclusions while I was delivering point number two. So I understand your initial reaction to S.T.I.C.K.

But let's talk about another word: *S.T.I.N.K.* That's the word that describes messages that are poorly planned and unprepared. None of us wants to serve up that kind of fare. Here's the good news: As you become comfortable with the S.T.I.C.K. method, you may even find it *saves* you time because it gives you a proven process to keep you on track in preparing your talks.

So before you close the book and write one of us a letter about our bad eating habits (Duffy), stop, take a deep breath, and check off the statements below that apply to you:

☐ I disagree with the S.T.I.C.K. actions as part of message preparation.

☐ I feel a little defensive because it appears S.T.I.C.K. will require a lot of time.

☐ I'm frustrated by my own lack of message preparation time.

☐ I'm excited to discover a practical way to help prep my messages.

☐ I hope I never have to eat a meal with Duffy Robbins.

☐ I feel I'm already good at message prep, and I'm looking forward to learning a few new things.

☐ I'm glad the acronym isn't S.T.I.C.K.I.T. because that would make it more difficult to lend this book to other leaders in the church.

A Typical Conversation with a Busy Youth Worker

Whenever I teach the S.T.I.C.K. concept to a group of youth workers, I usually have the following conversation in one form or another. In fact, I've probably had this dialogue (or versions of it) 100-plus times. It goes something like this:

> **Frustrated Youth Worker:** "I teach too often to take a lot of time to prepare."
>
> **Me:** "Why are you teaching so much?"
>
> **Frustrated Youth Worker:** "Because I oversee junior high, high school, and college, and someone has to teach them."
>
> **Me:** "Are you the only teacher in your church?"
>
> **Frustrated Youth Worker:** "No...[pause]...but...[pause]...I..."
>
> **Me:** [interrupting] "But you're the best teacher, right?"
>
> **Frustrated Youth Worker:** "I didn't want to say it like that."
>
> **Me:** "It's okay, you probably are the best teacher. But let me give you a few questions to consider:
>
> 1. Could there be another teacher in your church who's waiting for an opportunity to teach and express his gifts?
>
> 2. Could you create one message and teach it in a slightly different way to your different audiences?
>
> 3. If you allowed someone else a chance to teach, could it provide you with more space in your schedule to prepare something healthier than a fast-food message?"
>
> **Frustrated Youth Worker:** [typically] "I guess so. But, it's not going to be easy."
>
> **Me:** "I understand! It won't be easy. But what you're doing now isn't easy either. Plus, you know in your soul that it's not good. It's also not easy or good for your teenagers to consume fast-food messages every week."
>
> **Frustrated Youth Worker:** "Why can't you be kind, supportive, and affirming like your buddy, Duffy?"

My biggest hurdle during my early years of youth ministry was the twisted thinking that I needed to be the one to teach every week. I thought that since I was the youth pastor, all the teaching was expected from *me* because of my job title. In addition to that self-imposed expectation, I also carried the unrealistic expectation that I needed to hit a "home run" with every message. Unfortunately it took me too many years to learn that both of these expectations were totally unrealistic.

I've since figured out that I can't hit a home run every week. Neither can you. And the expectation of teaching every week...well, everyone hopes for and expects good teaching, but I've discovered that the good teaching doesn't need to come from me every week.

The main issue is that teenagers get good, solid biblical teaching—whether it comes from me or from someone else. I needed to adjust my expectations, deal with my own pride and insecurity issues, rethink how I was managing my time, and encourage other volunteers to help with the teaching. — *Doug*

Through dozens of similar conversations, I've learned the objections aren't with the S.T.I.C.K. concept. They can usually be traced back to issues of *time management.* So before we jump into S.T.I.C.K., let's briefly look at how we might help you get UNSTUCK and free up some additional prep time.

Finding Time to Prep

Most of the frustrations connected to youth workers not having enough time for preparation can be resolved by taking a close look at three simple ideas:

1. Delegation
2. Adaptation of messages
3. Planning

Of course, it's more complicated than that, but here are some ideas on how to potentially gain more than fast-food prep time.

Delegation

If you assign some teaching to volunteers on your team, then you might be able to raise up more communicators within your church body who could develop their gifts of teaching. And you might even discover an added benefit to this kind of delegation—when teenagers hear the same voice week after week, they often mentally check out. I've noticed that when I don't speak for a few weeks and then come back, there seems to be a lot more interest and enthusiasm among the students. Variety can be a great thing for a teenager's spiritual growth—and for your own health and survival in a long-term ministry situation.

Adaptation of Messages

If you prepare one message and take some time to figure out how to tweak it according to the unique needs of your other audiences (by changing some illustrations and context), you'll very likely be able to teach the same message to different age groups. I do this on a regular basis at my church. I'll reteach a message to adults that I've taught to teenagers and vice versa. Making some changes to one message is a lot easier and more time efficient than creating a new message altogether.

Planning

We've already said a lot in this chapter about planning, and the benefits of thinking about your messages several months ahead. And, again, at first it seems like a daunting task. But the more you can move your ministry toward long-range engagement and away from hand-to-hand combat, the more you can begin to make the kind of strategic decisions that allow you to survive and succeed in the battle.

If you spend a little more time on planning specific messages or thinking long term about an upcoming message series, you can give your teachers the kind of advance notice of date and text or topic that might make them more willing to say *yes* when asked to speak. And when another teacher takes one of your teaching slots, you just opened up some time for additional S.T.I.C.K. work. In the chapters ahead, we'll explore the S.T.I.C.K. elements in more detail. For now, there are two important ideas to remember: (1) Doing the right thing is more important than doing things right, and that requires adequate planning. (2) But doing things right *is* important. Our students can *taste* the difference. And that requires the time and intention of careful preparation.

That leaves us one more issue to consider before we move to the actual preparation of the message (S.T. I.C.K.). We can't cook without the proper ingredients. In the next chapter we'll talk about how to gather the materials we need to put this message together.

Before you move too quickly to the next chapter, take a few minutes and answer the following questions:

1. How much time do you currently spend on message preparation?

2. Who are other teachers (or potential teachers) within the church body who might do a good job if they were given proper notice?

3. Do you know what is currently expected of you as a teacher? If so, what are those expectations?

4. Do you feel as though you're the only speaker that your teenagers will listen to? If so, is this a good thing? What's the downside of speaker variety?

CHAPTER SEVEN

Gathering Material to Make Your Prep Easier

When I [Doug] was about 12 years old, my friends and I woke up early on Saturday mornings and rode our bikes to our "jobs." Our workplace was a little unconventional. We spent the morning digging through the huge, gross, dented industrial trash containers in the back alleys of supermarkets and other businesses in search of aluminum cans. We were scavengers.

If you're younger than me (which you probably are), you might need a quick history of recycling. In the early '70s, home recycling wasn't part of our family's language or lifestyle. This was before Al Gore invented the Internet and made movies about global warming. Today we recycle because we care about the environment. It's just something we expect to do. But back then, we recycled for one purpose—money. We'd gather aluminum cans, fill plastic bags with them, and then transport them to the recycling center in exchange for cash. By noon we could triple our weekly allowance just by gathering aluminum cans. It was the good life!

Plus, these Saturday scavenger hunts through the trash would net me prize-winning stuff that my misguided parents thought was junk. They'd often say, "There was a reason you found that in the trash can!" Little did they know that I also found some legitimate treasures. I hit the jackpot one Saturday when I found a pool stick that required only a little bit of glue, a "perfectly good" bicycle tire, a lamp, and a fish tank that I still own to this day. All of these treasures became mine simply because I looked for them.

"One Person's Garbage Is Another's Person's Gold"

While I don't want to draw too straight a line between collecting trash and message preparation, I would have to say that those mornings in the dumpster taught me valuable lessons about constructing a talk: If you want to develop effective messages on a regular basis, you have to become a scavenger—you have to develop the habit of gathering.

Every effective speaker understands the need for more ideas, statements, ads, illustrations, phrases, titles, cartoons, graphics, articles, books, and quotes—anything that might contain potential content for your messages (the keyword is *might*). The goal of gathering is to have on hand plenty of material that you *might* use when you begin to prepare a message. In this chapter we want to explore how to gather it, what to do with it, and how to use it in your messages.

But first let's talk about the benefits. Suppose you already have a pool stick, a bicycle tire, and a lamp. What are the benefits of scavenging behavior?

Gathering Gives You a Head Start

Most of us have been there: We sit down with a teaching assignment, a Bible, a blank sheet of paper, and a desperate prayer, *Oh God...please give me something worthwhile to say. I want to serve you well; and if I can't serve you well, then I'd at least like not to humiliate myself and my family.* And then we beg God to ignite our brain cells and inspire us with something compelling. It's the worst part of message preparation because there's nothing that causes paralysis like a blank piece of paper and a deadline. How many times have we thought, *I can't speak to teenagers. I've got nothing to say?*

God is the only One who creates something out of nothing. As you listen to effective communicators, you discover that they don't begin with blank pages and their Bibles. Typically, they began their message prep with their Bibles *and* file folders full of content and ideas to jump-start their preparation.

Now try to imagine this scene:

> You're sitting down to create a message on friendship. Your text is 1 Samuel 18 (David and Jonathan). You've read the passage several times, but you're stuck on where to go with it. You're staring at a blank page, praying for something to miraculously appear in your mind. And in this moment of despair and discouragement, the *something* becomes a *someone.* An angel of the Lord walks into the room and hands you a three-inch-thick file folder stuffed with ideas, articles, photos, stories, quotes, and so on, and says, "Fear not, for behold I

bring you good tidings and great resources." Now bathed in bright radiance, you begin to look through the folder.

You see an article that appears to be ripped from an airline magazine. It's titled "Great Friends Are Made Not Born." You immediately think, *That could be a good title.* You don't even take the time to read it, but you write down the headline. Next, you grab a pamphlet describing the importance of small groups that was picked up at a church three years ago. About halfway down the page, there's a circle around a well-written paragraph with the word *Friendship* as a headline. You set the pamphlet aside for now, but you recognize that the paragraph might serve you in a later stage of your message preparation.

The next item is a newspaper photo ripped out of a *USA Today*. The photo shows five 90-year-old women sitting and talking. The article describes their lifelong, post-high school friendship. You love the photo, and you think this could serve as an option for your title graphic.

Some of the items you look at don't do anything for you, and you set them aside. You pause at a Charlie Brown cartoon that looks like it was torn from a Sunday newspaper. You read it and determine it's cute, but it's not funny. There may be a point in your message where it could be used as an illustration, especially if you decide that your message really needs a cute, unfunny cartoon. But for now, you put it in the "maybe" pile.

Then you come across a page photocopied from a C. S. Lewis book. It's a letter he wrote to a friend, and in the letter he describes his understanding of friendship. It's good, vintage Lewis, but it might not work for the group you're speaking to. However, you're not sure, so you set it aside.

Then, near the back of the file, you see the cover of a *Seventeen* magazine from 18 months ago. One of the article titles highlighted on the front cover reads, "Are You a True Friend? A Test to Help You Find Out." There's got to be something useful in there that will trigger an interest in your teenagers. You decide it's a keeper.

Can you imagine a scene like that? Are you interested in finding out how that could happen to you on a regular basis? If getting that kind of head start on your message prep every week gets you even mildly excited, then you need to think about becoming a scavenger. If you cultivate the habit of gathering, then you won't have to *imagine* that scene; it will be a regular part of your ministry life.

Gathering Sparks Your Creativity

One of the most freeing truths I've learned is that so-called "creative people" aren't typically creative "on demand." Self-described creative people will usually readily admit that they're dependent on certain externals to stimulate their creativity. That means those of us who believe we're not creative can feel a little better about ourselves. Just because we don't create, that doesn't mean we aren't creative.

I discovered the secret of these creative types when I invited some of them into my message-preparation process. Granted, they were definitely more creative than me; but when I tried to tap into their expertise—creativity—I found them needing (1) more time to think, and (2) inspirational environments. They responded to my requests with comments such as:

- "I'll get back to you with some ideas."

- "Let me think about it for a while."

- "I need to find a location where I'm inspired."

- "I need time for my mind to percolate."

- "I'm not creative; I simply plagiarize others' ideas."

- "How much are you paying me for this?"

- "I'll get back to you after I've smoked some weed." (Note: This last one happened before I worked at a church.)

Even creative people sometimes need a push to really get their creative engines going. And for a lot of us, that folder of gathered materials is just the push we need to get the message-prep process in motion. Building on the creative work of others, we're able to go places we wouldn't have gone otherwise.

Here's an example of borrowed creativity. I [Doug] have a friend named Ty Mattson who makes a lot of money working as a big-shot graphic and content designer. (Except when he works with Christian publishers—he designed this book cover.) Ty was recently paid (well) by a large, multimillion-dollar company to show and tell the benefits of living in a new housing development. Ty produced an award-winning brochure that now sits on the counter at Home Depot stores across the country.

I know what you're thinking: *But Doug, I don't own a hardware store, and we did our series on the power of tools and leaf blowers last Fall.* I know. But on the counter of your nearby hardware store is free content just waiting for you to build on it (no pun intended). I recently used portions of that brochure when I prepared a message on "developing community." I didn't create the concept, but that doesn't mean I couldn't use it in a creative way.

Imagine having a file full of those kinds of creative prompters. You're sure to become more creative.

Gathering Opens a Door into Your Students' World

Another benefit of taking time to gather material is the relevancy and "current factor" you'll have with teenagers when you use material from their world. I'm definitely not cool anymore. (That ended when I was about 23 years old. Actually, some would argue I never was cool.) I'm not going to fool a teenager into thinking I *am* cool by getting tattoos and piercing my neck-fat. But when I'm able to use something that a teenager recognizes (an ad, for example) to help communicate an important message, it helps me cross that bridge from my world to their world. It's surprising how the simple act of using something we've gathered from our teenagers' world so clearly demonstrates our concern for them.

Of course, they probably won't tell you that. It's a rare teenager who approaches you after a message to say, "Thank you for caring enough to use material from 'my world' to communicate with me; I want you to know I deeply appreciate your attempts at relevancy." That never happens. The responses are usually more along the lines of—

- "Did that really happen to your dog?"

- "Where is that story about Bono in the Bible?"

- "Can I borrow a dollar?"

- "You wear your pants too high."

I may not always receive verbal appreciation; but as I'm speaking, I can sense that examples from their world are better at capturing their interest.

During a recent Sunday morning message, I used a headline that I'd ripped out of *People* magazine a few years ago, and it was amazing to see the nonverbal response when I flashed it up on the screen. It was obvious my teenagers were interested. They're much more fascinated by a Hollywood story than a canned illustration of Sir Winston Churchill that I could read from the book *10,000 Illustrations for Preaching* (subtitled, *Quotes You'll Never Use by People You Don't Know*). I wouldn't have had that headline if I weren't a devoted gatherer and a client of Hair No More (where I read *People* magazine as I wait for my haircut).

But isn't it a lot of work? you wonder. *How do I go about exploring the dumpsters?*

Seek and Ye Shall Find: How to Gather Material

The real key to gathering is that it's 90 percent "habit" and only about 10 percent "hunt." You don't have to go out of your way to gather. You just need to be alert. You can gather "on the go." If you've made gathering a habit, you don't have to set aside time during your week to go scavenging. It becomes a natural part of how you go about your day. Let me get more specific.

Skim Everything

The keywords to keep in mind during the gathering process are *skim* and *code*. While gathering material, make a commitment to only skim it. Don't read it. That diminishes the pressure to consume, understand, and agree with every word of every item. Skimming allows you to pick something up, look it over, identify how it "might" be used (code it), and then keep moving. (More on a coding system later.)

Skimming requires a liberal discernment filter. You really don't want to think about whether you WILL use it, rather *Could I ever, possibly, maybe, if I was really desperate use it?* If so, gather it. You don't need to know how you're going to use what you gather; you just need to think that you "might" use it someday, somewhere, somehow. If you have to take the mental energy and time to discern whether you'll use each item you gather, then you'll probably quench the gathering impulse. Just grab it, cut it out, and move on. (Later, when you get a chance, you can either write to the folks at the library or explain to your friends why their books and magazines were returned with missing pages. Just kidding! I'd never do that to anyone...except my pastor.)

Try it. Make it a goal to collect each day at least five items that you might be able to use while preparing a message. You'll be amazed at how much potentially useful content you see around you on a daily basis. Instead of passing it by, pick it up.

At first, this impulse may not feel natural. You might feel as if you're always "on" and constantly "working" on your message. But soon the habit of gathering will become so common that it won't even feel like an effort—like when you walk by a vending machine and—without even thinking—check the change return slot to see what little provision the Lord might have provided.

Don't Just Collect It—Protect It

At this point, you're probably thinking, *Won't I end up with a pile of junk that I'll never be able to use?* My answer: It's only a pile of junk if you're never able to use it. If you don't have a plan for all of the materials you gather, then you'll end up with a lot of paper stacks—basically a mess. So to make this work, you need to do something with what you've gathered.

I'll admit that I do end up with a large pile of material, but it's stashed away in a box in my office. The bigger the pile, the better it is! And while some of it may be junk, most of it has the potential to be helpful. So here's what I do: I code it, I pile it in a box under my desk, and I get someone else to file it. It's that easy. Here's how it works for me.

Code it. For me, the most difficult part of the gathering process is immediately coding what I've gathered. This step is a little more tedious than finding and collecting. And discovering is a lot more fun than describing. But if I don't code something immediately, then my volunteer will come in to do the filing and inevitably say, "Where do you want this to go?" Then I'll have to stop what I'm doing and figure it out. And if I'm going to do that, I might as well file it myself. So I go with my gut and quickly give each item a code word.

Another reason why immediate coding is difficult is because my mind wants to show off to one of my multiple personalities and prove that it can come up with multiple categories for whatever I've gathered. I often struggle to identify just one topic for coding.

Right now I have a sheet of paper in my back pocket that I picked up in my son's chemistry classroom. (Tonight was his school's open house—a very boring night when parents visit the classrooms and teachers pretend to enjoy it.) I gathered this newsletter because of the headline, "Friends Matter," and I was curious to know what a chemistry teacher had to say about friendship. (You don't typically think of chemistry teachers as being highly social creatures.) My son told me the newsletter was about how to tap into the power and potential of studying in groups—"Friends Matter." Ah, a clever chemistry teacher (friends = study group; matter = chemistry).

Now, my dilemma with the newsletter is this—I could code it several different ways: "friends," "community," "school," "studying," "chemistry," or "bad puns." There are six options, and I haven't even read the newsletter. But since I've tried to discipline myself to give only one coding per item, I choose "friends."

Here was my mental process to that particular coding:

1. I already have some awesome chemistry illustrations from my four-week series on creation and evolution called "Atom and Eve."

2. I've only taught on the topic of studying once (that was the weekend after my oldest daughter got a D- in Introduction to Music).

3. I wasn't being serious about "bad puns." It was just my attempt at writing with a little humor (which you can now put in *your* file under "not funny").

4. If I plan to do a message on either "school" or "community," there's a good chance I'll also pull out my "friend/friends/friendship" file when I do.

On very rare occasions, I'll code something with two topics, but I try not to do this because I don't want a redundant filing system. Also, that requires extra work for the volunteer to make a photocopy of the items—one for each file. Typically, one keyword works.

This same principle of coding can work with anything you read in a book that you think might be useful in a message. How many times have we all read a book, marked it up, and thought, *Wow! That's a great quote; I can't wait to use it,* but then put the book back on the shelf? Then when it's prep time, we can't remember which quote would go with which message. If I read something in a book that I might want to use, I'll simply code it, mark the page with a paper clip, and set the book aside for my volunteer to photocopy and file.

Pile it. This is my favorite action! Whatever I've gathered and coded, I now drop in a pile (in a box) under my desk. I love dropping things in there! I want that box to be overflowing when my volunteer comes into the office to file. I want my volunteer out of breath and sweating by the time the filing is done. Plus, when I drop something in the box, I also know it's no longer in my pocket, on the countertop, in my car, in my briefcase, and it won't get destroyed in the laundry when I forget to empty my pockets and my wife asks, "Doug, why do you have a picture of five elderly women in your pocket?"

There is nothing fancy, spiritual, or creative about this pile. It's just a box that collects whatever I gather. When I first started the discipline of gathering, it used to stress me out when I thought about all the time and effort it was going to take to file everything. This was a terrible fear because it served as a filter for gathering. I'd pick something up or tear something out of a magazine and think, *I could see myself using this....* But then the filing fear would arrive, and I'd think, *Do I really want to take the time to file it?* To which there was always the same answer: *NO! I don't want to file anything!* I still don't want to file anything! I don't even like to file my toenails. But once I realized that I didn't have to be the one to file things, I got rid of that prohibitive fear filter.

File it. It's been said that filing is a way to lose things in a more organized fashion. Unfortunately, for most of us, that's how it usually plays out. Having all your gathered content sitting in a pile won't help you much. The key to retrieving the "paper gold" you've collected is to have it organized in a way where you can actually access it and recycle it.

The reason I've become so good at gathering material is because I learned one key secret to effective filing: "volunteer." Several years ago there was a sweet old lady (former librarian) who would come into the church office and volunteer to help with anything that needed doing. She was a saint who did my filing for many years. After she passed away, I convinced my mother to come into the office and take over my filing. That was a little more complicated. (Try explaining to your mom why a box piled high with materials on sex, teenage sexuality, sexually transmitted diseases, and back issues of *Seventeen* magazine is sitting under your desk.) Anyway, the mom-season was short-lived and painful. Thankfully, I introduced her to another minister who didn't speak on sex as often as I did, and he was much easier to work with. Now Mom and I are both happier.

I'm convinced that God has someone in your congregation who either has the spiritual gift of photocopying and filing (service/helps) or is at least interested in combing through documents and clippings on sex, teenage sexuality, and sexually transmitted diseases. As difficult as it may be to believe, some people are wired to love this type of service. Most people would rather stab themselves in the eye than file (like me). But there's someone out there who'll feel valued and encouraged by helping you. Ask for help through your church bulletin, and then develop a relationship with this person. Ask this volunteer to come into your office once a month and file. Don't assume you can't find someone—you can! Again, I really believe there's someone in your church who's waiting for an opportunity to serve in this behind-the-scenes and helpful manner.

Regardless of how you end up organizing all that you've gathered, it's important to store everything in a place that's easily accessible. I'm a little odd in that I don't have one place where I always prepare my messages. Sometimes I'll prepare at home, and other times I'll prep at the church office. Sometimes, during the quiet hours, I'll prep at Taco Bell. And on occasion, I'll even use the hospital cafeteria (which is a great place to work because the food is cheap and it's easy to hide there). But regardless of where I prepare, I know all of my materials are at the church office, and I can access those files when needed.

One more comment for you computer geeks who may be appalled that I haven't mentioned the words *scan, download,* or *Bill Gates* in this chapter: I'm often asked if I file my content electronically. As much as I wish I had a snappy, savvy, technological response to this question—regrettably, I do not. Perhaps you suspected this when you heard about the box under my desk. I'm sure there are easy ways to use scanners and organize information so it's readily available in a digital format. But when it's time to prepare my message, I want to touch a stack of papers and filter through them without staring at my computer screen for long periods of time while searching for material.

There are probably some very clever people who've developed a system whereby everything gathered can be scanned and transported into a mobile phone by simply using the keywords *gerbil slayer*. I'm really happy for their technological wizardry, and I encourage them to write a book and show everyone how prehistoric I am for feeling more comfortable with tactile objects. But at this point, I prefer to stay with the pile-and-file method. I admit it: I'm old school.

How to Use Your Gathered Material

This entire gathering process is done every day for weeks, months, and (for some of us) many years. If you've collected some material, the idea is that when you're working on that friendship message (1 Samuel 18), you can go straight to the "friendship" file and find a few ideas to jump-start your preparation. Depending on the topic, you might also poke around the filing cabinets for other folders that fit that same topic (e.g., "community," "small groups," "chemistry class study groups"). Once you grab your folders, you're armed with content. And when you have content, it can provide you with some confidence. You start to feel as though you have the material you need to work on your message.

Then once you sit down to study for the message (chapter 8), you simply plop the file folders on your desk knowing you have several potential ideas close at hand. It's like a dumpster that's chock-full of aluminum cans. Instead of creating something out of nothing, you're creating something out of something. Now that blank page doesn't look so big, does it?

How to Create Messages That S.T.I.C.K.

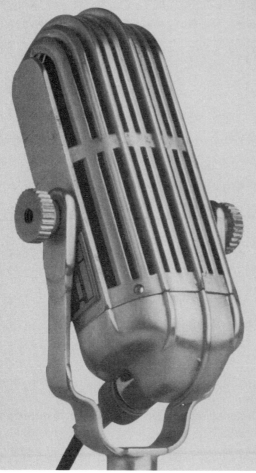

CHAPTER EIGHT

Study: Improve Your Content and Increase Your Confidence

In the world of youth workers, as most of us are well aware, nothing spells excitement like S-T-U-D-Y. It's right up there with terms such as *meeting, to-do list, budgeting, elder board, senior pastor's kids,* and *colonoscopy.* It's intriguing, isn't it, how many of us believe we have the gift of teaching or preaching, but how few of us seem to have the gift of studying?

Why Study?

It would be a lot more fun—and maybe closer to the truth—if we began the S.T.I.C.K. preparation process with **S,** as in—

- **S**tart with a great illustration.

- **S**earch for a cool video.

- **S**urf the Internet for a sermon already prepared.

- **S**teal a message from your favorite author.

- **S**ee if you can postpone your message until next week.

But the fact is, there's no substitute for taking step one, STUDY the Word of God.

Study Stirs the Heart

Teenagers are attracted to passion, passion requires fuel, and there is no better fuel to keep the fire burning in your own heart and mind than biblical truth. That's why study is so important. It ignites an intellectual passion that's deeper than mere emotional passion, but every bit as contagious. The best teaching always comes from the depths of your own spiritual life. When you speak from what God is doing in your life, there's a transparency and an authenticity (*ethos*) that will connect your listeners (*pathos*) to your message (*logos*).

Study Strengthens Your Sense of Confidence

When you study, you gain a sense of confidence and clarity, a sense of conviction that this is what God wants to say to these teenagers in this moment of history.

Study Stimulates the Entire Preparation Process

Knowing and understanding something significant from the biblical text will pave the way for the other elements of the S.T.I.C.K. process (which we'll cover in the following chapters). It's easier to *think* about your message (S.**T**.I.C.K.) *after* you've studied the biblical text you're going to teach. Likewise, it's much easier to *illustrate* something (S.T.**I**.C.K.) when you know what that *something* is.

We all know it's tempting to build a biblical message around an illustration, but generally speaking, it's not a good idea—even if it's a really strong illustration. Illustrations are vital to illuminate your message and engage your audience. But we can't illuminate a message if we don't know what it is—and what's the point of engaging the audience if we have nothing to say?

And finally, beginning your message prep with study time will give you a better sense of the most natural way to *construct* (S.T.I.**C**.K.) your message. So it just makes good sense to start with STUDY.

In this chapter we want to give you some practical ideas to help you study and to guide you through a study process that can make your messages more enriching for your audience *and for you*. Ready to study *STUDY*?

Two Premises

There are two premises that drive this book and undergird much of what we say in this chapter. Our first premise is that "All Scripture is God-breathed and is useful for teaching, rebuking, correcting and training in righteousness, so that all God's people may be thoroughly equipped for every good work" (2 Timothy 3:16-17).

Second, we assume you're reading this book with the hope and intention of becoming more effective at teaching the Bible to teenagers. If it's not about that and your primary motivation for reading *Speaking to Teenagers* is simply to become better at giving announcements or to learn how to tell more engaging stories... uh, well, this chapter may not be especially helpful for you. But if you want to become better at teaching the Bible to teenagers, then you'll need to develop disciplines that will help you study God's Word so you can teach it with clarity, conviction, and confidence.

Words of Caution

The apostle Paul warns, "Knowledge puffs up while love builds up. Those who think they know something do not yet know as they ought to know" (1 Corinthians 8:1–2). It would be nice if Paul were pleading for more ignorance because then most of us could feel like we're well on our way to sanctification. But he doesn't seem to be saying, "Don't gain knowledge" (i.e., "Thou shalt not study"). He seems to be saying, "Be careful how you use your knowledge."

As a man who devoted much of his early life to study, Paul knew all too well the possible dangers of even something as good as diligent study becoming something potentially bad. What might those dangers be for people like ourselves—youth workers who study the Bible so we can communicate it to teenagers?

Danger #1: Impressing Professors

When I was a seminary student, my homiletics professor was very difficult to impress. He's even more difficult to impress today because he passed away several years ago. He was a good man, a great preacher, a very tough grader, and someone I really wanted to impress when I was a young communicator. But even today, I've got to force myself to remember he's no longer my audience and I'm not competing for a grade. When we study, we want to study for our real audience—that group of teenagers to whom we plan to speak, not the imaginary audience we want to impress.

We've all heard youth ministry speakers who might have been very effective had their audience been a panel of seminary and college professors. Unfortunately, the profs couldn't make it to youth group, and the teenagers who did show up were left confused and disconnected—and therefore bored with the content. It's nice that you still remember how to parse verbs and can articulate the historical context for the use of mud as Jesus' healing agent of choice (John 9). But it's far more important that you study with the intention of gaining knowledge so teenagers can recognize that God's Word is understandable, relevant, and has the power to transform their lives even in the twenty-first century.

Always approach study with your specific teenage audience in the forefront of your mind (*pathos*), not some imaginary academic elite. Jesus sent out the disciples with the command "teach others to obey," not "teach others to conjugate Greek" or "teach others the historical background of the Essene community" or "teach others the value of a good Bible college or seminary education." You get the point. All of that may be helpful, and it may be a part of your study. But the ultimate goal of study is to persuade—to move an audience toward practical life change.

Danger #2: Impressing Teenagers with Your Intelligence

When I first began to see the importance of studying and adding depth to my messages, I had to literally beg God for discernment on what was and what wasn't important information for my teenage audience. I felt this tension because I was so excited about all that I was learning, and I wanted to reveal it all to the kids I loved so much. It's taken me many years to figure this out, but I've come to realize that if teenagers can't understand my content, then they won't be motivated to study God's Word on their own.

When I confound them with too much data, history, dates, and extra-biblical theories, they're not enthused for more; they're confused more. And the only words that spark enthusiasm are when I say, "And my last point is...." Be very careful about how much of your study makes it into your actual message.

Constantly check your motives as a teacher. If you study so teenagers will say, "Wow! You're really a smart youth worker. It's such a pleasure to sit at the feet of the intellectually elite and bathe myself in your academic and scholarly work," well, you've got the wrong motive. Repent of your pride, get counseling for your insecurity, and stop studying to impress others with intelligence that's probably "borrowed." Instead, study so you can impress a 14-year-old that God's ways are worthy enough to change his ways.

When we get to K (Keep Focused), we'll challenge you to carefully cut some of the material you've uncovered through your study. We're not saying, "Cut it so it'll be simplistic," we're saying, "Cut it so it'll be simple enough for your teenagers to understand." It's a delicate balance to study and really plumb the depths of a text without making your message so deep that students can't figure out what you discovered. Even a well-prepared meal is no good if it can't be digested. In the end you'll probably need to cut some of your background information, research, and theories to make sure your message is edible for a teenager. However, at this point it's critical that you study for as long as your schedule will allow.

Danger #3: Emphasizing Head Knowledge While Experiencing Heart Failure

Most churched teenagers don't need *more* Bible knowledge; they need to be challenged to put their knowledge into action. Good biblical teaching requires more than opening the frontal lobe and disseminating Bible information. (See chapter 3 on persuasion.) Biblical knowledge that is void of spiritual transformation is what ticked off Jesus (*ticked off*, by the way, is the Greek translation of the Hebrew word *tic-tac*—meaning "no longer refreshing"). Jesus displayed anger toward those who were "religious." He called them "whitewashed tombs" (Matthew 23:27); they looked good on the outside but they were "full of the bones of the dead and everything unclean." It's a vivid picture of head knowledge without heart transformation.

When you take the time to study God's Word for a message, think *wisdom* more than *knowledge*. You do a disservice to your students when you neglect the heart in favor of the head. Make it your goal to communicate God's wisdom so teenagers may know God and love him. Help your students gain understanding so they can make wise choices and live the preferred life God has designed for them. "Be shepherds of God's flock that is under your care, watching over them" (1 Peter 5:2).

Now, before you read any further, think: *Which of these dangers do I need to avoid so I can be faithful with how and what I study?*

Steps to Effective Study

The goal of study is to gain a greater understanding of Scripture so you can—

    a. Allow the text to speak for itself, untarnished by your assumptions and preconceptions

    b. Identify the timeless message that God has for his people

    c. Consider what these timeless truths mean for your life and for the lives of your students

Where to start?

Step One: Determine the Text

As you begin your study, you'll want to think in terms of two different types of messages—*textual messages* and *topical messages*.

The approach you use will determine the focus of your study. The following two exercises will help demonstrate the difference between the two approaches.

Exercise #1: Take a moment and read through the following passage. As you read, briefly jot down the possible topics that are suggested in these two verses.

> From there Elisha went up to Bethel. As he was walking along the road, some boys came out of the town and jeered at him. "Get out of here, baldy!" they said. "Get out of here, baldy!" He turned around, looked at them and called down a curse on them in the name of the Lord. Then two bears came out of the woods and mauled forty-two of the boys. (2 Kings 2:23–24)

Use this space to jot down the topics that come to your mind as you read through the 2 Kings text.

What did you come up with? Here are our lists. (Oddly enough, there were some minor differences in what we took away from the passage.)

Doug	Duffy
Speaking to Build Up	Speaking to Build Up
Dealing with Anger	Dealing with Brats
Respect for the Elderly	Respect for the Bald
Animal Rights	Animals Did the Right Thing
Learning to Forgive	The Justice of God
Purpose-Driven Mauling	Enjoy the Silence

FIGURE 8-1. POSSIBLE TOPICS SUGGESTED BY THE TEXT

Exercise #2: Okay, now do a second exercise. Take the "Dealing with Anger" topic from Doug's lists and in the following space, jot down five Bible passages that address that one issue.

What did you come up with? Here's our list:

- "Do not repay anyone evil for evil. Be careful to do what is right in the eyes of everyone." (Romans 12:17)

- "A gentle answer turns away wrath, but a harsh word stirs up anger." (Proverbs 15:1)

- "He looked around at them in anger and, deeply distressed at their stubborn hearts, said to the man, 'Stretch out your hand.' He stretched it out, and his hand was completely restored." (Mark 3:5)

- "My dear brothers and sisters, take note of this: Everyone should be quick to listen, slow to speak and slow to become angry, because our anger does not produce the righteousness that God desires." (James 1:19–20)

- "In your anger do not sin": Do not let the sun go down while you are still angry, and do not give the devil a foothold." (Ephesians 4:26–27)

These two exercises, when done back to back, demonstrate the difference between using a textual approach to speaking and using a topical approach to speaking. (Actually, the first exercise vividly proves the importance of sound exegesis and careful STUDY. Both of us read more *in* to the passage than we probably got *out* of it; but we were having a little fun.)

The difference between these two approaches to study is simple (Figure 8.1):

- With *textual messages*, the text suggests the topic (Exercise #1).

- With *topical messages*, the topic suggests the text (Exercise #2).

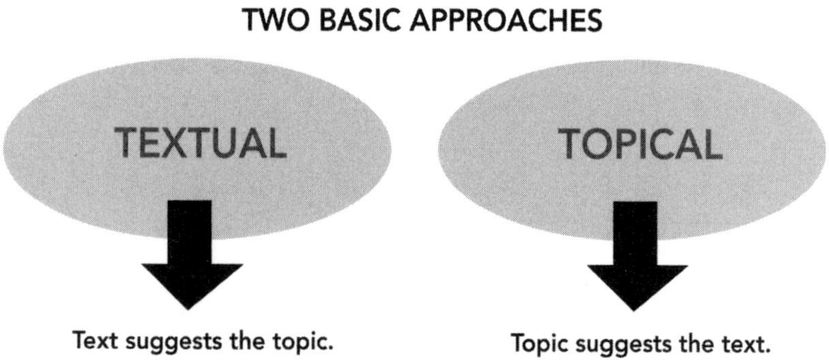

TWO BASIC APPROACHES

TEXTUAL

TOPICAL

Text suggests the topic.

Topic suggests the text.

FIGURE 8.1

Both approaches are good and useful; and although you may occasionally hear someone say they believe one is far superior to the other, both approaches have unique advantages and disadvantages.

TEXTUAL

- Points students back to the words of Scripture;
- Points youth workers back to the words of Scripture (it forces us into the text);
- Makes it harder to duck texts that are "inconvenient" or hard to talk about;
- Helps students learn how to feed themselves from Scripture instead of giving them a diet of ready-made processed talks;
- Offers a more balanced diet of truth—topics are suggested by the text rather than by the whims or hot topics of any one group or youth worker;
- Can get bogged down in more sophisticated theological-textual questions that, in fact, might just "muddy the water" for a teenager who is asking, "What does God say about....?"
- Can—it doesn't have to—make it more difficult to speak to student's felt needs. Obviously, there is a point at which the Bible speaks to every aspect of the human condition, but it doesn't do that in every passage, or even in every book. So, it can feel a little less student-sensitive, a little less responsive to students' needs.

TOPICAL

- Allows for flexibility. You can adjust and shift topics to meet the needs of the group;
- It's easier. That doesn't make it better; but it does require less study, and that's just a fact;
- It approaches the text the way our students live. They don't read the Bible to find out what it says; they read the Bible so they can do what it says. Now, obviously, they can't do what it says without finding out what it says, but again, one approach is directed more toward concepts, and one is directed more toward the concrete;
- Allows your teaching to be more needs-based;
- Requires a little less work to make it relevant because with topical, the topics are chosen because of their relevance. Whereas with a textual approach, the topics come to us because they are there in the text;
- Can develop in our students an appetite for "how-to" Christianity—can reduce all Christian truth down to a "fix it" guide. Could end up skipping over truths that might, in time, transform the mind (Romans 12: 1) but don't immediately have relevance for a teenager's life;
- When we teach from a topical menu that jumps around from topic to topic, it can allow us to avoid hard topics that we don't feel comfortable or competent to talk about.

If we were to hear just one talk in a series of five, then we might not know whether the message was topical or textual because the actual delivery could be very similar with both approaches. In every textual message, there is going to be a reference to some real-life topic. And in a topical biblical message, there will be some reference to the text. When it comes to the delivery, it's really more a question of emphasis. But in terms of planning, it can make quite a difference (Figure 8-2).

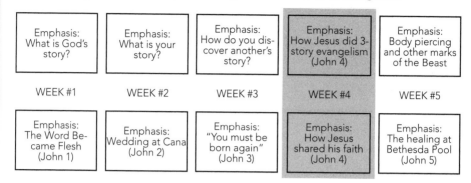

Speaker #1: Tom Topical is doing a five-week series on evangelism.

Emphasis: What is God's story?	Emphasis: What is your story?	Emphasis: How do you discover another's story?	Emphasis: How Jesus did 3-story evangelism (John 4)	Emphasis: Body piercing and other marks of the Beast
WEEK #1	WEEK #2	WEEK #3	WEEK #4	WEEK #5
Emphasis: The Word Became Flesh (John 1)	Emphasis: Wedding at Cana (John 2)	Emphasis: "You must be born again" (John 3)	Emphasis: How Jesus shared his faith (John 4)	Emphasis: The healing at Bethesda Pool (John 5)

Speaker #2: Tammy Textual is doing a five week series on the first five chapters of John.

FIGURE 8-2. NOTICE THAT IN WEEK 4, BOTH THE TOPICAL MESSAGE AND TEXTUAL MESSAGE WILL SOUND PRETTY SIMILAR.

We don't want to say one is better than the other, but we are willing to say that one without the other isn't so good. In his book *Communicating for a Change*, Andy Stanley frames the issue by saying there are three approaches to speaking. As you read through them, it's quite clear that each approach has a distinctive way of determining which text(s) you'll study.

Teach the Bible to people. This would be a purely textual approach—going through Scripture book by book and chapter by chapter so listeners can find out what it says. This is akin to a guide walking people through an art gallery so they can look, admire, and maybe develop an appreciation for what they're seeing.

Teach people the Bible. This approach is a little more audience-sensitive, but it's still largely textual. Its intent is still teaching what the Bible says, but it asks the question, "What can we do to make the Bible more interesting to people who may not know anything or care anything about God?" So speakers who use this approach add in media tools, engaging outlines, and any other device that might help them listen, admire, and develop an appreciation for what they're reading.

Teach people how to live a life that reflects the values, principles, and truths of the Bible. This third approach still points us to the gallery of God's truth: history, wisdom, poetry, narrative, and teaching. But it asks this question, "What if the point isn't getting people to *look* at God's truth, but to *live* it? What if people are so blown away by what they've seen that they not only admire God's Word, but they also want to see what it would look like lived out in the living color of their own lives?" This is, in effect, a different focus. This is teaching the Bible not so our students can hear it and admire it, but so they can *do* it (James 1:21–23). It still requires that we get students into the text, but it recognizes that we really haven't done our jobs until we've gotten the text into our students' lives. It's this type of speaking that offers a balanced diet of topical *and* textual teaching.

To make this as practical as possible, let's assume that whether your approach is topical or textual, you've been led to a specific text. Write that text in the space below. We'll come back to it in the coming pages as we continue through the Study process:

Step Two: Beg God for Insight

There are several ways to approach Bible study, but the one element they all have in common is the necessity of prayer.

It's vital to begin your study time by begging God to give you wisdom and insight that is much greater than your own. God loves the teenagers that you'll be teaching more than you ever will! Right? Ask God to clear your mind, focus your thoughts, inspire your creativity, and ignite an insight that becomes such a strong conviction that you can't wait to share it with the teenagers whom you also love.

We realize that writing about prayer as an early step in this process sounds simple—and it is. But it's still an area we all struggle with. Prayer is often taken for granted. Too many times we find ourselves justifying our lack of pre-study prayer by thinking, *God surely knows I need his help to say anything significant. God knows I'm desperate. I don't need to tell him I'm feeling frantic to finish this message before the teenagers arrive later tonight...uh...*

Well ..oh my...before they arrive in 15 minutes.

Then during youth group we quietly mumble a prayer as we grab our Bible and approach the stage, *God, please bless this message.* And maybe we pull it off; maybe we don't. But by bypassing specific and intentional prayer, we essentially leave God out of the entire communication process.

I can clearly remember the day when I changed my study time to include a more intentional focus of begging God for his insights rather than my own. There was such a sense of peace and confidence and connection that I can remember thinking, *Why haven't I always done this? No wonder I often feel I lack confidence in my messages. It's because I didn't connect to the One who cares about communication more than I do.*

This prayer time is deeper than simply asking God for his blessing (i.e., "Dear Jesus who turns water into wine, let's see what you can do with this watered-down mess of a message!"). Prayer causes us to be fiercely dependent on God's intervention in the studying, thinking, illustrating, constructing, and simplifying process.

I'm embarrassed to admit that I've had to learn how to beg. Deep within my soul I've come to experience that I'm merely going through the motions of a public speaker if I'm talking about anything that I don't genuinely sense is God's message. Please don't overspiritualize that last sentence—I don't pretend to be inspired every time I teach, nor do I believe I say exactly what God wants me to say every time I teach. But I've made it a goal to never teach teenagers (or anyone else for that matter) without the security and confidence that I went before the God who knows my heart, my audience, and my capabilities and begged the Holy Spirit for something that is so much deeper and more powerful than I could conjure up through my own power and insight. I literally *beg* God to help me.

Step Three: Read (and Reread) the Text

Read and reread your chosen text several times prior to going to outside sources (i.e., commentaries and so on). Read your text slowly. Read it quickly. Read it in multiple translations and paraphrases. Read it backward (for example, read verse 8, then 7, then 6). Read it with a Scottish accent and pretend you're William Wallace and your face is painted blue.

The key here is repetition, because it's within the repetition that you discover the good ideas that you wouldn't consider with one superficial read. Don't be surprised if the reading and rereading also helps you to think about how to organize and construct your message. Typically you'll find that the more you read a text, the clearer an outline becomes.

I've made it my goal to read and reread my selected text *at least* 10 times. Why? Because—especially when I'm already really familiar with a text—it's within those multiple readings that old words sound new, or an old combination of words will trigger a fresh idea, or a different translation or paraphrase will help me to think of a passage in a new way.

During this read and reread process, I have next to me a spiral-bound notebook and several different translations and paraphrases of the text I'm studying. Sometimes I'll actually pull the Bibles from the shelf; but more often than not, I'll simply use my Bible software and print the different translations and paraphrases of the same text. I feel this method is a little more efficient, and it lets me freely scribble my notes on the photocopied pages of the biblical text.

As I read and reread the passage, I'll mark it up with my pen. It's very messy. I'll circle words I think may be important, I'll write a question mark when I'm confused, I'll flip back and forth between the translations to compare and contrast the different uses of language. Occasionally, when I have time, I'll even look for hidden codes in case I decide someday to write fiction. But if at any point I begin to think of an outline, a teaching direction, an illustration, a big idea, a small-group question, a personal application, or anything else that might serve as content, I immediately record it in my notebook so I don't forget it. Then all of my thoughts are in the same place.

Because I've gone through this process many times, I regularly create a decent teaching outline or potential message just by reading and rereading the same passage several times. But I have to fight the temptation to cut my study short and begin constructing my message just because I think I've "got it." Instead, I force myself to listen to the thoughts of those who've studied this passage before me.

Every time I teach on this subject, I'm always asked how I came up with the number 10. It's a good question, and there is a deeply spiritual answer. I created a biblical equation that goes like this—10 Plagues of Egypt (Exodus 7–11) multiplied by the Parable of the 10 Virgins (Matthew 25:1–13) minus 66 books of the Bible minus 12 disciples minus 10 of Joseph's brothers (Genesis 37) minus Mary and Joseph (Luke 2) = 10.

$$
\begin{array}{rl}
 & \text{10 Plagues of Egypt} \\
\times & \text{10 Virgins of the Bible} \\
- & \text{66 books} \\
- & \text{12 disciples} \\
- & \text{10 brothers} \\
- & \text{Mary \& Joseph} \\
\hline
= & \text{10}
\end{array}
$$

Step Four: Allow Commentaries to Enlighten You

One of the basic doctrines of the Reformation is *sola scriptura:* "We have but one sacred text, and that is the Bible." But it's one thing to anchor our doctrine in Scripture alone; it's quite another to *read* the Scripture alone. Every single heresy that the church has faced has been perpetrated by someone who read and reread the Scripture alone. The Holy Spirit has a history, and as we continue our study of the passage, we want to know what's been said about this passage by other brothers and sisters in Christ throughout that history.[78]

One of the great treats of living in the twenty-first century is that we're surrounded by volumes of thought written by brilliant scholars and theologians who preceded us. By consulting their insights and comments, we can expand our understanding of the passage beyond the biases of our own ethnic and socioeconomic perspectives. Here are four quick suggestions for using commentaries in your study routine.

1. Collect them. I wish someone would've encouraged me to begin building my library at an early age. Very generous and kind members of my immediate and extended families have helped me collect ugly ties, hideous Christmas sweaters, fancy grilling tools, and more underwear than I could ever use in a lifetime. Had I known as a young man what I know now, I would have asked them to skip the Pep Boys gift cards and buy me commentaries.

If you don't have study materials, begin making a wish list of different commentaries. Ask respected Bible teachers what commentaries they reference and poke around their libraries to see them firsthand.

There are so many types of commentaries that finding the right ones can become confusing. As you slowly discover the types you like, investigate whether each comes from a series or if it's a stand-alone book. If it comes in a series (covering all 66 books of the Bible, or 27 New Testament books, or 39 Old Testament books), you might want to begin the process of collecting that series.

One word of caution here: Just because a collected set looks good on the shelf that doesn't mean each of the commentaries in a set are of equal value. Buy the commentary based on the author or the general editor of the series. Don't just buy a set because it's a set. Usually a good series has a strong general editor. Identifying a trustworthy and respected editor is part of the collecting process. (See www.speakingtoteenagers.com for our message board on favorite commentaries.)

2. Filter them. Not all commentaries will be helpful to you. You may buy a set of commentaries at a bargain price and discover the reason they were so inexpensive is because the author didn't believe in Jesus. I'll say it again: Not all commentaries are created equal! Most of us have seen academic commentaries that are thorough and scholarly but offer very little help to the person trying to communicate biblical truth to teenagers. I went to seminary, and I consider myself fairly intelligent; but I've read some commentaries and thought, *Huh? I must be the dumbest seminary graduate there ever was because I have no idea what that means.*

And then there are those commentaries at the other end of the spectrum—where the entire commentary is filled with stories, illustrations, poems, and devotional thoughts, but it doesn't really dig into the text. In that sense, commentaries are like grilling tools (I should know)—some of them look really good, and some actually help you prepare an edible meal that will feed others.

3. Compare them. As you filter through the commentaries and discover the ones that fit you best, you might find it wise to grab a few other commentaries that represent theological positions different from your own. For example, both of us would probably most accurately be described as conservative evangelicals. If you've read any of our books or heard us speak, you already know that. But when studying a passage, there is occasional value in knowing how those to your theological right or left would likely interpret the selected text. By doing this, you gather theological context. It might even be worthwhile to use their positions as points of discussion.

And by knowing others' theological positions it increases your *ethos* profile. It enhances your own credibility when you say things like, "I believe the Bible teaches this, but not everyone believes like I do. Some pastors, for example, teach ABC. Those pastors are called heretics." Chances are, you won't spend a lot of time studying outside your theological comfort zone. (I would estimate that less than 10 percent of my study time is spent on theological positions that are different from mine.) But the time you do spend can offer you the value of a different perspective.

4. Enjoy them. At some point you'll discover a style of commentary that fits with your theology and your style of learning. When you find that set of commentaries, they can become like good friends. You'll look forward to seeing what *your friend* has to say about a particular Scripture passage. It's a good thing to be drawn into study and to learn to enjoy your study time.

What I've found to be true about my own study time is that I always learn something I didn't know prior to cracking open the commentary. The new depth not only allows me to think a little deeper, but it gets me excited to keep coming back and continue my learning. The more I learn, the more excited I am to teach. And when that excitement becomes passion, it makes me a better communicator.

Step Five: Go Beyond Commentaries

Spending time in commentaries will help you learn more about your primary text, but you'll want to save additional study time for three other sources that can provide further insight.

1. The Bible. You'll probably benefit from consulting a concordance just to survey other passages of Scripture that might speak to the same topics or themes as your primary text. Basically, you're asking, *What else has God said about this topic?*

As you read through your commentaries, be sure to write down all the additional Scripture passages referenced. Most writers will cite specific, relevant passages in the body of their commentaries. I always write those "additional" passages in my spiral notebook. Then when I close the commentaries, I spend a little more time reading the different biblical references I just collected.

By doing this you gain a bigger picture and a better understanding of the totality of God's Word. It's unlikely that you'll use all of these verses in your actual message, but this added study will give you the confidence of knowing more of God's Word that complements your chosen text.

There have been many times when I study for a verse-by-verse message that could easily become a topical message because of all the additional Scriptures I've discovered. For example, I recently taught a six-week series from Colossians 3:12–17 that I called, "Dressing Up for a Life Change." During the week when I was studying the peace of Christ (verse 15) I was directed to more than 15 additional "peace verses" that were referenced in just one commentary. So if at some point in the future I choose to do a one-time topical message on peace, I now have several additional peace Scriptures—that's plenty for a strong topical message.

Since I was teaching one verse a week in this series, I only used Colossians 3:15 as the primary text. But I made it known to my teenagers that there were several other verses I wanted them to read during the week to gain a fuller, biblical understanding of peace. I usually provide those additional Scripture references on the back of the students' notes or outline.

2. General wisdom. This includes books, tapes, articles, and any other media or curricula that might help me better understand or better teach this passage. This is material I search out specifically for *this* message (as opposed to the *gathered* material we referred to in chapter 7). After studying the commentaries, it's worthwhile to find out what other teachers, preachers, and writers have had to say about this passage or topic. Basically, you approach these sources with the question, *What have others already learned that I might be able to use?*

When I beg God for greater insights, I do so with the realization that there are many intelligent men and women who've already written or said better things than I could say or think about this passage, even on my best day. Why not make use of their insights?

But isn't that stealing?

Yes. Welcome to youth ministry. We prefer to call it "research." Remember the words of Ecclesiastes 1:9, "There is nothing new under the sun." The only thing that keeps you from learning from others is your pride.

3. The Super Files. These are the materials you've *gathered* (chapter 7) in that little vault called your filing cabinet, just waiting to overflow and refresh you with additional insight. I now retrieve that file and go through it. At this point, I'm really just looking through the files for any type of content that might fit in the genre of "research" or "content" (basically, the material that will help with the meat of the message). The photos, cartoons, flyers, and quotes are all materials I would term "fluff," and I'll return to them when it's time to CONSTRUCT and ILLUSTRATE my message.

The Stop and Start of Studying

At some point you've got to stop studying! But when do you have enough material to put this message together?

We said at the outset of this chapter that the goal for studying is understanding what God wants to say to this group of teenagers in this moment of history. That's important! But we also affirmed the added goal of gaining confidence as a speaker—feeling that you genuinely have a firm grasp of the text or the topic on which you've chosen to speak. That's also important! The basic idea is that you'll stop studying when you feel you've met both of those objectives. This kind of discernment may be tough at first. Try thinking of it this way: Don't stop studying when you have enough understanding for a message; stop studying when God is finished with your heart.

When you get to this point, you more or less recognize that even though you could learn more, your study time needs to be folded into the other demands and priorities of your life. There will always be more you *could* do, but don't be discouraged by that. This is not a dissertation; it's a message to some teenagers whom you and God dearly love. If you've done your homework, you can trust God to do the heart work.

Start Studying: The Earlier the Better

One last practical tip before we close out this chapter. I begin my study time early in the week—actually, it's the first thing I do during my workweek. I take Mondays off, so I block out two to three hours on Tuesday morning for my study time. I wish I could study longer; but during this season of my life, that's the most time I can afford and still be faithful to my other responsibilities and priorities.

After my morning study time, I'm usually racing off to a staff meeting, which typically, in turn, creates a series of follow-up, one-on-one meetings and other boring realities. If I feel the need for more study time, I'll try to squeeze in another hour or two on Tuesday before I go home. Frankly, in my world this rarely happens since I still need to get caught up on all of the pastoral tasks and administrative details that came up at church over the weekend.

The main reason I begin my studying early in the day is because it gives me more time to spend *thinking* about (T), *illustrating* (I) and *constructing* (C) what I've studied. Whether you're a volunteer or a paid youth worker, managing your preparation time will be a constant battle. But if you want to create and deliver more than fast-food messages, then you've got to find the time to devote to your preparation. As you'll see in the next chapter, thinking about and reflecting on what you've studied is another essential step toward creating effective messages.

CHAPTER NINE

Think: Take Time to Reflect on Your Audience and Content

A youth ministry friend who read the first draft of this book told me he casually mentioned to his senior pastor that he was going to be out of the office for a couple of hours because he needed to get in a place where he could think about his message before youth group. The pastor looked at my friend as though he were demon possessed and said, "The church is not paying you to think. We're paying you to educate our teenagers by challenging *them* to think. If I were you, I'd get back to your office and start *working* on your message, rather than just *thinking* about it."

Well, honestly, we've read and reread that pastor's remarks several times, and we can't actually figure out what the pastor meant by all that. But what seems clear from the pastor's response is that this pastor doesn't place a high value on thinking. (And frankly, I've heard some of this pastor's messages, and they *also* make it clear that this pastor doesn't place a high value on thinking.)

Unfortunately, either my friend didn't explain himself well, or the senior pastor just didn't understand that taking time to *think* **is** *working* on your message.

Now a confession: This was a tough chapter to write, and here's why: How do you challenge friends and peers to do something as basic as *think* without insulting them? Thinking seems automatic. It would be like including a chapter called "Breathe" or "Eat" or "Steal Illustrations from Your Fellow Youth Workers." Some things just seem so obvious. And yet this element of the S.T.I.C.K. process is often overlooked in the progression of message preparation. We've all heard too many misdirected and ill-conceived messages to believe otherwise.

Perhaps there's a piece of you that just wants to skip this chapter and move on to illustrate because you're thinking, *Is this "Think" chapter going to be worth my time? The title is so riveting!* It's totally understandable if you feel that way. Firing the gun is a lot more fun than taking aim. Slopping on the paint is much easier than laying down the drop cloth. Stepping on the accelerator is way faster than consulting the map.

Basically, stopping to *think* just feels like a great big speed bump on the road to Message Land. But what if stopping to *think* actually helps you *get* to Message Land and get there in a better way? And what if it makes the trip more valuable for everybody who's traveling there with you? And what if *not* stopping to think is keeping some of your students from climbing on board? As we've mentioned in previous chapters, youth workers tend to be doers. And that's often a good thing, but in the words of an old proverb, "Doers who do but do not *think*, tend to be do-doers." And that's not such a good thing.

I Was Taught to Study...Not to Think

As this section's header amply demonstrates, we're both well-educated— thanks to four years of college and three years of seminary. And we're grateful for what we gained from our academic journeys—careful instruction in Bible and theology and thorough instruction in homiletics. But while we were being educated on sermon preparation and delivery, no one taught us the importance of *thinking*.

You might be wondering, *Well, what schools did you guys go to?* Our schools have politely asked that we not say. But they were good schools. They just never challenged us to think in the way we've described in this chapter. Maybe they thought it would be insulting to the students. Maybe they thought it was too obvious, like "breathe," "eat," and "take the minimum number of Hebrew credits."

But *thinking* well is an absolutely essential part of the message preparation process.

This Type of Thinking Is Wider Than Your Schedule

My youth ministry buddy who had a run-in with his senior pastor was trying to do the right thing by taking some time to think. But he was probably going about it the wrong way. When we talked about his close encounter with his pastor, I realized where he may have gone wrong was trying to attach a time allotment to his *thinking* because this kind of *thinking* isn't something that happens on a schedule.

For example, had he done his study early in the week (or several days prior to his message, if he's speaking midweek), his schedule would have allowed a built-in margin for thinking about his message and his audience. It would begin at the point where he stops studying, and it would end at the point when he actually delivers the message.

So in a sense, you don't set aside a portion of your schedule for thinking about your message. You develop the discipline of thinking about your message as you go through your day—all day, every day—while you're sitting in meetings, talking with others, and just living your life. You're not doing anything differently or setting aside time. You're just rearranging your schedule with the idea that if you slide your study time to a point earlier in a seven-day cycle, then there will be more time to *think* about the message in the remaining four, five, or six days leading up to your message. This allows time for the knowledge you gained through study to percolate in your brain, drip into your heart, overflow into everyday experiences, and make its way into conversations where you can "test" your thinking.

This thinking time should happen naturally anywhere you are—driving in your car, exercising, even daydreaming at school or in a church staff meeting. If I'm driving in the car and my wife says, "What are you thinking about?" about 90 percent of the time I respond with, "I was just thinking about our marriage and how much I love you!" The other 10 percent of the time I say, "I'm just thinking about my message." Here's the point: Don't feel pressure to try to quantify an amount of time for thinking; just be thinking all the time. The best way to give yourself that think-time is to provide breathing space between your study time and your delivery time. That's when the percolation happens.

On page 134 you can see one example of how I try to implement these S.T.I.C.K. actions on a weekly basis. I've attached a very general time allotment to each action—except for *think*. It's impossible for me to really know how much time I spend actually thinking about my message and my audience because I don't have a set schedule where I sit at my desk and say, "Okay, I'm now going to take 30 minutes to think. Ready, set, think!" First, if another staff member overhears you saying things like that to yourself, it's likely to frighten them.

Second, ideas need more than 30 minutes to percolate and incubate. It takes, from conception to birth, 187 days for a baboon to be born, 31 days for a chipmunk, 420 to 450 days for a giraffe, 11 to 14 days for a finch, and 225 to 250 days for a hippo. Do we really believe it's possible for an idea to grow from conception to delivery in 30 minutes? It almost never works that way. Thinking should be a much more natural and organic part of how we live life after the study time is finished.

Let me give you an illustration of how this *think* time works for me. I've mentioned that in my weekly routine I usually try to grab at least a couple of hours of study time on Tuesday mornings to prep for my Sunday message. By doing this, I can think about my message for several days between study and delivery. One Wednesday I sat down for an hour to *construct* my teaching outline (S.T.I.C.K.). I felt pretty good about how I intended to organize and communicate the content, but several components were still either missing or incomplete: I didn't have an opening illustration or personal application, I was still uncomfortable with several of the transitions, and I didn't know how I was going to conclude the message. Other than that, this baby was really coming together!

Fast forward to Thursday night. I was watching my daughter's volleyball game, and one of her teammates made a very aggressive attempt to chase down a ball. In doing so, she ran her head directly into the volleyball net. She tried to duck, but she was moving too fast and her head caught the lower part of the net. This accident bounced her entire body backward—like you'd see in a cartoon—and she fell flat on her back. My immediate thought should have been, *Wow, I hope she's okay—maybe I should hold a prayer meeting!*

But that's not exactly what happened. (At this point in the story, you gain a little glimpse into my immaturity.) You can probably guess what immediately came to my mind—and if you can't guess, it's likely because you're (a) more spiritual, (b) a caring and tender human being with a pastoral heart, (c) not desperate for illustrations, or (d) a senior pastor who's wondering why I wasn't at the office trying to "grow the youth group." Of course I thought, *That was funny! That will make a great introduction to my message this weekend.* And what's worse is that I sat there wishing I'd captured it on video so I could show it as part of my message.

As it turned out, the girl was fine (I prayed silently from the stands), and within seconds she pulled herself from the floor to the sounds of my daughter's hysterical laughter. (The apple doesn't fall too far from the tree.) Meanwhile, up in the stands, I silently thanked God for giving me the opening illustration for my Sunday morning message on compassion and hurting with those who hurt.

Here's the point: I didn't insert *volleyball time* into my calendar under a "Think About Message" heading. But I was "working" on my message because I'd allowed myself a gestation period. From the time I began to study and prep on Tuesday, the message was percolating and brewing in the back of my mind. In that sense, this type of *thinking* is not unlike the *gathering* process we talked about in chapter 7. It's a thought process focused on what *might* be useful, what *might* be helpful, what this *might* become.

You probably won't have the gestation period of a guinea pig (that's 68 days) to prepare your Sunday night message. We understand that. But don't look at this type of *thinking* as something that happens intentionally on a given day and at a given time in your weekly schedule. (That's preparation.) Look at it as a type of passive message development that happens while you go about your normal routine. The first type of thinking is preparation; this type of *thinking* is gestation. So allow yourself some space between conception and delivery. You might be amazed by what comes out!

This Type of Thinking Is Higher Than Your Learning

When I did a synonym check on the word *think*, my software suggested several alternative words that might help define what we're talking about here.

- *Reflect*
- *Consider*
- *Deliberate*
- *Mull over*
- *Ponder*
- *Envision*
- *Contemplate*
- *Chew over*
- *Baboon gestation*
- *Meditate*

Of all the words on this list, *meditate* might be closest to this phase of the message-preparation process. It's probably even better than the word *think*—but when we asked youth worker focus groups what they thought, not one of them was inspired by the concept of S.**M**.I.C.K. And when we dropped the element of *thinking* altogether (S.I.C.K.), people agreed that was somehow even less motivational.

To meditate on something is to think about it—to chew on it over and over so it becomes central to your thoughts. Someone put it this way: "If you know how to worry, you possess the necessary skills for meditation." When you worry, you're simply thinking about something over and over and over. That's what it means to meditate.

King David pointed to meditation on the Word as a source of the depth and insight that made him a great teacher: "I have more insight than all my teachers, for I meditate on your statutes" (Psalm 119:99). All of us understand that insight is a rare jewel and that it will probably require more of us than simply watching a volleyball game. This type of *thinking* focuses on the big, deep, and wide picture of God and his ways.

This Type of Thinking Is Wider Than Your Content

There's so much involved in good communication, so many variables, that you've got to think beyond just content. You need to be thinking about your heart, your feelings, your target audience, their feelings, the content, the teaching environment, and what teenagers will take away from your message. For a speaker to focus only on content would be like a chef who focuses only on food. Of course the food is important, but what about the atmosphere? What about customer tastes? What about presentation? What about the food temperature? There's a lot to think about.

Here's a starter list (not exhaustive) to get you thinking about some things we need to be...thinking about.

- Audience: Who will receive your message? What are their needs?

- Environment: How does the setting help or hinder what you're trying to communicate?

- Connection: What is your ethical profile with this audience? How can it be improved? (See chapter 4.)

- Delivery: How do I communicate the content in a convincing, persuasive way?

- Translation: What sort of signals are you getting from the audience? How might that impact your delivery?

Most youth workers are typically preoccupied with two questions: What will I say? and Will they care about what I say? Those are great questions to think about, but they're not enough if you're going to develop and deliver messages that stick and make a difference in a teenager's life.

What Should You Think About?

I engage the same study disciplines noted in the previous chapter. I read and reread, I consult the commentaries, and I research other resources. But still, there are many times when I hit an "intellectual wall" after studying. I don't know what to do with what I know. When this happens, I don't try to force an outline; instead I just give myself time to think. I reflect on the text, and meditate and mull it over in my mind and heart. That allows time for God to inspire me with something that's better than what I could come up with on my own. It always happens: Think time leads to better messages.

Think about God's Word

About 75 percent of the time when I read a passage of Scripture, I can immediately come up with how I might want to teach it. When I illustrate this to youth workers, the rookies are easily impressed. At first they think I've got some special gift. It's not a gift; it's simply a skill I've developed over 25-plus years of teaching the Bible every week. But the other 25 percent of the time, I have no idea what I want to say about a particular text. And the ideas only come through meditation—thinking about and reflecting on God's Word.

Sometimes when I'm stuck, I'll take the Scripture passage and write it on a 3 x 5 card and carry it with me. I pull it out during the day and think about it while I'm standing in line somewhere, pumping gas, during commercials, staff meetings, whenever. Basically, I want to make sure that before I teach God's Word I've been *thinking about* God's Word.

Think about the Teenage World

I'm convinced that being a dad in a house full of teenagers has made me a better Bible teacher to teenagers now than at any other time in my entire youth ministry career. Never mind that I'm the age of my students' parents or that I don't have the energy or the "cool factor" that I had in my early 20s. Living in the same space as teenagers (what I've recently started calling "myspace") has given me great insight into their world.

Before I had teenagers of my own, I thought I was a good communicator. I hung out with teenagers. I knew their language, their thoughts, their problems. I was...like...omigosh...Mr. Relevant! But honestly, now I look back and laugh at myself for thinking I knew so much about teenagers. In retrospect, I knew so little about family dynamics or how teenagers respond when they're at home, or how they approach homework or how they react to discipline and experience emotions when they don't get their way. I may have known a lot about "their world" (adolescent culture), but I didn't know a lot about them. I'm sure that when I was younger, I had good content and decent connections to their hearts; but I didn't really know my audience like I do today.

Now I think about teenagers all the time. They're constantly in my home, asking questions, being loud, being silly, being wonderful, being inquisitive, and often being obnoxious. But here's the important point: If I'm willing to *think*—not just as part of some scheduled reflection time in my office on Wednesday mornings, but in an ongoing everyday way—then these same teenagers are also prompters of God's truth and reminders of how his Word plays out in their everyday world. And that has changed the way I teach.

Think about Connecting to Their World

Of course we all know that in order to apply biblical truth to the lives of teenagers, we must be aware of not only *who* they are but also the *world* they live in. If you want to rescue a drowning person, it helps to know something about the drowning person; but it also helps to know something about the tides and currents that impact the struggle to stay afloat. Part of your ongoing thinking process should be focused on what a truth would look like in the life of a teenager.

Think about questions such as *What difference does this Scripture text make to a 12-year-old?* and *What is a 14-year-old going to walk away with from this message?* You want to constantly make this request: *God, help me to see this message in the way a teenager would hear, see, understand, and feel it.*

Sometimes a simple conversation with a teenager can help you think more deeply about your message—which questions need to be answered, which ideas need to be clarified, and which needs need to be emphasized. Sometimes a teenager will be at my house, and I'll say, "Are we going to see you at church this weekend?" This simple question often opens the door to talk about the potential message. I'll usually give a brief overview of what I'm thinking about to see what confuses, what causes questions, what triggers interest, and basically get an early gauge on how my message might be perceived.

Think about Your Specific Audience

I've coached several sports—actually, prior to their high school years, I coached every team on which my children played. (And when my kids played sports in high school, they asked me if I could coach their opponents' teams.) As I coached my players on the skills and fundamentals of a sport, I discovered that kids "get it" at different times throughout the season. Some have more practice, natural ability, or life experience that helps them achieve certain skills more quickly than others. Other kids are just more methodical, and they need more "reps" to take the skills and turn them into game day. One ingredient of a good coach is the ability to notice the different talent levels of his players.

I've discovered an interesting parallel between coaching and speaking to teenagers. A good communicator will recognize that teenagers are at different places within their spiritual journeys and take the time to think about and recognize the unique faith commitments within those spiritual journeys. It's another area of reflection during my *think* time.

Most of us have at least three primary "audiences" within our youth ministry that we need to *think* about when we reflect on a message:

1. The teenager who is a committed follower of Jesus

2. The teenager who is struggling to keep his commitment to Christ

3. The teenager who doesn't know anything about Christ and has sincere questions

Each of these teenagers is in a very different place spiritually. It's important to think about those three "places" and remember that we don't speak merely to Christians or non-Christians; we speak to teenagers, and *then* we consider where they are on their spiritual journeys.

The terms that help me remember these different audiences while I'm speaking are S-words: Sold-Out, Stumbler, and Sincere Seeker. Every week those three audiences are at youth group (and probably yours, too), and they appreciate it when I take the time to address them and acknowledge their current spiritual commitments. It's another opportunity for them to realize, *My youth pastor knows me.*

Each of these sub-audiences requires your thought because when it comes time to challenge them to apply what they've heard, the application is often different for each phase of spiritual commitment. You're going to challenge a kid who is Sold-Out in a different way than you'd challenge a Sincere Seeker or a Stumbler or a Senior Pastor (who tells you to go back to your office and stop thinking so much).

Think about "The One Thing"

The bad news about speaking the good news to teenagers is that oral communication doesn't always have a lot of staying power. You're doing well if they can remember the message after the closing prayer. The best we can hope for is that a teenager will be inspired to pay attention, to consider the content, and to remember something that will cause reflection and application.

The miracle is that every now and then, it works. We speak, teenagers listen, and God stirs their hearts to respond. It's an enterprise that requires the deep work of God. We do the possible. His Holy Spirit does the impossible. But we need to constantly think about how we can work in concert with God.

As we *think* throughout the preparation process, we want to listen to God's Spirit for the one main idea that God would have us communicate from a given text. We're convinced that one of the key elements for crafting messages that matter is to clearly articulate one solid idea, one main thought, one "remember this" point to an audience. In your thinking process, go after that one compelling thought, the essential action, the basic principle that your students might take home with them. If you can send them home with one thing that sticks, you've done a good job. (More on this in the next chapter.)

CHAPTER TEN

Illustrate: Add a Little Color to Your Messages

A Parable

Once upon a time there was a youth worker who cared very much about his youth group. He cared that the students' souls were parched and their hearts were dried up. And he hurt because when the teenagers arrived each week for church, they were always desperately thirsty. But what burdened him most of all was that it didn't need to be that way. He knew what few of them would admit—more than anything else, they needed water.

So the next week at youth group, he gave them water—lots of it! He brought in a high-pressure fire hose he'd picked up while in seminary, and he delivered a strong, powerful spray. He really let them have it. And when he finished the power-wash with a word of prayer, he expected to see everyone quenched and satisfied. What he saw instead was a group of teenagers thoroughly drenched, completely soaked, and still desperately thirsty. He believed they were apathetic for the water.

So discouraged was he by his failure to get them to drink that he asked one of his volunteers to give the students water the next time they gathered. Of course, this volunteer hadn't been to seminary, and she'd never had the chance to buy a fire hose or collect a shelf full of nozzles. But she still had a deep affection for the students, and she knew the Source for water.

When the students arrived at church that week—still looking thirsty and dehydrated, but now wearing raincoats and other protective gear—she simply gave them glasses full of water and invited them to drink. And you know what? Most of them did drink. It wasn't the water that made them turn their heads away; it never had been. It was the way the water was delivered.

The lesson of the parable? Choose one:

a. Teenagers need to invite Evian into their hearts.

b. With the right equipment, we can do baptism *and* crowd control at the same time.

c. If we want to offer students the Living Water, then we need to present it in a way that lowers the pressure, allows them to breathe, and gives them a chance to drink.

If you answered "c," way to go! And one way to do that is to make good use of effective illustrations. Let's start with some basic assumptions:

Assumption #1: For a lot of youth workers, the default approach to communication is the power-wash—a direct spray of content.

Assumption #2: Most youth workers don't use enough illustrations.

Assumption #3: Teenagers want and need more relevant, real-life illustrations when they listen to messages.

Assumption #4: Illustrations work—they're extremely effective in making the point and in making the point stick.

In one study conducted with 2,000 students, about 10 percent more information was retained when speeches used a variety of illustrative devices, figurative language, analogies, stories, and so on. This was true whether the audience was listening to a live speaker or merely an audio recording.[79] To borrow from the apostle Paul, illustrations provide a "visible image of the invisible" (Colossians 1:15, NLT). In other words, illustrations help teenagers see.

Illustrations are one of the main pivot points in effective communication, and they're essential to making messages stick beyond the spoken word. Whenever I hear an incredible speaker, I think, *I need to work harder on illustrations*. Whenever I hear an average speaker, I think, *I need to work harder on illustrations*. Whenever I'm listening to a speaker who uses great content but basically hoses kids down, I think, *More illustrations please! You're killing them!* And when I hear a master communicator use illustrations to refresh the audience with opportunities to "taste and see," I think, I *need to learn to use more illustrations and learn how to use them better.* So often the effectiveness of a message relies on the speaker's ability to find illustrations and use them well.

Jesus is arguably the greatest teacher ever. As we study his teachings, it's immediately apparent he understands the power of good illustrations. As a matter of fact, we're told Jesus never spoke without using a parable or story (Matthew 13:34). Dramatic stories, vivid word pictures, provocative parables, and object lessons—like a carpenter who skillfully uses his tools to shape rough timber into a smooth chalice, Jesus uses illustrations so his listeners can drink.

Of course, you could argue, "Yeah, well, I'd have amazing illustrations too if I had the ability to turn water into wine." And that's certainly true. But this chapter isn't about doing the miraculous or how to turn water into wine. (That's in our next book.) This chapter is about turning fire hoses into drinking glasses—from water sprayed to water offered.

Opening Windows, Searching for Gold

The operative principle here is simply this: When creating a message, you always want to look for places in your content where a teenager might say, "Show me what you mean. You're pointing to something that isn't really visible to me, and I want to understand. Give me a window so I can see what you're talking about."

When you give them an object lesson to stand on so they can look through that window, or a personal story that opens the curtains wider, or a video clip that makes the window cleaner, you create ah-ha moments that allow your students the chance to glimpse what they couldn't see before.

For a lot of us, this action step in the S.T.I.C.K. process is the toughest part of the weekly message-preparation regimen. But there are two ways we can help ourselves here. First of all, we can develop the habit of gathering illustrations (chapter 7). That won't *always* give you a lot of gold, but at least it gives you a mine to dig in. Second, we can begin our study process far enough in advance to allow the maximum amount of time between conception and delivery. Having adequate time to dig is only helpful if you know where the gold is buried. And learning where the gold is buried is profitable only if you have the time to do the necessary digging.

As you mine for illustrations, it might make more sense for you to shift the order around a bit. For example, in my case, the sequence usually plays out like this:

1. **Tuesday morning: S**tudy the text.

2. *Tuesday morning (off and on) until the delivery on Sunday morning:* **T**hink about what I studied.

3. *Wednesday morning:* **C**onstruct an outline or a flow for the content that I'll be teaching.

4. *All week (informally) and Friday morning (formally):* Now that the basic structure (or content) of the message is built, I think about where I need illustrations (informally: all week) and pick the specific illustrations on Friday.

5. *Saturday night or Sunday morning:* Cut content, double-check to make sure I **K**eep a clear focus. (You'll be introduced to a helpful checklist on page 186.)

While we sincerely believe that each element of the S.T.I.C.K. process is critical, we don't believe it's critical that you do each element in the sequence implied by our S.T.I.C.K. acronym. We just used it to make it easier to remember (and because T.I.C.K.S. wasn't really an image we wanted to hang our hats on).

One of the main benefits of *thinking* (**T**) about your message throughout the week is that illustrations are happening around you all the time. And when you know the essence of what you're going to teach four to six days before you teach it, the illustrations are a lot easier to spot—because it sharpens your awareness.

For example, I [Doug] drive a white 1999 Toyota 4Runner. Prior to this, I drove a white 1991 Toyota 4Runner. Being a creature of habit, I likely would have bought a white 2007 Toyota 4Runner, but there was this little formality called "college tuition" that has messed with my eight-year vehicle buying cycle. Anyway, when I first drove that car off the lot in 1991, I was so excited! I didn't know anyone who had a white 4Runner. In my mind, I was unique because I honestly believed I was one of only a handful of people who owned this car.

Of course, no sooner did I leave the dealership than I saw another white 4Runner, and then another, and then another, and then another. By the time I got home with my new and *totally unique* white 4Runner, I'd seen 197 white Toyota 4Runners. They were everywhere! Dealerships must have had a blowout special that day, and they all hit the road at the same time. Or maybe there's another possibility: They'd been there all along, but I just hadn't noticed them.

You don't notice what you're not looking for. Until I was looking at the world from *inside* my cool, one-of-a-kind, white Toyota 4Runner, I wasn't conscious of the white Toyota 4Runners I passed every day. I didn't notice them because I wasn't looking for them.

When I've done my study work early in the preparation process, it allows me time to go through my week and look at the world from inside that text. It allows me to see illustrations and ideas that I might have routinely passed by. And the reason is simple—now I know what I'm looking for. The key is giving yourself some space between study time and delivery date. The more space you allow, the stronger your illustrations will become.

Develop the discipline of observing, capturing, and recording "life as it happens." When something unique or odd or wonderful or painful or intriguing or embarrassing happens, write it down or record it into your phone or some other handy audio device. You don't want to forget it.

Imagine your child is running to give you a hug after work; but just before she gets to you, she trips and bangs her face and knees on the sidewalk. Your first thought should be, *Is she okay?* But later on, you might further consider what happened: *Wow, my first response to her fall was not condemnation or anger at her clumsiness; it was grief, love, and a desire to restore her. That's just like God's love for us! Man, that's good! I need to ask my daughter to stop crying so I can tell her about this illustration, and then she can help me remember it.* Or (for the more technically inclined), *My voice recorder is in my study. I think I can grab it on my way to get the first-aid kit.*

Now, that's a little exaggerated—obviously I'd grab the first-aid kit and then the recorder. But you get the idea: Just like you'd do with your new habit of gathering (chapter 7), you want to always be on the lookout for illustrations. You're constantly watching, looking, thinking, and wondering, *Will that preach?*

Amazing Stories

At a May 3, 2002, meeting of the Annual Conference of the Society of General Internal Medicine, doctors were given the stunning results of research that looked at the aftereffects of a five-day campaign that featured Katie Couric, then cohost of NBC's *Today Show*, to raise the public's awareness of colon cancer. (In 1998, Couric's husband, Jay Monahan, died of colon cancer at the age of 42.) And at the heart of that campaign was Couric's live, on-air colonoscopy.

To determine the campaign's effects, the University of Michigan researchers examined colonoscopy rates drawn from a database of 400 endoscopists across the United States, as well as from a managed-care organization between July 1998 and December 2000 (89 weeks before Couric's procedure and about 40 weeks after).

The data showed that the average number of colonoscopies performed by each doctor increased from 4.76 to 6.13 a week. The mean age of patients having colonoscopies decreased significantly, and the proportion of women increased significantly. Said Dr. Peter Cram, lead author of the project, "Our study shows that the number of colonoscopies increased by 19%, and was sustained for 40 weeks."[80]

Now, you may wonder if you have somehow fallen asleep and stumbled into a different book—and now that you're reading about colons and disease, you're wondering how to stumble back out. But in fact, this study vividly demonstrates two realities: (1) the persuasive power of story, and (2) that guys our age are particularly interested in colonoscopies.

Biographical or autobiographical stories can be an amazingly strategic form of illustration. Both of us love to read histories, and they're obviously a deep well of poignant and powerful stories. But we also like to draw from a wide range of fields—adventure, missions, current events, sports, military, and colonoscopy research.

Let's talk about some very simple elements of good storytelling.

Watch Your Waste Lines

Don't waste a lot of time getting into the story. Some of the common time wasters are:

- Telling the audience that you have a story to tell. (e.g., "Let me tell you a really amazing story...")

- Asking permission to use the story. (e.g., "Do you mind if I tell you one quick story?")

- Documenting the story. (e.g., "This is a story I got from a friend of mine who...well, I guess she wasn't really a friend; more of an acquaintance, but I'd known her for about a year, although I really knew her brother better than I knew her, although I didn't know the brother as well as I knew their parents—who are great people! They came to my wedding and bought me a sweet filet knife that I used last night when I tried to cut the gum out of the carpet that Pete—who's sitting over there and who I like to call "the Pete-ster"—threw up last weekend when he and the Droopy boys spent the night in my living room. Anyway, this story came from Steve...")

- Needless background facts. (e.g., "I wasn't even going to use this story, but I came across it in a back issue of *Gun Running & Today's Christian Woman*, and I thought it might make an interesting illustration someday.")

"Woo" Is More Important Than "Wow"

Always begin with a hook line—something that gives your teenagers a reason to listen.

- Give them a verbal heads-up. (e.g., "Sooner or later you learn that the color pink doesn't go with every kind of footwear...") It doesn't tell the whole story, but it signals to the audience something about what's coming.

- Or you might use a rhetorical question. (e.g., "Have you ever had one of those days when your hairpiece kept falling off?")

- Start as far into the story as possible without leaving the audience behind. Don't make them listen to the first four episodes if they can understand the story with a quick jump into episode five. (e.g., "I still can't believe it happened; even the guy who owned the restaurant was amazed...")

Hopefully, that opening line in the story will introduce some tension. You want to say enough to hook the audience, but not so much that they take the bait and swim away. Essentially you want to woo your audience with this question: "Do you want to know what happened next?" When they're not asking that question anymore, story time is over.

Point to the Point

Before you begin telling the story, you want to offer a connecting line—the line that links the story to the content of your message. There's nothing more bewildering for an audience than a story that's lost and looking for a point. A story needs to be connected at both ends, going into the story and coming out of the story.

For example, "I don't care how long you've been in a church; it almost never makes sense to go to war with a friend in your small group. One of the basic lessons of human relationships is, 'Never anger the snake when it's wrapped around your leg'...[then you give the snake illustration]...and it was a lesson he learned the hard way, but he learned it: The only thing more difficult than making peace with a small group member who's driving you crazy is being at war with a small group member who's driving you crazy. 'Never anger the snake when it's wrapped around your leg.'"

Speak in Specifics

Compare these two introductory lines: (1) "A few years ago..." or (2) "On September 1, 2007..." One just sounds more real, doesn't it? Or how about these two lines: (1) "One day a group of teenagers were down at the local fast-food joint..." versus (2) "There were three of them, two guys and a girl, Rick, Keith, and Megan, and they were all seniors. They were sitting in their favorite booth at Taco Bell..." The story becomes much more interesting when we add specifics.

Get It Right

It was a Sunday morning service at my old church in Barrington, Rhode Island. I [Duffy] was preaching to a congregation of folks who've grown up around seafood—some of whom made their living digging clams in the waters of Narragansett Bay. I'd planned to use an amazing illustration about how pearls are formed; it was a wonderful story about how God turned an irritant (sand) into something beautiful (a pearl). It was going to be my knock-out punch in a sermon about dealing with pain. But to really contextualize this story, I decided that instead of using the word *clam* I would use *quahog*. I was so proud of myself because this was a locals-only term.

Just when I expected sniffles of emotion and recognition, I instead heard stifled giggles, and a few not-so-stifled chuckles. I couldn't figure it out. Then after the sermon, someone told me that my illustration—the one I'd intended to be poignant and moving—had instead been humorous because I'd talked about quahogs having pearls. Since I wasn't a local, I didn't know what all native Rhode Islanders knew—quahogs don't have pearls.

Raucous laughter wasn't really the vibe I was going for—it kind of spoiled my ending. But this personal humiliation taught me the importance of checking my facts before telling a story.

It's a Good Story, But Is It the Right Story?

Even a well-told story is no good if it's a story your audience doesn't want to hear. For example, "I don't know if I've ever told you young people about the first time I got diarrhea" or "Most of us probably don't think much about hydraulic pressure." Make sure you know your audience well enough to know what stories you can tell them.

Personal Stories

There are three other variations on the story motif: The interview, the testimony, and what we call "failure stories." Let's look at them.

The Interview

Interviews are great illustrations because they're so simple to use. When you know a teenager is doing something in her life that relates to what you plan to talk about, access her opinion or advice through a short interview. Interviews like this add another voice to your message and break up the content with something teenagers would rather hear than another adult talking to them.

Let's say you're teaching on friendship: You might ask a pair of friends to share a few practical ways they work on their friendship and then tie it into your message. Tip: Give them the questions ahead of time so they don't feel put on the spot or spend all of their allotted time trying to say something coherent.

Testimonies

Testimonies are similar to interviews except that, typically, with a testimony you wouldn't ask questions of the person speaking. Teenagers are natural storytellers. Just sit in a Starbucks some afternoon and listen to their conversations. Every teenager has a story to tell, and every one of those stories has something to offer. When you can get teenagers to tell their stories, you'll be amazed at how much more memorable and impressionable your message becomes. In fact, what you'll likely find is that teenagers won't remember much of your message when someone shares a powerful testimony. But they'll remember the testimony, and they'll probably be able to connect it to the big idea of your talk.

The key to finding testimonies within your youth ministry ranks is to encourage all of your students to write their personal stories and turn them into you to read and file. Don't discount the stories that seem "normal" or "bland"—no drugs, no abuse, no near-death car crashes, no colon stories, no upper-tier Amway sales, and so on. The radical testimonies are the ones that seem to get the airtime, but I love presenting stories of teenagers who've been making good decisions. I think there's tremendous value in having them share about their journeys with Jesus. Plus, even a "good-kid" testimony, if it's well written, will include the reality of loneliness, feelings of inadequacy, fear, and so on. When you get your students to write their stories, you can read them and file them under the different topics about which you'll be teaching throughout the year.

These real-life stories and testimonies are easy to use and a powerful way to enhance your messages. Personal is always more powerful. Consider the difference between the illustration books for speakers and preachers and the popular, never-ending, money-making, ridiculously titled series of books called Chicken Soup for the Soul. If you've ever read one of these books, you know they're essentially page after page of real-life stories and personal testimonies. When you compare the stories in the Chicken Soup series with the stories found in books like *1000 Illustrations for Speakers*, there's really no comparison. Why? Because the Chicken Soup books are filled with real names, real faces, and real lives. Most speaker-illustration books lack that personal connection. In fact, one of the projects we now have in development is a new book called *Chicken Soup for the Colon*. But, seriously, put your illustration books on the lower shelf and begin writing and collecting your own illustration book full of real-life stories. Personal is always more powerful.

Failure Stories

Today I drove past a car that was stalled on the side of the road. I hate to admit this, but as I passed it, I wasn't even tempted to help the person because I was running late for a meeting and definitely in a hurry. I thought, *Oh, bummer for that person*, and then I kept on driving. When I got to the restaurant, not only was I late, but the person I was meeting was even later. Now I felt guilty for not stopping to help the old lady trapped in the burning car. (Just kidding, she wasn't that old.) To relieve my guilt, I grabbed a napkin and wrote: DELAYED EMPATHY/CAR BROKEN DOWN. This will now become a personal illustration that I can use when I talk about being sensitive to the needs of others.

That story serves as a prime example of a failure story, and failure stories are always a big win with teenagers. Teenagers appreciate it when you honestly share from your fragile and broken life. Not only does it offer a real-life illustration, but it's more powerful because you're *not* the hero of the story. This illustration is much more powerful than one you could read or memorize from an illustration book titled *Mean People: True Stories of Unkind Humans*. It's powerful because it's personal.

Teenagers need to hear more failure stories from the men and women they admire. When teenagers know you're not perfect, it will increase your *ethos*. We're not suggesting you never tell stories about you making the right choice, nor are we suggesting that you pursue failure so you'll have an arsenal of illustrations. But we do want to encourage you to communicate from your weaknesses as much as, if not more than, from your strengths. When you share honest failures you inspire teenagers to keep going in their spiritual journeys. You give them hope that they can fail and still "succeed" as followers of Jesus Christ.

Are there limits as to how much information you should share in your failure stories? Absolutely. There are some important boundaries you shouldn't cross. Here are some simple guidelines:[81]

1. Self-exposure must have a purpose. Transparency is not just about saying everything we feel or think. Up front at a youth group meeting is no place for a leader to work out his issues. We don't speak just to get something "off our chests." The goal must be edification, not self-expression.

2. Make sure every confession of failure is joined with a clear intention to do better. The glory of the gospel is that by the death of Jesus *for* us we are saved "just as we are." But as glorious is the fact that by the life of Jesus *in* us, we are not bound to stay as we are. (See Romans 5:9–10; 8:8–17.)

   We should be honest enough to admit that ours is a "messy spirituality," to use Mike Yaconelli's term. (*Messy Spirituality*, Youth Specialties/Zondervan, 2002) But the great news of God's sanctifying Spirit is that little by little—he helps us clean up our messes. It's true: God loves us as we are, but he doesn't intend to *leave* us as we are.

3. Our transparency must point students to Jesus. We don't share our problems so people will notice how much we've given up, how wild we were, how humble we are, or how honest we're willing to be. The nature of real transparency is that it allows students to see *through* us so they can see Jesus more clearly.

4. Some confessions simply aren't suited for public consumption. Talk to your prayer group of peers. Talk to your pastor. Talk to your counselor. Talk to your spiritual director. But don't dump a load on the youth group that they shouldn't be asked to bear.

A Special Word about Personal Stories

If you're going to use someone's personal story, it's essential that you ask for permission to share it in front of others. This is absolutely necessary if it involves anyone within your youth ministry or your family. You could destroy your credibility if you tell a story about a teenager without first asking for permission—even if it's a positive story.

While this seems like a no-brainer, it's also important to remember that this principle holds true even if the illustrations are about your own children or other family members. You don't want your own children to feel hurt because you lacked discernment.

Last weekend I was planning to tell a story about my oldest daughter, and the night before I was supposed to use it, I ran it by her. Much to my surprise, she didn't feel comfortable with me retelling that story. Now typically, she's quite willing to give me permission to tell stories about her, so this is no reflection on her. But for some reason, this particular story made her uncomfortable. The good news is that she gave me permission to tell you *this* story about her being uncomfortable with me telling *that* story.

It can get really ugly if you tell a story without permission. I once told my youth group about a friend who made some bad decisions, went through a messy divorce, and basically screwed up his life. But as I was telling his story, I made a dumb, needless comment about his ex-wife. (I said something like, "She wasn't innocent in this relationship, either.") It wasn't until after my message that I learned that my friend's ex-wife had remarried, and her stepchildren had been sitting in my audience. Even though I didn't mention any names, the children knew I was talking about their stepmom. Obviously, they were very offended that I would lump their stepmom into the same category as my friend—who really was the main character of the story and a total idiot. They felt like I'd made their mom sound bad, too—like she was guilty by association. I was totally caught off guard by this situation because I honestly meant no harm to the ex-wife or her family. I hardly even thought about her.

In reflection, that was the problem—I hardly thought about her. There was nothing in my friend's story that required me to mention his former wife. It was my own stupid mistake. The whole illustration was about his life, his bad decisions, and the sad consequences connected to those bad decisions. But by not thinking through all the details of the story and then speaking carelessly, I made a bad blunder, and I paid for it with relational conflict following the message. The fallout and the follow-up conversations were very painful. Bottom line: If the illustration isn't about you, get permission. And then, just to be safe, *even with permission* it's a good idea to change some of the details of the story so it can't be traced back to anyone in particular.

But stories are only one of the brushes with which we paint the vivid pictures that make our message content come alive.

Add Brushes to Your Tool Kit

There are many ways to paint a picture. Let's talk about some additional tools for developing effective illustrations.

Shameless Plug: We have a two-volume set of drama books called *Spontaneous Melodramas* that offer creative, entertaining ways to get students inside a biblical narrative through easy-to-do drama. Each book contains 24 different scripts—12 from the Old Testament and 12 from the New Testament.

The idea behind a "melodrama" is that a narrator reads through the script while the cast spontaneously acts out their parts as they're hearing the action the script dictates. If there's a speaking part, they speak it. If there's an acting part, they act it. The feedback we get from youth workers who've used these books is that the melodramas are a really fun, user-friendly way to introduce teenagers to a passage of Scripture-- and of course, teenagers always enjoy being in the front of the room.

Each of the melodramas offers a twist on a familiar biblical narrative. So, for example, the story of Samson and Delilah (Judges 16) uses a soap opera motif—"The Young and the Hairless." And the story of the demoniac (Mark 5) who was so demon-ridden that he identified himself as "Legion, for we are many" has a Disney motif— "101 Damnations."

Drama

If there's one thing we've all observed about drama, it's that teenagers will pay more attention to their peers who are attempting to act than an adult who is trying to speak. Even bad drama grabs more interest than a good talking head. Drama can be a great illustrative tool.

For example, right in the middle of your message, you could insert a short sketch (where you might normally have used a story or an illustration) and say, "Here's another way you could look at it...watch this." Then sit back and allow a couple of your teenagers to use their skills (or lack thereof) to act out the situation. (Good Rule of Thumb: Watch the length. Short, bad drama is *always* better than long, bad drama.)

There are more drama scripts available on the Internet than you could ever possibly use. Some cost a few bucks; others are free. But you should have ready access to a pretty wide range of topics.

Movie Clips

It doesn't take much youth worker genius to recognize that teenagers would rather watch a movie than listen to a sermon. And it doesn't take much watching to recognize that quite a few movies are nothing more than visual sermons. There are at least a dozen great books on the market (and at least that many Web sites) that can help you find good film clips to use.

I'll often use a movie clip to illustrate relational principles—those seem to be the easiest to use without a lot of elaborate setup or contextualization. Whether it's anger or love or conflict or mistrust, there are lots of clips that illustrate and put flesh to the content. (Good Rule of Thumb #2: Some movies put too much flesh to the content—stay away from those clips.)

A movie clip is almost always a big win because kids connect so well with this medium.

It increases your *ethos* profile when you take something from a teenager's culture and use it to teach a truth from God's Word. Sometimes even bad Hollywood theology can be used as an example to teach good biblical theology.

One additional note on using movies: I don't believe the use of a video clip condones watching the entire movie any more than serving pizza at an overnight endorses childhood obesity. But we're not so naive that we can't understand the concern. What we do clearly understand is that lots of parents don't want their teenagers watching movie clips at youth group that the teenagers wouldn't be allowed to watch at home. So use discernment here. Remember, it's not always what we say, it's also what they see and hear that makes all the difference.

Music

Using music as a tool of illustration has the dual benefit of waking up your students and communicating with them through a medium that's near and dear to their hearts. Music can be prerecorded or it can be live. Again, the same principle applies to music as to drama—teenagers love to hear other teenagers sing.

The only caveat we need to add here is this: One big difference between drama and music is that while bad drama is still better than no drama, bad music is just...bad—bad for the audience, bad for the singers, and bad for the message. Live music that starts off being a wonderful testimony of God's faithfulness can, by the end of the song, degenerate into a vivid illustration of the problem of evil. That doesn't help you very much, and it only humiliates the "singers." Again, a lot of discernment and wisdom is required in youth ministry leadership—so beg God for it and then use it.

If you decide to play it safe and go with prerecorded music, make the words available through your talk outline or through onscreen media so students can follow along.

Humor

When humor works, it can be a powerful means of communication in general and of illustration in particular. The human brain has a built-in bias for novelty. Research has even documented specific health benefits of laughter. Dr. Arthur Stone and his colleagues at the State University of New York found that "having fun, pleasant experiences improves the functioning of the body's immune system for three days—the day of the event and two days after."[82] (That may help explain the nasty cold you've picked up while reading this book.) All of us love to laugh, and most of us know the power of getting teenagers to laugh—especially at church!

There are five basic categories of humor to consider:

Exaggeration

This would be any kind of overstatement related to people, places, sizes, the way people feel or act, and personal experiences. *Delivery Tip:* There are two ways to play exaggeration. One is to deliver the line with a sense of awe or surprise or disgust. For example (from the last chapter), "By the time I got home with my new and *totally unique* white 4Runner, I'd seen 197 white Toyota 4Runners. They were everywhere! Dealerships must have had a blow-out special that day, and they all hit the road at the same time."

The other way is to deliver the line in an even, understated tone: So it becomes more about irony than about disgust.

Surprise

Surprise means making use of unexpected or unusual feelings, events, or facts. One of the most valuable lessons you can learn about humor is that, at its core, it's about surprise. That's why timing is such a huge piece of doing humor well.

Delivery Tip: Think about how to structure your delivery line so it offers the maximum surprise. Always move the punch line as close to the end of the sentence as possible. If you can, make it the last word(s) in the sentence.

Setup is crucial to maximize the element of surprise. One standard gag technique is to offer two or three serious items followed by a final item that's absurd. That sets up the surprise. For example (from chapter 5), every time you speak to teenagers, they're asking questions like this:

- *Does he really understand me?*

- *Does she care about me?*

- *Does he even like me?*

- *I wonder when he started losing his hair?*

Absurdity

Absurdity is when you use materials that are illogical in thinking or in language (see latter comment about 'losing his hair' as an example). *Delivery Tip:* These lines are often best delivered deadpan with a matter-of-fact tone. The best way to kill absurdity is to laugh at your own jokes. No matter how funny you think you are, try to restrain yourself.

Human Problems

These are situations in which a person appears foolish or is simply the victim of everyday life. This could be anything from the *Candid Camera* technique of allowing us to "see ourselves in the act of being ourselves" to the third-person report of something that happened to someone else. For example, "Until she stood up fast, she didn't realize the Port o' Potty was standing on slanted ground...."

Delivery Tip: Use your words well. Paint the most vivid portrait possible.

Sarcasm

Sarcasm includes teasing or bringing attention to someone's faults, and it's the lowest hanging fruit on the humor tree. That's why everyone quickly reaches for it (especially teenagers). But it can also be very hurtful, and it can breed mistrust.

Delivery Tip: Ration your use of sarcasm very carefully. Restrict it to nonpersonal entities (such as corporations or objects), ideas, or iconic pop-culture figures that represent ideas. We're not saying you won't get a laugh if you direct your sarcasm toward students or leaders in your group. We're only saying the laughs may come at too high a cost.

The one absolute exception to this rule is self-deprecating humor. Anytime you can make fun of yourself, you'll win your audience. When you don't take yourself too seriously, you strengthen your *ethos* profile. When you tell the story about the time you tripped and fell while getting out of the car, your teenagers will think *dork*, but you'll become far more believable and trustworthy in their minds.

Remember, *ethos* connects with trust, and teenagers are asking, *Can I trust you?* Teenage audiences appreciate people who don't take themselves too seriously. So when you fail and have enough courage to point the laughter at yourself, teenagers are more apt to like you and trust you.

Funny Versus Not Funny

Having identified five categories of humor, let's make it even simpler now and reduce it to two *types* of humor: That which is funny and that which isn't. Blessed is the speaker who can discern the difference. In your use of humor, remember that comedy isn't what makes *you* laugh; it's what makes your audience laugh. If you're going to use humor, you need to make sure teenagers can identify and relate to it.

For example, I tried showing to my teenagers a video clip from the old TV series *Get Smart*. When I was a child, I loved that show and its bumbling spy character, Maxwell Smart. But my youth group didn't quite appreciate its comedic value. They were thinking, *Why was that TV show in black and white? Why is the spy-guy talking into his shoe? Why not just use a mobile phone? This is really stupid and not funny.* Translation: "*You're* stupid and not funny." So the most fundamental rule of humor is to use humor that teenagers will understand. *Delivery Tip:* If they're not laughing, it's not funny.

Headlines

Talk about the gold right before our eyes. Newspapers are a constant source of illustrative material. If you can make reading the news part of your daily schedule, that's great. If you can't, do so as often as possible. I'm constantly ripping headlines out of our local newspaper. Today's read: "Some dollar coins missing 'In God We Trust'." Obviously, I don't know how or when I'll use that headline, but I'll use it. It was a good one! And regardless of when I choose to use it, it will still feel current because it's a headline. Sometimes the date is important, but most of the time the headline is the real illustration and the date is irrelevant. You can simply say, "I found this in the newspaper, and I thought it was interesting, especially since we're talking about trusting God."

Now, we realize most teenagers don't wake up early and run to the driveway screaming, "I can't wait to read the newspaper!" In that sense, it's not like showing a video clip. But teenagers know enough to understand that in our culture a headline is kind of a big deal. So look for headlines that are intriguing, shocking, absurd, or funny. It's a great way to give your audience a little breather, or an additional connection to the content in your message.

Short Readings from Books

For most teenagers, their first conscious experiences of someone holding them close and nurturing them was in the context of Mom or Dad reading them a story from a book. Now 14 or 15 years later, that probably doesn't happen every night. But the *ethos* of that moment still feels pretty vivid. Sometimes *reading* a story to your audience can be even more effective than telling it.

I'll occasionally read a good story to my students. What I've found is that whether it's serious, humorous, or inspirational, a story breaks up the message both in content and delivery. Reading from a book gives my speaking tone a different sound. It's kind of a throwback to "story time with Mrs. Francis" (my kindergarten teacher).

Typically, I'll have a stool nearby. So at a couple of key times during my message, I'll grab the stool, move it to a slightly different location on stage, and then sit and read the story. I realize this isn't groundbreaking communication technique (a lot of people move stools when they know they'll be speaking to a large audience). But there's something about reading a story with a more intimate voice—or from a "storyteller's setting"—that serves as a great way to deliver a solid illustration. A few simple suggestions:

- Feel free to edit a story to meet the context and time constraints of your message.

- Be very conscious of length. Although it doesn't sound like a long time, an 8- to 10-minute story may push your teenagers to the edge of their listening capacity. It doesn't have to be, but it could be. We're just saying, be aware.

- Don't overlook the power of children's stories. About twice a year, it might be a good idea to spend an hour or so just looking through the children's section of your local bookstore in search of a winner.

- Bolster the impact of stories by using onscreen media. Especially with children's stories, artwork is often an important element.

Pictures

With the Internet and some of the amazing photo editing software that's now on the market, pictures have become a youth ministry art form. The largest file on my computer is my Pictures file. It contains hundreds of pictures that I've either found or received over the years. They're a great resource to either give your students a humor break or illustrate a story or an idea.

For example, imagine I'm telling a failure story about when I was in a car accident, and then I say, "Here's what my car looked like," and I show a photo of an abandoned car stuck in a tree. The story was true, but the exaggerated photo is just a gag to add humor to my story. The best part is that with humorous pictures, you don't have to *be* funny to use humor.

With the simplicity of small digital cameras or camera phones, it's easy to snap on-the-fly photos of humorous license plates or T-shirts or bumper stickers that you see as you go about your normal schedule. For example, I could tell the story of seeing a VW van filled with hundreds of Christian bumper stickers, or I can tell the story of the "evangelism van" and show the picture of the van. Guess which one is a stronger illustration?

Because of the comedy value of pictures and photographs, it's easy to overlook the power of pictures to provoke serious reflection on a topic or an idea. If you were to teach on poverty, for example, your teenagers may not have an adequate mental picture to draw from without your offering some real-life imagery. Without the picture to portray an image of poverty, it's too easy for them to think about it only in the context of their own world. (i.e., poverty = a teenager who doesn't own a car, takes a bus to school, can't afford designer jeans, and listens to a low-end iPod.) Using a picture can help you redefine important concepts.

Eavesdropping

I could fill a book with conversations I've overheard between teenagers. I spend a few hours a week in fast-food restaurants either reading or working (like right now), and I'm amazed at what teenagers will talk about with their friends, even though that creepy "old guy" [Doug] is sitting in the booth right behind them. I suppose it's because I look like I'm working that they don't think I can actually hear what they're saying. Their painfully honest conversations always give me fresh illustrations that I can use during my messages.

For example, "I was sitting in Taco Bell earlier this week, and I heard three high school students talking. One told the other...." Then I retell the conversation.

I usually leave out the incriminating details, but I can echo back enough of the conversation that my teenagers know I'm not making it up. They know that particular conversation because they've heard it or spoken it before.

This is one of those types of illustrations where I always get the feeling that my teenagers are thinking, *Gosh, he really knows our world.* Well, one of the reasons I know their world is because they talk so loudly about their sins. Most adults don't talk about their sins publicly; and if they do, they definitely use their "inside voice."

Object Lessons

I think it hit me for the first time on a frosty New England morning several years ago. It was Sunday morning, and I'd just finished preaching what I felt was a fairly effective sermon. Now people were streaming down the aisles on their way out of church. I was in my "thanks for coming" mode, where I shake hands and respond to the various comments as people walk down the front steps of Barrington Baptist Church. "I appreciate the encouragement." "I'm glad you found it helpful." "No, ma'am, I'm fine, I just haven't been getting much sleep lately." "Good to see you too." "Yes, honey, that is my real hair; shouldn't you be in the nursery?"

Then came an epiphany.

I realized that two out of every three positive comments—er...uh...maybe I should say, two of *the three* positive comments were not about the sermon I'd just preached. They were about the children's talk that I'd given at the beginning of the service, a simple little illustration using a glove and my hand. (I know you're thinking puppets—but, oh no, it was so much more.) And it was amazing. Middle-aged guys in three-piece suits were walking out saying, "Hey, thanks for that little talk with 'Gary the Glove.' It [sniffle] really [wipe eyes] touched me!"

Such is the power of a good object lesson. Here are a few suggestions about how to use them well:

- **Remember that even good object lessons won't teach themselves.** There is no such thing as an object lesson that's so good its only instructions are "just add audience." Every now and then someone will come up to me after a seminar for youth workers and complain that they tried an object lesson I'd suggested and, they groan in frustration, "It didn't work!" Then I have to explain, "That's right. *Ideas* don't work. *Youth workers* work. Ideas are the tools that youth workers use to do their work." To complain that an idea doesn't work is like a carpenter complaining to Home Depot that a hammer doesn't work. An object lesson is nothing more than a tool. Even the best object lessons may need to be tweaked to fit your specific group.

- **Remember that the object of an object lesson is for kids to learn a lesson.** An object lesson is a way of focusing the mind and the heart on some truth you want to teach from the Scripture. It's not an end in itself. If you just stand up with a pair of boxers and say, "You know, kids, life is like a pair of underwear... Now let's close in prayer," you're not going to accomplish very much spiritually, and you're probably going to frighten the kids in your group. Just doing an object lesson without taking the time to process that object lesson and without helping your students reflect on what they've seen is going to leave them remembering an object instead of the lesson.

- **Remember to keep it simple.** The power of an object lesson is its simplicity. Resist the temptation to show your kids all the deep symbolism you've uncovered in "the mystery of the hula hoop." One of the best ways to ruin an object lesson is to try to make more of it than it is. If you can, make one truth visible to your students; that's enough. Don't squeeze the analogy so much that you end up suffocating it.

- **Remember it's only an object lesson.** One of the many lessons marriage has taught me is that my wife takes windows *very* seriously. For example, before I was married, I believed a window was something you looked through. I didn't realize that, at least from my wife's standpoint, windows are actually points of architectural flourish, stages that showcase various window dressings, and greenhouses that breed growing things. Now, I'm not complaining—our house looks great. But I must confess that every now and then, I feel just a twinge of temptation to pull out a machete so I can see outside.

Object lessons allow us to view what we otherwise might not have seen. And in that sense, they're a great tool. But we'd better not get so carried away with the object lesson that we clutter up the truth that it's showing us. *An object lesson is not for decoration; it's for illustration and illumination.* It's a way of letting the light through so teenagers can look across the landscape of God's truth. But it's possible to make an object lesson so elaborate and intense that everyone is distracted from the truth you want them to see.

I [Duffy] remember one of my youth ministry students at Eastern University giving a talk in which he broke a china plate to illustrate his point.He smashed this plate on the floor of the classroom, and shards of glass scattered like shrapnel, literally cutting one of the girls in the front row. Another young woman was so caught off guard by the sudden slam and crash of the plate that she began to cry. I'll admit it was a powerful illustration. It's just that, to this day, nobody can remember what he was trying to illustrate.

Jesus was constantly pointing at stuff, holding it up, using it, and explaining to people, "This is like the kingdom of God." But every time he picked up a grain of wheat or cursed a fig tree or washed filthy feet, he didn't do it so people would become intrigued by wheat, sympathetic toward figs, or aware of foot hygiene; he did it to point people to God. Remember that the point of an object lesson is not to have kids look at it, but to look through it.

Make Sure Your Illustrations Point to the Point

Whatever method of illustration you choose, you'll want to be very careful that it clearly connects with your content. We've all heard "great" communicators who do nothing more than tell a series of unrelated stories that connect to nothing. Entertaining? Maybe. But enlightening? Not likely. There's no main message. There's no take-away value. There's no personal application. We all agree that people are wowed by a good story, but good stories don't equate to good communication. Make sure you have a purpose for your illustration.

Along those lines, be careful with overly dramatic illustrations. The problem with illustrations that contain graphic details or highly emotional endings is that the teenager will remember the illustration more than its intended point (e.g., the child who got run over by the train, the lady who loses her leg in a skiing accident, the firefighter who was burned while trying to save the church, the youth pastor who loses his hair while bobbing for razor blades, or the two bears that attack 42 young men (see 2 Kings 2:23–24)).

We're not suggesting you steer clear of emotional stories. We're just warning you that the more dramatic the illustration, the greater the risk that it'll distract from the very point you want to make.

Preaching the Words

If someone were to look back over the last century and a half and study the speeches that have shaped our national consciousness—e.g., Abraham Lincoln's "Gettysburg Address," Winston Churchill's "Battle of Britain" speech, Franklin Delano Roosevelt's post-Pearl Harbor "Day of Infamy" speech, Martin Luther King, Jr.'s "I Have a Dream" speech, Ronald Reagan's commemoration of the fortieth anniversary of the D-day invasion, Pedro's campaign speech in *Napoleon Dynamite*—we might begin to see that all of these speeches have one trait in common: Each speaker took very seriously the power of words—in particular, the power of *word pictures*.

We've spent the bulk of this chapter talking about how we use words to illustrate important truths. If illustrations are the pictures, then words are the brushes we use to paint those pictures. Effective illustrations require that we use those brushes well. Great communicators have always known this: Words matter.

Watch Your Speech

It was December 8, 1941. Just 24 hours earlier the American Naval base in Pearl Harbor had been the target of a massive, deadly attack. The cost in human life was staggering. American casualties were 2,403 dead and 1,178 wounded. President Roosevelt sat down behind a microphone to address America; its citizens were reeling with shock, outrage, and uncertainty. The speech he gave that day, cowritten by his speechwriters Samuel Rosenman and Robert Sherwood, became known as the "Day of Infamy" speech, one of the best-known orations in America's collective memory.

What most people don't realize is that the word *infamy* did not appear in the original draft of the speech. The original phrase was, "Yesterday, December 7, 1941—a date which will live in world history—the United States was simultaneously and deliberately attacked by naval and air forces of the Empire of Japan."

In his second draft, Roosevelt crossed out *world history* and edited the first line to read, "Yesterday, December 7th, 1941—a date which will live in infamy—the United States of America was suddenly and deliberately attacked by naval and air forces of the Empire of Japan."

He also replaced the word *simultaneously*—an accurate word, but lacking in power—with the word *suddenly*, which is vivid and more immediate to the mind. Roosevelt understood the power of words.[83]

In speaking to teenagers, we cannot underestimate the importance of words— in particular, the *right* words. Changing even one word can have a surprising effect on the persuasive impact of a phrase.

In one experiment that demonstrates this point convincingly, University of Washington psychologists Elizabeth Loftus and John Palmer showed people film footage of an automobile accident. After viewing the film, subjects were divided into two groups and asked questions about what they'd witnessed. One group was asked, "How fast were the cars going at the time of impact?" The other group was asked, "How fast were the cars going when they smashed into each other?" Subjects who were asked the question using the word *smashed* gave consistently higher speed estimates than those who were asked the question using the word *impact*.

One week later the subjects in both groups were asked whether they recalled seeing any broken glass in the accident. Loftus and Palmer found the same effect: Even though there was no broken glass at the scene, those who were asked the question using the word *smashed* were more than twice as likely to report broken glass than those who were asked the question using the word *impact*.

What that means is we need to choose our words thoughtfully and carefully. People in the persuasion business understand and capitalize on this reality. That's why we hear movements described as "pro-choice" and "pro-life." It goes back to the biblical idea that the names we give things have real significance.

For example, I never use the phrase "make love" when talking with teenagers about sex, because it's a patently deceptive phrase. If the act of sexual intercourse actually *made* love, this would be one amazingly loving planet. I don't want my teenagers to buy into the notion that somehow having sex will *make* love. Biblically speaking, sex is not about *making* love; it's an expression of love shared by two people who've *made a lifelong commitment*. Why is that a big deal? Because words matter.

I'm also very careful with euphemisms such as "adult language" or "adult video" because it suggests that somehow profanity and pornography are markers of adult behavior (i.e., if teenagers want to act grown-up, then they should use four-letter words and watch skin flicks). If Loftus and Palmer's research suggests anything, it suggests that these kinds of phrases shape perceptions in the minds of our students.

Here are some other practical suggestions:

1. Use precisely the right word. Don't just say it was "round" when you can say "oval," "egg-shaped," or "about the size and shape of a marble." These are words that paint vivid pictures on the wall of the brain.

2. Use specific words, instead of generic words. Rather than use the word *house*, what about using a word that projects a picture in the mind: *hut, lean-to, mansion, tepee, loft apartment, shanty*, or *shack*? Again, remember that the more specific your terms, the more you have to factor in the emotional dimension of the message. If you're describing a "house" in New York City, you might use the term *three-floor walk-up* or *one-story brownstone*. Both are vivid images, but if you don't live in a city where that terminology is used, the first phrase sounds like a dance and the second one sounds like an elaborate name for a rock.

3. Use descriptive words. "The wind whined." "The cold clawed." There's a risk of getting carried away here. The phrasing has to sound like you, or it will just sound silly. But sounding like you doesn't mean it has to sound bland. (See chapter 14, oral style versus written style.)

Try this for practice: Imagine the scene when Jesus enters Jericho (Luke 19). Visualize it in your mind, and then, as vividly as possible, use real words to describe what it might have been like.

4. Use specific verbs. People don't just "walk"; they "swagger," "stumble forward," "stagger," "step gingerly," "move haltingly," "limp." Each of these verbs gives us a vivid mental picture.

5. Use short, vivid words. Speaking to teenagers is not the time to brandish your extensive vocabulary. Stay away from words that require translation—even simple translation. That's why Roosevelt dropped *simultaneously* and went with *suddenly*. While both adjectives were accurate, *suddenly* draws a more vivid and immediate image than *simultaneously*. For example, instead of phrases like, "he passed away," we might use phrases like "he died." Rather than say, "The countries have contiguous borders," why not say, "The countries share a border"?

6. Use words that are familiar to your audience. Beware of using Christianese. Words such as *consecration, salvation, glory, grace, sanctification, judgment day, Christology,* and *glossolalia* are appropriate parts of the faith vocabulary, and some of them are very important terms. While it would be beneficial for our students to understand and use such terms, to speak them before they have any meaning to the teenage audience is like giving safety instructions to American preschoolers using Chinese. It's cool that the instructor is fluent in Chinese, but these instructions are too important to be misunderstood.

7. Use sound words. Speaking of words that are widely unfamiliar, I've been waiting since high school to bust out the word *onomatopoeia*. I remember learning that it refers to words that are also sounds: *buzz, gong, howl, drone, bang, hiss*. These are the kinds of words that can really add color to the black-and-white words of an illustration, and they also allow students a two-dimensional vehicle for hearing your talk.[84]

Let's face it: Crafting effective illustrations is hard work. But they're worth every effort, and every second effort that you put into finding and using the right ones. Unless you just want to power-wash your students with biblical truth, illustrations are a great way to lower the pressure, allow them to breathe, and give them a chance to drink. Use them widely and wisely to help your messages stick.

CHAPTER ELEVEN

Construct: Organize and Pull It All Together

One of the occupational hazards of speaking every week and trying to learn more about communication is an inability to listen to another speaker's message without some form of critical analysis. I don't mean to critique others, and I don't want to; but most of the time, I just can't help it. During the sermon, when I'm sure God is trying to speak to me about my soul, I'm evaluating illustrations, listening for voice technique, watching for transitions, and trying to understand the structure of the message.

It's not a mean critique; it's more of an interested one—the same way interns stand in an operating theatre and stare down on a surgeon operating on someone's heart. I'm not trying to be critical of these communicators as they wield their biblical scalpels; I just want to learn how I can be a more effective surgeon of the soul. And I'm intrigued by the variety of ways that speakers choose to organize and communicate their thoughts.

As I write this, it feels like I'm confessing a sin or sharing a deep, dark secret. I'm quite sure my own heart could use some work on that operating table. But my guess is that lots of speakers suffer from this same type of Attention Deficit Disorder. It comes with being a student of communication.

Most of the great speakers I've heard—the ones who've used words to penetrate my heart and move me to some form of action—are the ones who had an obvious plan for their content. They didn't just stand up and start speaking. The good ones have given careful thought to the way they combine diligent study, focused thinking, and their gathered illustrations to come up with a focused message that results in maximum impact.

On the other hand, I've also heard very engaging speakers who used excellent voice and gesture technique and told amazing stories, but when it was over, they'd said nothing significant. Not because they were lacking in skill, but because they failed to organize their content in a way that made sense to the listener.

While working on this chapter, I witnessed precisely this kind of thing firsthand at a youth ministry conference. After the speaker had completed his presentation and we closed out the session, we all exited into the lobby. Not surprisingly, I was immediately surrounded by people evaluating the speaker. What *did* surprise me a little was the amount of positive feedback I was hearing.

One friend looked at me and exclaimed, "Wasn't he great?!" Since this was more of a statement than a question, I didn't feel obligated to be completely honest with my answer. So I said, "He had some incredible speaking skills!" This was absolutely honest—his delivery *was* excellent. But had I been more forthcoming in my evaluation, I would have said, "Honestly, I can't categorize him as a 'great speaker' because if you look beyond his delivery, what we heard tonight was some pretty thin content and a very weak structure. But I really liked his shirt!"

My friend's immediate appreciation was directly connected to the speaker's impressive presence and delivery. And it was completely understandable. He was attractive and funny; he walked the stage with confidence; he was likeable, enthusiastic, a widely respected author; and he definitely wore a cool shirt. In a lot of ways, he was the perfect "big crowd" speaker. But his message was so scattered—there was no clear focus and no big point or challenge to take away.

He simply told a series of unconnected stories, and each one had a different theme. None were strong or convicting; none challenged us to action. They were good stories—really good. They were all entertaining, polished, humorous, and detailed. But by themselves, they were nothing more than well-told, unrelated stories.

Aside from a couple of self-promoting moments, I really enjoyed his personality; and I was cheering him on in prayer, hoping he'd pull everything together and leave us with a message, a challenge, or at least a good reason for listening to him for 45 minutes. Instead, he left us with a book and T-shirt promotion, a powerless message, and a strong reason to get back to my hotel room and work harder on this chapter. He needed this book—he was a great speaker who communicated poorly.

But I wish you could have seen his shirt.

What's Lying Around the Construction Site?

Imagine a construction site that contains several pieces of building material just lying around—some heavy, some technical, some colorful, some unique, but none of them with great value on their own. The pieces are essentially worthless until someone builds them into something. Of course, getting all the proper materials on-site is critical. But it's just a pile of random stuff until someone comes along who can assemble the pieces into something useful. That's the key to constructing a good message—it's more than having a lot of great materials; it's knowing how to do good construction.

When you have content that you've gathered, studied, thought about, illustrated, and prayed over, what do you do with it? This is what *construct* is all about. It's the step that requires you to pull it all together and put the meat on the bones. So how do you organize your material and build something special?

There isn't just one way. Some people organize everything into one point. Others use three points. John Bunyan, the great seventeenth-century preacher and author of *The Pilgrim's Progress*, once preached a sermon titled "The Heavenly Footman" in which he developed 38 distinct points. (Although, from what we can tell, he didn't do a lot of youth ministry.) I'd argue that once you've done the hard work that we've discussed in previous chapters, there are many different ways to construct your message.

When you use message construction, your outlines will be clear. Your mind will begin to immediately filter your research into your default "construct blueprint." If you have a construct that works for you, you can read a passage of Scripture and your mind will be trained to match the content with your construct: *That's definitely a concluding application point, or If I say it like this, it could become my main idea.*

There's no rule that you must be loyal to the same construct every time, but having one that works for you is a time-saver, a stress reducer, and a key component of creating messages that stick.

Key: Discover a *Construct* That Feels Natural for You

Virtually every time you hear a message, you're introduced to a different style of message construction because constructing and organizing a message is personal and unique to the speaker. That's probably one of the main reasons I'm a critical listener—I love to see how other people organize their material. It's so personal.

Most likely, your current message construction blueprint contains a combination of—

- How you were taught (you tend to teach the way you were taught)

- What "feels" comfortable to you

- What supports the way your brain works (linear, story, random principles, etc.)

- Styles used by other speakers you admire

- And a collection of other miscellaneous ideas you've picked up along the way

Plenty of speakers believe there's only one right way to construct a message. Our approach is a little more flexible. We want youth workers to learn a way that feels right for them. If your organization style feels right, then you're going to be more comfortable and more passionate; you'll also have more fun while you're delivering your message.

But having said that, effective communication is not just about being comfortable, feeling passionate, and having fun. The key to effective communication is saying something with clarity and focus so others can hear it and respond. You might have a blast as you deliver your message, but if the blast results in a bomb, then you've wounded your audience and you're right back where you started—surrounded by lots of pieces of disconnected material.

Many communicators have never identified their favorite styles of message construction. Because of that they essentially start from scratch with a new organizational "system" every time they prepare a message. If you don't have a particular default *construct*, you're not alone. And this is a good time to begin exploring one that might become a fit for you.

We don't believe our job as authors is to identify "the one" construct that will always work for you, although we'll present several options in this chapter. But regardless of what construct option you choose (or create on your own), we do believe it's our job as authors to help you shape your message according to the principles of *inductive communication*.

Inductive Communication

Do you remember the episode in Jeremiah 18:1–6, when God sends Jeremiah on a field trip to the potter's house?

> This is the word that came to Jeremiah from the Lord: "Go down to the potter's house, and there I will give you my message." So I went down to the potter's house, and I saw him working at the wheel. But the pot he was shaping from the clay was marred in his hands; so the potter formed it into another pot, shaping it as seemed best to him.
>
> Then the word of the Lord came to me. He said, "Can I not do with you, house of Israel, as this potter does?" declares the Lord. "Like clay in the hand of the potter, so are you in my hand, house of Israel."

Have you ever thought about why God would summon Jeremiah to go to a different location to receive the Word of the Lord? Was it hard to hear at Jeremiah's house? Were there too many distractions? Was God outside of his area code? Could there have been bad reception? Or might it have something to do with God's intention to use his message to make the maximum impact in Jeremiah's life?

We've already referred to concepts like *environmental factors* and *pre-exposure* and how they can impact a listener. These ideas didn't originate with us. God wanted to get Jeremiah's attention with an object-lesson metaphor about the potter and the clay. It only makes sense that God would want Jeremiah to hear that message while standing in the potter's house where he'd see the potter's hands working the pot, smell the smells of the pottery shop, and hear the sounds of wet hands slapping and shaping and molding the wet clay. God didn't *just tell* Jeremiah the Word of the Lord; he wanted Jeremiah to *experience* the Word of the Lord. That, in a nutshell, is inductive communication.

Most of us who took college speech classes were told to construct our messages like this:

- Tell them what you're going to tell them.

- Tell them.

- Then tell them what you told them.

This would properly be called *deductive communication*. It's constructed like a syllogism: $a = b$, and $b = c$, therefore $a = c$. We're not suggesting that this approach *never* works. (Of course, by the power of God, anything is possible.)

But communication research is quite clear that most people don't learn this way—mostly because we don't live this way.

Some examples:

- We don't buy new software and immediately go home and read the instructions word for word. Instead we buy new software and immediately go home and start punching keys on the keyboard and fussing until we figure it out by trial and error.

- Most of us aren't that interested in the problem of evil; but we're very interested in how God could allow a dear friend to die at a young age.

- You don't really care about the concept of electromagnetic waves operating at 2.45 GHz (corresponding to a wavelength of 12.2 cm, or just over 4-3/4 in.); you just want to microwave your popcorn during commercials.

In real-life situations, our concern isn't usually with the concept; it's with the concrete.

Please understand, *we're not saying concepts are unimportant.* Some of them are *very* important. Scientific concepts, theological concepts, developmental concepts, communication concepts—they shape the way concrete events and experiences happen. Concrete without concepts are just random chunks of life. We might as well just say, "Stuff happens!"

When we construct something, we want it to be built on the foundation of sound ideas and concepts. In fact, we've included concepts in this book because we want it to be based on sound theology and good communication research. We need concepts. But we also understand that you didn't buy this book to learn theology and grasp some more concepts about effective communication. Your purchase was for a very concrete reason: You want to become a better speaker.

Deductive communication deals mainly in concepts; inductive communication deals mainly in the concrete. One explains while the other explores. Our audience needs concepts *and* concrete, word *and* flesh. Note Luke's description of his purpose for writing his gospel in Acts 1:1: "I wrote about all that Jesus began *to do* [concrete] *and to teach* [concept]" (emphasis added).

But as Jeremiah 18 so clearly demonstrates, it's the concrete that leaves the lasting impression. God didn't want to just teach Jeremiah a concept. Jeremiah could have learned those concepts at home. No, God wanted to teach Jeremiah a concept in a way that would leave a vivid impression on his heart and on his mind.

That means in most cases, we'll best guide teenagers into new truth through the doorway of concrete life. Our talk will be structured so we *explore* a truth before we *explain* a truth. That style requires frequent use of illustrations, stories, object lessons, images, sounds, smells, textures, and any other tool of concrete life that will help us bring teenagers to the threshold of new commitment or life-change.

There are countless examples of inductive communication in Scripture. Maybe we should begin with the Master Teacher himself. Do this little assignment: Read through the Sermon on the Mount (Matthew 5–7). As you read, take note of Jesus' use of inductive elements in his own speaking style. Watch for illustrations, parables, concrete examples, and metaphors drawn from everyday life. Note too his approach to the sermon: Is he talking *about* an idea or *to* the crowd? What does he do to draw in the audience?

We'll wait while you read. When you come back, we promise we'll be right here waiting at the end of this paragraph.

Welcome back. So...did you see it? It's like a buffet of inductive communication. In fact, in the book *Inductive Preaching*, authors Ralph Lewis and Gregg Lewis provide a meticulous, stunning analysis of the Sermon on the Mount. In this sermon (which is about 20 minutes long if it's read at the pace of normal oral delivery), we see the following:[85]

Words	2,320 (18–20 minutes)
Images, Illustrations	348 or 1/6 words (e.g., salt of the earth, house built on sand, lilies of the field, etc.)
Comparisons	142 or 1/16 words
Verbs for Energy, Action	404 or 1/6 words
Pronouns to Clarify and Relate	320 or 1/7 words
2nd Person Pronoun for Directness	221 or 1/10 words
Present Tense (relevance for right now)	approximately 65%
Future Tense	approximately 30%
Past Tense	approximately 5%
Varied Viewpoints	42 different aspects of happiness
Knock-Knock Jokes	0
References to *American Idol*	0
Data from Colonoscopy Research	0

Jesus' public teaching and preaching are saturated with elements of inductive communication. And what's more, there isn't one instance of Jesus using the speaking model I learned in college: Tell them what you're going to tell them, then tell them, then tell them what you just told them, and then raise a guy from the dead. (Okay, just the first three.)

In fact, it's tough to recall even a single instance of Jesus saying, "Our topic for today is...." He was more likely to say, "Suppose one of you has a hundred sheep and loses one of them," than he was to say, "Our theme for today is the lost-ness of man." Granted, the Gospels don't give us every word Jesus spoke (read John 21:25 to understand why). But judging from the words we do have, Jesus appeared to be an inductive communicator.

Of course, it isn't just in Jesus' ministry that we see inductive communication. Let's look at some other examples.

2 Samuel 12:1–14

It's now been several months (maybe as much as a year) since that fateful spring day when King David began his affair with Bathsheba. David's own account of these days tells us it hasn't been all romance and passion, either. We know from Psalm 32 that he's been haunted by the guilt of his adultery, betrayal, and murderous deeds. So in 2 Samuel 12:1–7, it must have been high drama when the prophet Nathan, sent by God, is ushered into David's royal chambers.

> When [Nathan] came to him, he said, "There were two men in a certain town, one rich and the other poor. The rich man had a very large number of sheep and cattle, but the poor man had nothing except one little ewe lamb he had bought. He raised it, and it grew up with him and his children. It shared his food, drank from his cup and even slept in his arms. It was like a daughter to him.

> "Now a traveler came to the rich man, but the rich man refrained from taking one of his own sheep or cattle to prepare a meal for the traveler who had come to him. Instead, he took the ewe lamb that belonged to the poor man and prepared it for the one who had come to him."

> David burned with anger against the man and said to Nathan, "As surely as the Lord lives, the man who did this must die! He must pay for that lamb four times over, because he did such a thing and had no pity."

> Then Nathan said to David, "You are the man!"

First, let's observe the obvious: Here is Nathan standing before mighty King David, King of all Israel, David the giant killer, David the warrior, David the guilty adulterer—talk about a tough audience! What is Nathan's introduction? A hokey little story about a rich man and a poor man...and their sheep (Little Bo Peep meets Donald Trump): *The rich man had a very large number of sheep and cattle, but the poor man had nothing except one little ewe lamb he had bought.*

Okay, it's an interesting concept, but why did Nathan start there? Because, of course, David grew up with sheep; as soon as Nathan mentioned *sheep* David probably thought, *Oh really? What kind of sheep? Wooly bully, short hair, long hair, steel wool?* Nathan began with sheep because he understood his audience (*pathos*), and he knew David would be intrigued and hooked by a sheep story. With someone else in another time and in another place, it might have been different—we don't know. It might have been, "Once upon a time there was a rich man who had a bunch of aardvarks...."

But then notice how Nathan used the parable of the two sheep owners to invite David to explore the injustice and outrage of a man who, although he has much, takes something precious from another man who has less:

> *Now a traveler came to the rich man, but the rich man refrained*
> *from taking one of his own sheep or cattle to prepare a meal for*
> *the traveler who had come to him. Instead, he took the ewe lamb*
> *that belonged to the poor man...*

Before Nathan can even explain the offense of David's adultery with Bathsheba, David is already angry and indignant that someone could be so selfish—that someone with so much could take something from someone who had so little. He's breathing fire.

> *David burned with anger against the man and said to Nathan,*
> *"As surely as the Lord lives, the man who did this must die! He*
> *must pay for that lamb four times over, because he did such a*
> *thing and had no pity.*

This is the point where Nathan moves from *explore* to *explain.*

> *Then Nathan said to David, "You are the man!"*

If we were to draw a diagram of how Nathan shaped his message to David, it would probably look something like a funnel (Figure 11-1).

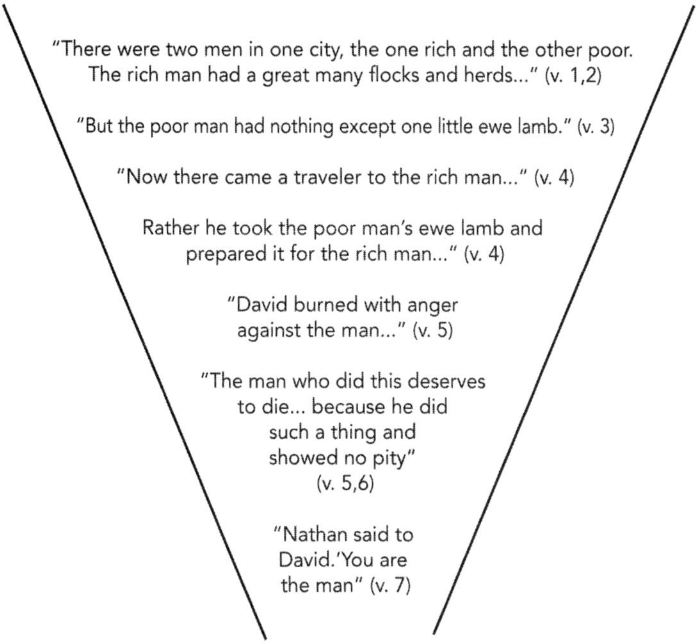

"There were two men in one city, the one rich and the other poor.
The rich man had a great many flocks and herds..." (v. 1,2)

"But the poor man had nothing except one little ewe lamb." (v. 3)

"Now there came a traveler to the rich man..." (v. 4)

Rather he took the poor man's ewe lamb and
prepared it for the rich man..." (v. 4)

"David burned with anger
against the man..." (v. 5)

"The man who did this deserves
to die... because he did
such a thing and
showed no pity"
(v. 5,6)

"Nathan said to
David. 'You are
the man" (v. 7)

FIGURE 11-1 2 SAMUEL 12:1-11 STRUCTURED IN THE INDUCTIVE FUNNEL.

Nathan was wise enough to understand what has been described earlier in this book as *reactance* (see chapter 4). Intuitively he realized David wasn't going to want to hear what he had to say. If he wanted David to listen to a message about sin, he had to get David to believe he was listening to a talk about sheep. Clearly it's not a deductive approach. This isn't Nathan saying what he's going to tell David, and then telling David, and then telling David what he just told him. That would have been a dead approach (maybe literally). And yet, if Nathan had used the homiletical approach I learned in college and in seminary, that's precisely what he would have done. "Good morning, David, our topic for today is adultery... Bathsheba and you!"

So many sermons and talks are structured with the assumption that the audience is willing and hungry to hear what we have to say. "Our topic for tonight is Jehoshaphat..." as if teenagers have been walking around school and asking their friends, "Wouldn't it be great if tonight's message was on Jehoshaphat?" That's an upside-down funnel.

FIGURE 11-2

It promises to gain the attention of every teenager in the room who is very curious about Jehoshaphat. But what about the other 98 percent of the teenagers?

Nathan's message in 2 Samuel 12 was wide enough on the front end (sheep), to make sure his audience was listening, but it was narrow enough on the back end to make sure his audience knew what and *who* he was talking about (Bathsheba). It was inductive communication par excellence. He explored before he explained. Experience (2 Samuel 12:1-6) came before exposition (2 Samuel 12:7-14). As you structure your message, make sure it's wide at the top end and focused on the back end.

Let's look at a New Testament example of inductive communication.

Acts 17:16–31

> While Paul was waiting for them in Athens, he was greatly distressed to see that the city was full of idols. So he reasoned in the synagogue with both Jews and God-fearing Greeks, as well as in the marketplace day by day with those who happened to be there. A group of Epicurean and Stoic philosophers began to debate with him. Some of them asked, "What is this babbler trying to say?" Others remarked, "He seems to be advocating foreign gods." They said this because Paul was preaching the good news about Jesus and the resurrection. Then they took him and brought him to a meeting of the Areopagus, where they said to him, "May we know what this new teaching is that you are presenting? You are bringing some strange ideas to our ears, and we would like to know what they mean." (All the Athenians and the foreigners who lived there spent their time doing nothing but talking about and listening to the latest ideas.)

This description of the idolatry and skepticism Paul confronted in Athens gives us a pretty vivid picture of the emotional element (*pathos*) of Paul's message in Acts 17. This was going to be a tough crowd (Figure 11-3). You get the sense this wasn't an audience that would turn mushy with, "Once upon a time, there was a poor man who had a pet lamb that shared his food." In terms of our earlier discussion of persuasion in chapter four, this crowd is mostly on the left end of the chart.

HOSTILE	BELIEVE AGAINST: DON'T BUY IT BUT NOT HOSTILE	NEUTRAL	BELIEVE FOR: BELIEVE IT BUT DON'T BEHAVE IT	WILLING TO ACT: BELIEVE & BEHAVE
Entertain	Inform		Change Belief	Convince		Move to Action

"What is the babbler trying to say?" (v. 18) = Skeptical

"He seems to be advocating foreign gods" (v.18) = Believe Against, but not Hostile

"May we know what this new teaching is...?" (v.19) = Not Hostile, Closer to Neutral

"Do you know any stories about baby sheep...?" = Did Poorly in Philosophy class

FIGURE 11-3. PAUL FACED A TOUGH CROWD AT THE AREOPAGUS (ACTS 17:16-21).

And that is precisely how Paul read his audience (as hostile):

> Paul then stood up in the meeting of the Areopagus and said: "People of Athens! I see that in every way you are very religious. For as I walked around and looked carefully at your objects of worship, I even found an altar with this inscription: TO AN UN-KNOWN GOD."

It was a bold, savvy approach. First, try to establish some common ground and get them in the funnel (i.e., "Dude, you guys are way religious!"). Then draw from the familiar: "I saw that idol out there on the main road, 'To an unknown God.'"

Clearly Paul isn't telling them what he's going to tell them and then telling them. Had he done that, his opening words might have sounded like this:

> For as I walked around and looked carefully at your objects of worship, I saw some women cooking over an open fire, and it reminded me of where you guys are headed if you don't get your idol-worshiping, pagan rear ends in gear and repent.

Somehow, Paul sensed that approach wouldn't be effective. So like an old experienced fisherman, Paul throws his lure into the water. Now it's time for the hook:

So you are ignorant of the very thing you worship—and this is what I am going to proclaim to you.

The God who made the world and everything in it is the Lord of heaven and earth and does not live in temples built by hands. And he is not served by human hands, as if he needed anything. Rather, he himself gives everyone life and breath and everything else. From one man he made all the nations, that they should inhabit the whole earth; and he marked out their appointed times in history and the boundaries of their lands. God did this so that they would seek him and perhaps reach out for him and find him, though he is not far from any one of us. "For in him we live and move and have our being." As some of your own poets have said, "We are his offspring."

At this point we can begin to see Paul woo his audience down the funnel—he's leading them into the narrow place where there isn't as much room to squirm. He's not preaching just to inform; rather, he's preaching to persuade.

Therefore since we are God's offspring, we should not think that the divine being is like gold or silver or stone—an image made by human design and skill. In the past God overlooked such ignorance, but now he commands all people everywhere to repent. For he has set a day when he will judge the world with justice by the man he has appointed. He has given proof of this to everyone by raising him from the dead.

If we apply Paul's message in Acts 17 to the inductive funnel, it would look like this (Figure 11-4):

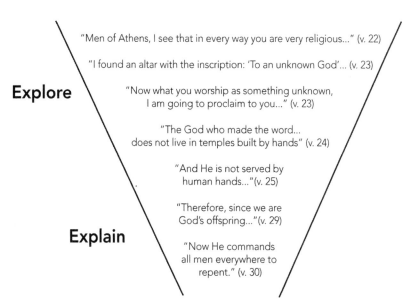

"Men of Athens, I see that in every way you are very religious..." (v. 22)

"I found an altar with the inscription: 'To an unknown God'... (v. 23)

Explore

"Now what you worship as something unknown,
I am going to proclaim to you..." (v. 23)

"The God who made the word...
does not live in temples built by hands" (v. 24)

"And He is not served by
human hands..."(v. 25)

"Therefore, since we are
God's offspring..."(v. 29)

Explain

"Now He commands
all men everywhere to
repent." (v. 30)

FIGURE 11-4. ACTS 17:22-31 AND THE INDUCTIVE BLUEPRINT.

The whole structure of Paul's message is a movement from *explore* to *explain*.

Construction for Induction

Inductive communication isn't just a way of getting your students' attention; it's a way of getting their attention so you can communicate the Word of God. Paul began his talk by pointing to a pagan idol (their world), but he finished his talk by pointing to Jesus (God's world).

> *In the past God overlooked such ignorance, but now he commands all people everywhere to repent. For he has set a day when he will judge the world with justice by the man he has appointed. He has given proof of this to everyone by raising him from the dead. (Acts 17:30-31)*

In putting together a talk, you always want to be conscious that the point of the funnel is to move teenagers to the bottom of the funnel. Our job is not to tell teenagers touching little parables about sheep and then close in prayer: "Raise your hand if you'd like to invite Fluffy into your heart." We tell them about sheep for one reason—so we can point them to the Shepherd.

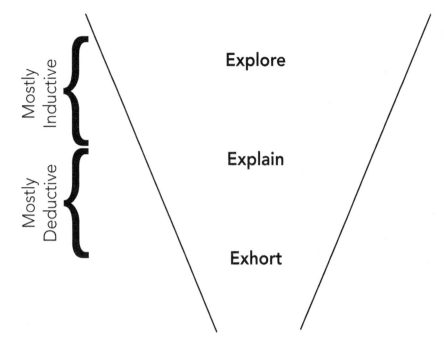

FIGURE 11-5. MOST MESSAGES WILL HAVE A BALANCE OF BOTH INDUCTIVE AND DE-
DUCTIVE COMMUNICATION.

That means most talks will be constructed with a combination of inductive *and* deductive material (Figure 11-5). The deductive elements are usually
more focused on the text and on application of the text. We see that reflected
in Paul's message in Acts 17. He explored; that's inductive (Acts 17:22-23).
Then he explained; that's deductive (Acts 17:24-28). And the reason he explored and explained (hold on to your pulpits, kids) was so he could exhort
(Acts 17:29-31)! It was all leading toward life change.

In very broad terms, the flow is illustration, then text, and then application. When I was first taught this type of thinking, I learned the progression
with these words, "Hook (Illustration), Book (Observe the text), Look (Interpret the text), and Took (Application)." It's a helpful group of words that
communicate the same thing.

Depending on how long you usually speak, you may have two or three
points in a typical message. *That's great—assuming those two or three points
all unpack one big idea that you eventually want to communicate.* If that's the
case, your message might actually be two or three funnels stacked within
one larger funnel; so each point is inductive, but the flow of the entire talk
progresses from explore to explain to exhort (Figure 11-6).

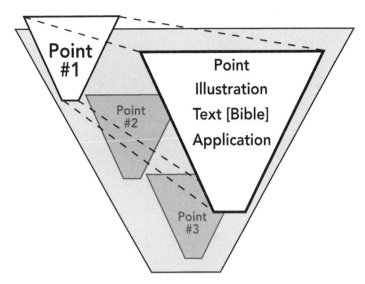

FIGURE 11-6. EACH POINT IN A LARGER MESSAGE SHOULD ALSO BE FUNNEL SHAPED.

That still gives you tons of freedom to build a message in the way that works best for you. But it gives you a basic framework by which to construct your talk. The diagram here—looking at the funnel from the top down (Figure 11-7)—reminds us that there are a lot of different ways to lead students first into a talk, and then into the text, and then to get the text into their lives.

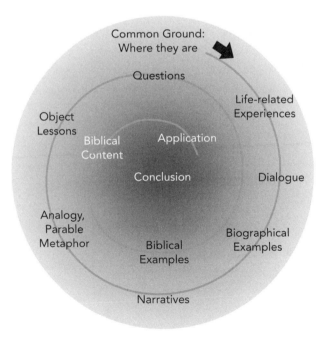

FIGURE 11-7. THE FUNNEL STRUCTURE ALLOWS FOR LOTS OF FLEXIBILITY SO YOU CAN BUILD YOUR TALK IN THE WAY THAT WORKS BEST FOR YOU.

Specific Samples

When I construct a message, I follow a very simple blueprint that I've been using for years. I've done it for so long now that my mind is trained to read a passage or study a topic and naturally organize it around these four questions: *Why? What? So what? Now what?* (Figure 11-8)

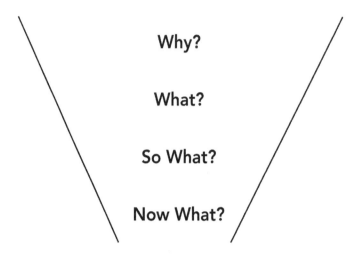

Why?

What?

So What?

Now What?

FIGURE 11-8

Let me expand a little...

Example 1

Why? I think about why my audience should listen to me. How am I going to persuade them that there are important reasons to listen?

What? I explain what we're talking about.

So what? I want my audience to understand why this message is significant to them in the twenty-first century.

Now what? I challenge my audience to do something with what they just heard.

It's really a simple construct, but it works for me. It fits how I think, and it typically meets the needs of my audience. I'd love to take credit for this blueprint, but I'm sure I learned it from someone over the years—I just can't remember who.

You could look at those same four questions and create a slightly different construct. Here's another way to say the same thing (Figure 11-9):

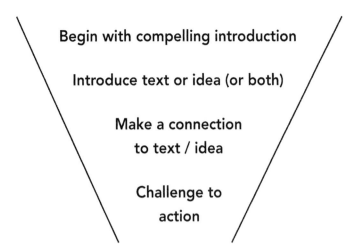

Begin with compelling introduction

Introduce text or idea (or both)

Make a connection
to text / idea

Challenge to
action

FIGURE 11-9

Example 2

1. Begin with a compelling introduction to hook their interest.

2. Direct their interest to the truth you want to communicate from Scripture.

3. Make a connection from your main subject to a teenager's life.

4. Challenge your audience to take specific action(s) or make specific commitments.

Or you could use a little more traditional approach but still use elements of inductive communication. The following outline summarizes your text into points and sends the audience away with a challenge. Note: Each point is inductive. Were we to diagram this message, we'd see probably three funnels within a funnel (Figure 11-10).

Example 3

Introduction: We all want to be loved. (Illustration: My first date.)

Point 1: God is love.

Point 2: God loves you.

Point 3: God wants you to love others.

Application: Go express your love today.

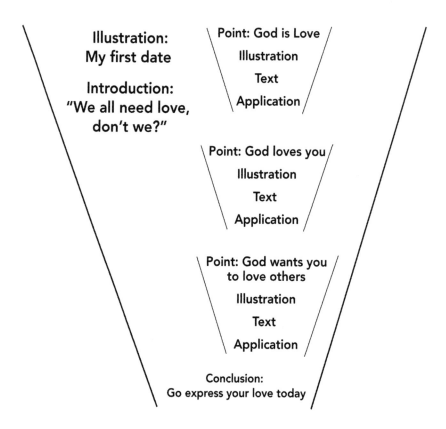

FIGURE 11-10

This structure shows the marriage of inductive and deductive styles. If it could talk, this structure would say, "There are a few things I want you to know, and there's one thing I want you to do. But I understand that my first task is getting you to (a) *want* to know what I want to tell you and (b) *want* to do what I want you to do." As you move through this message, you begin a new funnel with each new point. And each new funnel invites your audience to listen to a new idea. Remember, it's explore before explain; concrete before concept.

Just One Point

In his excellent book *Communicating for a Change,* Andy Stanley suggests another model for organizing your message. Andy's goal is to get you to organize your material in such a way that you leave your audience with one compelling point. Obviously the notion of *"one* compelling point" is not a new challenge. Many speaking/preaching instructors share that same goal—to have one point; one big idea; one clear take-home; one term, phrase, or challenge that's memorable. But Andy makes this point so well.

He writes,

> You pick one idea, principle, application, or insight and build around it. In any one sermon you are going to say a dozen or more helpful, potentially life changing things. And we've all had people tell us how much something we said meant to them and we don't remember saying it. We can't control how and where information lands with our audience. Their life experience forms a grid through which they filter everything they hear. All I'm suggesting is that instead of choosing two or three or four ideas to leave with your audience, just pick one.[86]

He suggests you construct your blueprint around the following five components: ME, WE, GOD, YOU, WE. (Figure 11-11) As you look at his very helpful map or blueprint for construction, it's quite clear that it's inductive in style.[87]

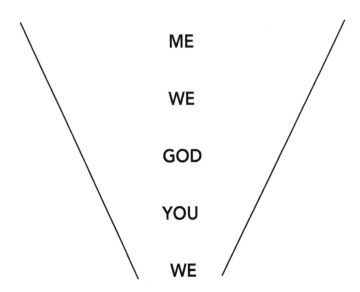

ME

WE

GOD

YOU

WE

FIGURE 11-11

I was anxious to read Andy's book. When I finished, I immediately called Duffy and said, "I think we're wasting our time writing our book on speaking. We should just write a short pamphlet that says, 'Read Andy's book.'" It's that good.

Andy forced me to rethink everything I've been taught about organizing messages. He wrote things such as, "Some of you reading this are going to be too afraid to try something new because you've settled in your own way. You know there's a more effective way, but you're stuck teaching how you've always been taught and you're afraid to try something new even if it might be more effective." How did he know? Was he listening to my messages? He was describing me.

His argument was so convincing, in fact, that I've accepted his challenge, and I've been experimenting with his construct style. (There are some similarities between it and my Why? What? So What? Now What? style of organization, and that made it a little easier than I thought it was going to be.) His map is changing the way I teach. I've been organizing my messages around ME, WE, GOD, YOU, WE for about a year (as I write this), and I really like it.

So maybe you're thinking, *Uh, then why did you and Duffy continue to write this book?* Well, mostly because Duffy is a little more difficult to impress than I am. Duffy hobnobs with presidents and kings and queens, and he realizes I'm not on those guest lists—and I'm duly impressed. But Duffy did read Andy's book, and he liked it.

Duffy wrote, "You're right, it is excellent and will be very helpful to speakers. But his entire book basically covers one of our chapters—the Construct chapter. Even if people were to construct around his ME, WE, GOD, YOU, WE thingy..." [That's an actual quote, by the way. I have the e-mail to prove it. "Thingy"—nice work, Professor Robbins. Now back to his e-mail...] "...they still have to know how to Study, Think, Illustrate, Keep Focused, develop delivery skills, and understand communication theory. So, my vote is that we keep writing the book so we can specifically help youth workers and, not to mention, we won't have to return the publisher's advance against royalty." Right! Now Duffy was making total sense—I hadn't thought about that whole returning-the-money part.

Anyway, here's why I think it was God's timing for me to read Andy's book. I was personally challenged to change, and the change has forced me to learn new skills. God used my struggle to change to help me remember again the importance of an open and teachable spirit. No matter how long we've been at this, we can always learn to do it better.. — *Doug*

ME

You begin by introducing a dilemma that you have faced or are currently facing (that's the "me"—i.e., "I wish I was a better friend," or "I struggle with building friendships"). The goal is for your audience to identify with you and hear that you're also human and have real-life issues and struggles. They identify with your *ethos*. This is where you want them nodding their heads and thinking, *Yeah, me too.* Once you've done that, you move to the WE.

WE

Now you communicate that you know you're not alone with this issue/struggle/situation/fear. You know you've got something in common with your audience. When you were sharing about ME, you knew they could relate because they also have the same or similar dilemma. You're basically broadening the tension and affirming the fact that you know this is important to them. Before you move on to GOD, you want your audience to identify with the tension and desire an answer. If they don't want an answer, then you're going to spend time answering a question they're not asking. In my construct (Example 1), this is what I called "So what?"

GOD

Next, you transition to the text to discover what God says about the tension or question you introduced in WE. The goal here is to point people to God's thoughts on the subject. Andy writes, "Don't just read it [Scripture]. Don't explain it to death. *Engage* the audience with it. Take them with you...Make it [the Bible] so fascinating that they are actually tempted to go home and read it on their own."[88]

YOU

This is where you challenge the audience to act on what they've just heard. In my construct (Example 1) this is what I referred to as "Now what?" This is the application. Many youth workers do a good job of describing the text, but they don't give students any idea of how they're supposed to apply it. This is where you're challenging your audience to apply what they've heard from God's Word.

WE

Close with several statements about what could happen if the audience embraced the particular truth on which you've focused in your message. Andy refers to this as simple "vision casting." An example of this might be, "Can you guys imagine what your junior high would look like if everyone walked out of here tonight knowing for sure that God loved them? Can you see how you might be different if you really knew God loved you? Can you imagine how that truth might impact your relationship with your little brother?" These are your dream statements for your group. You're imagining out loud what WE could do together if WE applied God's Word.

Some Assembly Required

Okay, if that's the blueprint, then what are the step-by-step instructions for *construct*? Here are some simple, but essential, steps:

1. Develop your takeaway (one key phrase, point, idea, action, truth to remember).

2. Discern why your audience needs to hear this key idea. (What might they perceive as valuable?)

3. Decide the clearest way to say it.

4. Discover how you might provoke their interest. *(I know they need to know this, but how do I help them realize they need to know this?)*

5. Determine what needs to be illustrated.

6. Deliberate over its connection.

7. Delay your final edits.

8. Depend on God's power.

1. Develop Your Takeaway

You're not ready for *construct*-ion until you know the purpose of your *instruction*. You can't complete your talk until you have one big idea. If you begin to construct without that one thought, then you're going to be building patios and balconies and installing windows before you even know how the rest of the building is designed.

As you construct a message, you'll want to begin thinking of one strong thought, phrase, principle, or action that teenagers might be able to remember when they get home. Chances are pretty good teenagers won't remember much of your message…at least not for very long. But before you judge them too harshly for their short-term memories, keep in mind that you don't recall too much from the messages you hear either. Right? So the question is, *What do I want them to remember or do at the end of my message?* Be realistic. Can you summarize it in a single sentence or phrase that is memorable or clear? Once you've got that one statement, be sure you repeat it several times throughout your message.

When you have that one thought, phrase, principle, or action you want them to get, you'll typically introduce that idea with a statement such as:

- "Here's why I really care that you get this…"

- "Here's what I really want you to know or do…"

- "The reason this is such a big deal is…"

- "If I could get you to remember only one thing, this would be it…"

- "If you miss everything else, catch this…"

- "*This* is why this issue is such a big deal…"

- "And so, when you go for your colonoscopy…"

As you're working on your message, keep focused on that one main idea. You haven't finished your message until you've made that one thought clear and compelling (and memorable, if you can). Begin and end your construction process with that one big idea.

Here are a few ideas:

- Conflict is inevitable, misery is optional, so in conflict I choose peace.

- Move past your past, God has.

- God's dream isn't something you chase, it's something you become.

2. Discern Why Your Audience Needs to Hear This Key Idea

Remember, communication is a two-way bridge. It's not just about what you want to say; it's about what they're willing to hear. What you're really asking at this point is this: *What's in it for them—not just from my perspective, but also from their perspective, from their end of the bridge? How will this one big idea speak to their lives?*

3. Decide the Clearest Way to Say It

My favorite way to test whether my message is clear is to consider if my outline could easily be taught by someone else a month later. If a teenager can pick up my message notes or an outline and reteach it without remembering how I taught it, then it's probably clear.

You might use a device like an acronym. Sure, they can be corny, and some of my sophisticated youth ministry friends tell me acronyms don't work with teenagers. But I speak to teenagers every week, and while I agree that some teenagers think they're corny, I disagree that they don't remember them. If I have to choose between corny and forgettable, uh...well...I'll choose corny every time.

For example, I was giving a message on decision-making, and I told my students, "When you're struggling to make a good decision and you feel like you're in a fog, remember these three letters: F.O.G." (When they feel like they're in a fog and they need help, they can consult their feelings, others (friends, trusted adults), and especially God— F.O.G.) Corny? Well, yeah. Memorable? Absolutely.

I've been guilty of acronym abuse, and I'm using this page of the book to publicly apologize for it. I'm really S.O.R.R.Y.

Sad I did it

Overwhelmed with grief

Remorseful

Really bummed

You've got to believe me

But there are times when it's the clearest way I can get teenagers to remember something. Now if you *force* words to fit your letters so you can make an acronym, then that's emphasizing cute more than clear. That can be a problem. That's the tail wagging the dog. When you have to choose, always choose clear over cute. Cute might make for fun presentation, but clear makes for good communication.

4. Discover How You Might Provoke Their Interest

A fisherman can't just stand up in the boat and yell, "Calling all fish! Calling all fish! I'd like you to get into my boat!" There has to be a lure. You can't just throw a party and expect people to show up; there has to be an invitation. And an architect can't just construct a building; he's got to figure out a way to get people to come inside.

We spoke in chapter 5 about a basic fact of communication: The audience is sovereign. It's the audience that decides whether you'll be allowed to cross the communication bridge, and it's the audience that decides whether it will move from its current position. So in constructing the message, you've got to give attention to the lure—the invitation. You've got to discover a way to get them into the building you're constructing.

You know what they need to know (the one big idea), but how can you get *them* to believe that *you* know what they need to know? The answer to this question will shape your introduction. Again, this is the top of the funnel, so you want it to be as wide and as inviting as possible. In terms of construction, this is the sign out front that invites people in, and it's the door through which they enter. You want a big sign and a wide door to get them into your message.

5. Determine What Needs to be Illustrated

The idea with this action is simply making sure your main points will *clearly* be your main points. Go back through your message and ask yourself, *Is there any place where I'm making a point that also needs a picture?* As we discussed in the previous chapter, everyone breathes better with an illustration. When in doubt, illustrate.

6. Deliberate Over Its Connection

I can't emphasize this action enough. This is where I always come back to messages that bombed and say to myself, *I missed it here! I didn't connect the content to my teenagers' lives. I scratched where they weren't itching. I thought they needed to hear it and could appreciate it, but I didn't do a good job answering the question* so what?

Be brutal on yourself here—this can make or break a message. *Will my description of this topic connect with a teenager's life, and am I saying it in a way that she'll "get it"*? I chose the word *deliberate* because I really believe that effective communicators need to spend some significant time struggling over connecting points from message to audience.

7. Delay Your Final Edits

This is the point of the message construction where you want to leave it a little long for now. Don't be too quick to edit material. Give it some time to simmer in your head and in your heart. There's still time to cut, but I'd rather have too much material than not enough. Relax. There's one more step in S.T.I.C.K., and when you get to **K**eep Focused, you can do some cutting there.

CHAPTER TWELVE

Keep Focused: Crafting for Clarity

The story goes that comedian George Burns was once asked, "How can I improve my speaking?" Burns deadpanned, "First, you need a brilliant introduction. Second, you should have a dynamite conclusion. Third, be sure that your introduction and your conclusion are not that far apart."[89]

For a comedian, Burns gave some pretty solid advice—it's clear, it's concise, it's accurate, and it's fairly funny. Let's be clear. As authors and youth workers, we don't want you to read that first paragraph and think, *Oh, Doug and Duffy believe that when speaking to teenagers, shorter is better.* We don't believe that! If you've ever heard one of us preach, then you know that's not true.

Nor, we should add, do we believe that a longer message is better. We both strongly believe *better is better*. And better usually means a message that's clear and focused. Before you consider yourself "done"...you need to make sure everything is focused.

The whole essence of a "stick" is that it has a sharp point on one end. That's what makes it S.T.I.C.K. And so it is with a well-constructed message. Its end must be whittled down to a sharp, clear, focused point.

Unfortunately, we've all heard them before: Sermons in search of a point, speakers who seemed determined to talk until they figured out what it was they truly wanted to say, unfocused messages that sort of left everybody thinking, *Wow, that would have made a good four-part series. Too bad it was a 10-minute devotional talk.* There aren't too many things more frustrating to an audience than listening to a speaker who lacks focus and intention.

The journey we've described so far requires you to study, think, illustrate, and carefully construct your message—each step is designed to help guide your thinking, your time, and your message preparation. Then once the initial hard work is complete (S.T.I.C.), there's one more critical element to make sure your *good* message becomes a *great* one—focus.

Keep Focused

In order for a good message to become a great message, focus is everything and everything must be focused—not just the message (*logos*) but also the heart of the speaker (*ethos*) and the target audience (*pathos*). That's why the most effective communicators are never finished with a message just because they have it composed. They're always tweaking their content, praying for their audience, and evaluating their own hearts to make sure they're focused.

To assist you with focus, we've put together a checklist of questions to help you define if you're spiritually, emotionally, and intellectually focused and ready to deliver the goods you've so diligently created.

Let's jump into the checklist, and then we'll briefly comment on each one:

My Focus Checklist

On this page we've listed the nine questions with their corresponding chapter numbers so you can reference the needed material later. On the opposing page, the same questions appear in a checklist format for you to photocopy and leave in the location where you're most likely to finish your prep.

1. Do I know the big-picture hurts and specific needs of my audience? (Chapters 2, 3, and 5)

2. Have I prayed for them? Do I have a spiritual burden and genuinely care that my students understand and apply this particular message? (Chapter 4)

3. Do I have a good grasp of the content I'll be teaching? (Chapters 5, 8, and 9)

4. Have I thought about how my content will connect and how it might matter to my teenage audience? (Chapters 2 and 5)

5. Do I have a clear, simple map for how I'll communicate my content? (Chapters 6, 9, and 12)

6. Do I have good illustrations, graphics, experiences, or exercises that will help me engage and connect to my audience? (Chapters 10)

7. Have I chosen the clearest, most powerful words? (Chapter 10)

8. Have I identified one main idea that I really want them to know when they get home? (Chapters 11 and 12)

9. What's in my message that isn't essential? (i.e., What can I cut?) (Chapter 12)

My Focus Checklist

☐ Do I know the big-picture hurts and specific needs of my audience?

☐ Have I prayed for them? Do I have a spiritual burden and genuinely care that my students understand and apply this particular message?

☐ Do I have a good grasp of the content I'll be teaching?

☐ Have I thought about how my content will connect and how it might matter to my teenage audience?

☐ Do I have a clear, simple map for how I'll communicate my content?

☐ Do I have good illustrations, graphics, experiences, or exercises that will help me engage and connect to my audience?

☐ Have I chosen the clearest, most powerful words?

☐ Have I identified one main idea that I really want them to know when they get home?

☐ What's in my message that isn't essential—i.e., What can I cut?

1. Big Picture Hurts and Specific Needs

I [Duffy] live in the countryside of southeastern Pennsylvania, near the old colonial town of Valley Forge. Not far from my house is a beautiful old covered bridge that, in its day, must have carried lots of traffic back and forth across the forge at Valley Creek. It's still a charming structure almost two and a half centuries after it was built. But there's a big sign on either end of that bridge that reads, NO TRUCK TRAFFIC. Any vehicle that weighs more than a few tons could easily turn that bridge into a covered ramp, a charming old boat launch that would lead abruptly down to the river because that bridge was designed for wagons and horses, not trucks.

Every time a youth worker speaks to a teenage audience, the goal is to build a bridge. But before that bridge can be built, the youth worker has to have a pretty good idea about the sort of traffic that might be expected on that bridge. What burdens or load is the message designed to carry? It doesn't matter if the message is beautifully conceived or a masterpiece of construction; if it won't allow the students to cross over, it's a bridge that falls short of its purpose.

If you're talking to a room full of teenagers, it's safe to assume there's a lot of hurt sitting in the audience. Before you invite students to cross that bridge, make sure you know enough about their hurts to ensure the proper message is in place. Make sure you understand the weight and the heaviness your students are facing.

Of course, there are the generic pains and longings that come with adolescence. You'll want to keep those in mind. But beyond those common concerns, there are the specific needs *your* teenagers are facing that are more unique to your particular church and community. It's safe to suggest that something unique is happening in your area this year, this month, this week, or even today that is unsettling to your teenagers and adding to the emotional baggage they'll carry into youth group.

Let's consider a few examples:

1. Your community is in the midst of a violence spree that has enhanced the usual level of fear that teenagers already feel.

2. A local school dance was capped off with a drinking-related car accident in which three teenagers were killed. Many students are now emotionally distraught as a result of the news.

3. The school district surrounding your church is experiencing a teachers' strike, and the teenagers are suddenly showing up to youth group happier, livelier, and more joy-filled.

All of these scenarios carry with them some realities that should influence your message. This idea of stopping to pause and be reminded of these hurts, needs, and realities of your audience will always help you focus your heart and your content.

2. Have I Prayed for Them?

You may have heard the old story about a former church member asking a current member, "How do you like the new pastor?" The current member says, "We love him! Like our former pastor, he also talks about 'going to hell' every week. But the biggest difference between the old pastor and the new pastor is the new pastor cries when he mentions hell because he doesn't want us to go there."

When you genuinely care for your students, it will be obvious in your speaking. We're not advocating tears, nor are we suggesting you scare your teenagers. But we do want to campaign for a genuine concern for your audience. Keeping focused is remembering whom you're speaking to and making sure you genuinely care about them. Remember that line from Wesley's journal (mentioned back in chapter 4): "My heart was filled with love, my eyes with tears, and my mouth with arguments."

When we spend time specifically praying for teenagers, something happens in the heart of the communicator—it becomes soft and tender, and it easily breaks for the audience. When I've spent time praying in general and in specific (actually praying for teenagers by name), I find that my talks reveal a unique passion and compassion that's different from the times when I've spoken and not adequately prayed for my audience. A prayerful approach brings me to the place where I can genuinely say, "*I so badly* want you to understand and apply this because *I care so deeply* about you, and I know God's Word and God's ways have the ability to redirect the course of your life."

Granted, I can say these same words without prayer, but the words "so badly" and "care so deeply" can't be said with the same spiritual emotion that I feel when I'm praying for my audience.

Speaking to teenagers is more than creating a message and then checking it off our to-do list. Speaking is a spiritual encounter between God's Spirit, God's Word, the audience whom God loves so much, and...you, the speaker. We're convinced that your posture of prayer can make up for a lot of weaknesses in other areas of your message.

3. Do I Have a Good Grasp of the Content?

It's tempting to quickly answer this question with a confident *yes* because of the time you spend studying. It's not unusual for youth workers to be overly confident and underprepared. This is a common disguise that many of us wear.

This is usually the part of my prep where I take time to refocus on my content. I want to make sure I know it really well. I know I can convince a group of seventh graders that I'm prepared, but I want to know in my heart that I'm *really* prepared. It's at this point when I usually give thought to the critics of my message.

Normally I don't spend a lot of time thinking about critics, but to sharpen my content, I'll spend a little time identifying the argument they might have after the message. I try to imagine where they'd find disagreement and how I'd answer them other than just, "Because I'm the youth pastor, that's why!" Typically, if I know my content well enough to defend it, then I know my content, and I'm ready to move on.

4. How Will My Content Connect and Matter?

This is the main question of focus that forces me to craft a *good* message into a *great* message. It's one thing to have a message that's understandable to *you*, and it's another thing to have a message that's understandable to the teenagers you hope to reach. One is good communication; the other is a classic "Zilwaukee"—a bridge to nowhere.

The typical question youth workers want to ask is, "Does this material make sense?" That's not too helpful; instead ask, "Can I see Cody [one of your teenagers] really applying this to his life?" The connecting points will cause teenagers to think, *Wow! He really knows me—that message applies directly to me. I wonder if he was eavesdropping on my conversations this week?*

In this book we've tried to make it very clear that persuasion with the goal of life-change is more than just information transfer. We don't need to scrawl one more line of Bible trivia on the wall of a teenager's brain. To use God's words, we want this message to be written on their hearts (Jeremiah 31:33). And that transformation won't happen if teenagers can't connect your teaching to the world they live in—no matter how dynamic you are as a communicator.

5. Do I Have a Clear, Simple Map?

It's really hard to get lost on a bridge. Once you start from one end, you typically won't face too many intersections until you get to the other side. But knowing where the bridge starts and knowing where it leads are two critical points on the journey. As a communicator, your task is to have a very clear idea about both the starting point and the end point of your message. Where can you help these teenagers gain access to the bridge? What is the intended end point? One of my favorite ways to map out a message for students is to provide them some sort of handout—nothing elaborate—just an outline for them to use while they follow along, write down what they want, and hang on to for future reference (or study additional Scripture references).

Here are some questions to get you thinking:

- Is my opening inductive? Am I taking my audience by the hand and inviting them to take the next step? Am I starting where they are?

- Is there a natural progression from concrete to concept?

- Are the transitions clear and smooth?

- Are my application points realistic and doable, or too intellectual and guilt-producing?

6. Do I Have Good Illustrations, Graphics, Experiences, or Exercises?

There must be something in the human DNA that makes all of us do it: When we cross a bridge, we turn our heads from side to side and strain to look across the water, or we open our eyes wide and marvel at the heights. When we cross a bridge, most of us are glued to the windows.

As a communicator, bridge-builder, and bridge-crosser, you want to give your students lots of opportunities to get near the window. You want to give them every chance to see how big and how high and how wide is the love of God. That's why your illustrations are so important. Good illustrations, clear graphics, vivid experiences, or active-communication exercises can motivate your students to stay on the bridge. They can also bring your message into sharp focus.

You might want to run through these questions to make sure you're not cutting corners and covering windows when it comes to the illustrations:

- Am I missing a key story that could really drive a point home?

- Is there an object or a photograph that would add "show" to my "tell"?

- Is there anything tactile that the teenagers can touch that will help them better understand and remember the truth of the message? Or is there any takeaway item that they can leave with to help them remember the message?

- Am I using any illustrations that my audience won't connect with?

- At this point it might be good to quickly revisit the voice question—will my voice be heard the most on this point, or is there someone else, something else, a video, or even silence that would speak more effectively than the sound of my voice?

7. Have I Chosen the Clearest, Most Powerful Words?

My [Doug's] pastor, Rick Warren, has been a friend, mentor, and partner in my journey to become a more effective communicator. He has an amazing ability to take complex subjects (doctrine, theology, Bible, etc.) and communicate them in words that are clear and therefore powerful. His book *The Purpose Driven Life* is the best-selling book in the history of nonfiction, and I'm convinced that one of the secrets to his genius is his relentless drive to use words that people understand.

In the prequel to *The Purpose Driven Life, The Purpose Driven Church*, Rick shares six questions that he considers when crafting his message. You might consider running through his list once you've chosen the words you feel are most important to your message.

1. What is the most *practical* way to say it?

2. What is the most *positive* way to say it?

3. What is the most *encouraging* way to say it?

4. What is the *simplest* way to say it?

5. What is the most *personal* way to say it?

6. What is the most *interesting* way to say it?[90]

Every week, at this point in my preparation, I can hear Rick's voice (this is a recurring subject during my therapy sessions) saying, "Doug, when you have the choice between cute words and clear words...always go with clear."

Many youth workers must believe they'll receive extra bonus points when an outline is clever or the words rhyme or the alliteration is snappy. Unfortunately, cute doesn't stick as well as clear does. Here's an example of the difference between words that are cute and words that are clear:

CUTE	CLEAR
Be sky high	Be positive
Be punch proof	Don't avoid conflict
Be true blue	Be honest
Your colon is rollin'	Your colonoscopy came back clear

8. Have I Identified One Main Idea?

My wife has a question that she's asked me a thousand times as we've driven to church together over the years, "What's your message about?" It seems like such a simple question, but it's not. In my early years of youth ministry I struggled to give her a clear and compelling answer. I'd say one thing, then try to explain it, then add a little more, and finally conclude by saying, "That makes sense, doesn't it?" More than once she'd say, "Not to me!" or "I hope it's clearer to the teenagers than it is to me because I don't know what you're trying to say." Thanks, dear.

Actually, one frustrating drive to church became a God-moment because I finally decided that if I couldn't answer her with a quick, clear explanation, then I hadn't focused my message enough, and I wasn't done preparing.

Communication experts refer to this concept using a variety of terms: *defining the big idea, reducing the sermon to a sentence, deciding the takeaway, articulating the main phrase that might reduce the need for marriage counseling...* whatever.

Here's one last image to force you to focus: If a teenager wanted to get a tattoo of your one main idea (and you'd better hope he doesn't), what would you want it to say?

9. What Can I Cut?

We saved this one for last because it's very difficult to cut material that you've worked so hard to create. Cutting material can be emotional because you'll most likely need to get rid of material that you've already likened to what God said on the sixth day, "This is good." It may be good. Actually, it may be *great* material, but if it doesn't help support the one main point, then it might not be necessary. Again, more isn't better; *better* is better.

The goal of cutting some of your content isn't to "dumb down" your message so it can be understood by a 14-year-old with ADD, but rather to clean it up and focus it so a 14-year-old can hear the message, understand it, and be capable of teaching it to a parent or friend. If that happens, that would be a sign of *better* communication.

Think about cutting like this: When I go to the doctor, I don't want the doctor to explain everything he's ever learned about my illness. I appreciate his intelligence, but I don't want to hear about all his medical knowledge and have him take me through his library of medical journals. I want a clear description of my problem and a realistic plan to get me better. Specifically, I want him to say, "I know what's wrong with you. I understand the root cause of your sickness, and I've got hope for you." For this doctor to deliver a focused and helpful message, I need him to cut some of his background material so his explanation is helpful and not exhausting. I'm trusting that he's very smart, but I'm not interested in medical concepts; I'm looking for concrete ideas and instruction about how I can be healed.

Look over your message and consider some of these questions:

- Does the message become unclear if I edit out this particular section?

- Am I holding on to this story just for the sake of pride or ego or an easy laugh?

- Which of my friends, who are emotionally unattached to my content, can make suggestions about what to cut?

One of the keys to cutting excess material is asking God's Spirit to continually guide your content. Prayer is really a part of each of these checklist items. Ask God to show you what must stay and what must go.

Keeping Focused and Watching the Clock

You'll notice we haven't said anything in this chapter—or in the book so far—about a specific time limit for your message. That's intentional. We don't want to prescribe a "one length fits all" time limit because every speaker, every group, and every speaking situation is so different.

As we noted in chapter 10, if you read through Jesus' Sermon on the Mount at a normal pace for public speaking, it'll take about 20 minutes. Obviously, Jesus was able to get pretty decent content on the table in that amount of time. So longer isn't necessarily better.

On the other hand, we know of at least one instance in which Paul preached all night long (Acts 20:7–12). And, as it happens, there was at least one "young" person (perhaps a teenager?) in the audience that night. (It was the first recorded lock-in in youth ministry history.) We also know from that Acts 20 episode that the only young person who was mentioned as part of the audience also dozed off and fell out of the window to the ground—and died. (Had Doug and his daughter been there, they'd have howled with laughter.)

What can we construe from this strange episode? Well, probably not too much. But here are some simple observations:

1. Shorter isn't necessarily more spiritual or more thoughtful. Paul preached a long time.

2. Paul didn't stop speaking until he'd said all that he felt God wanted him to say, even though it was a long sermon and even though there were "young" people in the house (at least one, maybe more).

3. If you preach long sermons while young people are in the house that may be what God is calling you to do. But you'd better be prepared to deal with some fallout afterward (but hopefully not the "to his death" kind).

Teenagers will listen to a good communicator for 45 minutes without complaint, but they'll also get restless within five minutes of listening to a poor communicator. It's really tough to pin it down to an ideal time. Here are some basic rules to keep in mind:

1. Your message is not the only element of the program, nor is it the only means through which God can complete his work. Don't allow your undisciplined use of speaking time short-circuit other facets of the program.

2. Just because teenagers are in the room doesn't mean they're listening. There's only one person who absolutely never complains about the length of the funeral sermon, and that person is dead. You could talk all day, and that person would never leave the room. But that doesn't equal engagement. Don't assume you can continue to present just because teenagers are still present.

3. Even an audience that wants to listen has physical limitations. All of those ears and minds and hearts are connected to bodies; and all of those bodies have bladders and bottoms. Like the wise old proverb says: "The mind can only comprehend what the seat can endure."

4. Remember that every time you give a message, you're making an unspoken covenant with your audience (chapter 5). One of the terms of that unspoken contract is that you won't take them for granted. If they're willing to listen to you for what they expect to be a 20-, 30-, or 45-minute message, don't punish them for their attention by giving them a bonus half-hour. I approach each message with the idea that I'm saying to this group of teenagers, "If you'll give me the allotted time, I promise to get you out by the allotted time." Now, if I need to pull an Acts 20 and preach longer than that (I never have), I assume God will make that very clear to me and, hopefully, to my audience as well.

Section 3

How to Deliver Effective Messages

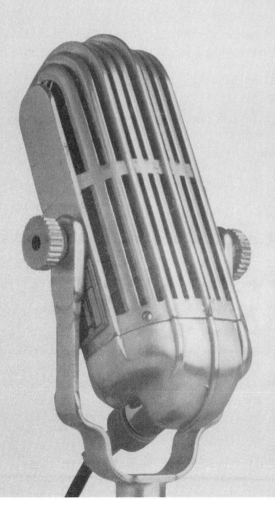

CHAPTER THIRTEEN

Prep for Delivery: Making the Space Work for You

There are disagreements about what makes the best environment for a hospital delivery room. Some say it should be a place of bright lights so the doctors can see clearly to do their work; others say the lights should be dim so the baby isn't immediately transported from his world of total darkness into an immediate world of paternal paparazzi. Some say the room should be warm to simulate Mom's tummy; others say the room should be cool to prevent Dad's fainting spells. Some say it should be a place of quiet to relax the mood; others want music playing to drown out the sounds of groaning, loud shrieks, and swearing. But what everyone agrees on is that environment is an important element of the delivery.

In previous chapters, we've talked about the dynamics of speaker credibility and audience analysis, all of which impact your talk before you actually start talking. But let's make this even more practical. What can we do to set the stage for effective communication? How can we prepare for the actual delivery?

Don't Overlook the Power of Pre-Exposure

One of our dear friends, the late Mike Yaconelli, had us in tears of laughter when he told us about the time he was planning to speak to his Young Life meeting from the book of Hosea. Knowing it was going to be a tough sell to get unchurched high schoolers to find value in words written centuries earlier by a minor prophet, Yaconelli came up with a creative plan. Prior to the meeting, he took three students with him into the streets of Yreka, California, where they stopped passersby and, on camera, posed this question: "If you were a prophet, would you marry a whore named Gomer?" As you might imagine, the responses were fascinating.

Later in the week when they had their meeting and Mike was finally ready to give his talk, his down payment on the students' attention span was a collection of those "man-on-the-street" interviews. It worked! The kids thought it was hilarious, and it definitely aroused their interest in the biblical narrative.

But even more ingenious was his decision to send out a postcard to all of his Young Life regulars before the meeting, and it posed this question:

IF YOU WERE A PROPHET, WOULD YOU MARRY
A WHORE NAMED GOMER?

COME TO BIBLE STUDY AND FIND OUT!

(Yaconelli joked that "no kids came, but a hundred parents showed up.")

It was a classic example of what communication theorists refer to as *pre-exposure*. The idea is to prime the audience by exposing them to the subject in advance of the actual message because pre-exposure will help an audience learn and process the message more quickly and easily when they do hear it.

Studies at Stanford University have shown that pre-exposure, sometimes called *priming*, can help students learn more quickly, process information better, and even increase their ability to remember information.[91]

What does that look like in youth ministry? Here are some simple pre-exposure ideas that can set the stage for your message:

- *"Be thinking about this."* E-mail all group members with a question to think about, a thought to ponder, or a case study to consider in advance of the upcoming meeting.

- *Weekly preview.* Send students an e-mail or post on the youth group Web site the passage of Scripture you'll be talking about. Invite them to read it in advance and send in reply messages with questions that could be incorporated into either your talk or a follow-up discussion.

- *Graffiti board.* Write on the message board of your Web site or the whiteboard of your meeting room a question or a statement relevant to your message topic. Invite students to write their own comments or thoughts on the board.

- *Posters or computer graphics.* As students arrive for the meeting, use posters or onscreen graphics to prime your students to think about the topic of your message.

- *Props.* Suppose the topic for your message is "Building Community." When students arrive for the meeting, they see pictures of the youth group in various kinds of activities posted all around the room. Or the theme is "Life Under Construction," so when students arrive, the room is decorated with construction materials—shovels, wheelbarrows, hard hats, yellow safety tape, and so on.

- *Music.* Use music that hints at the theme of your message. Have it playing as students arrive.

- *Aroma.* What about using scent as a tool for pre-exposure? Torie is a youth worker who plans to speak about "Jesus as the Bread of Life." Utilizing the church kitchen, she arranges for fresh bread to be baking as her students arrive. The aroma of fresh baked bread fills the building before she ever utters word one. And Torie's youth group doesn't just hear with their ears; they hear with their noses.

- *Setting.* On occasion you may even want to have the group meet in a different place so the setting offers an opportunity for pre-exposure. Examples:[92]

TOPIC	SETTING
Childlike faith	Nursery
Spiritual warfare	Local National Guard armory
Jesus walking on water	Lake or swimming pool
Death	Funeral home
Importance of serving others	In Duffy's backyard, right next to his pile of uncut firewood

Pay Attention to Room Design

Not only does the meeting space and seating design communicate a message, but sometimes it also has the capacity to interrupt yours. So as you set the stage for your talk, you'll want to give some thought to room arrangement.

Consider—

- *From where you'll be teaching, are there blind spots that will prevent you from seeing some of the students, or prevent them from being able to see any visuals?* If the meeting space is one you share with another group or ministry, think about objects, charts or posters, or other phenomena (another group, outside noises, etc.) that might distract from the message.

I remember speaking at a Florida water park where the stage was at the base of a massive water slide. Throughout my message, screaming kids careened down the slide every few seconds. "So, kids (scream!) (splash!) I know life sometimes can be (scream!) (splash!) really tough (scream!) (splash!), but Jesus is there for us (scream!) (splash!)." It was a difficult environment for the kids to focus.

- *Be aware of the lighting in the speaking area.* Make sure, first of all, that your face is visible. It's one of the most expressive parts of your body. Second, make sure the lighting doesn't wash out any images you show as part of a media presentation.

I took my youth group to a denominational youth event, and the room was so bright that the movie they showed was little more than faint shadows flickering on the screen, occasionally highlighted by badly written dialogue that was poorly spoken. The good news was we had several kids make decisions that Sunday afternoon. The bad news was they decided to never attend another denominational event.

- *Give some thought regarding the best place to put the front of the room.* Rooms are often designed with an obvious front space, maybe defined by a stage, a whiteboard, or a permanent screen. But strategic use of the room may suggest that chairs be reset for a more advantageous use of the space. For example, it's almost always advantageous for the speaker to arrange the room wide rather than deep (see diagrams below). Experience tells us that students who are the least eager listeners often place themselves in the back of the room (Figure 13-1).

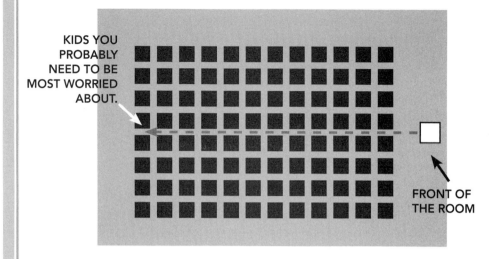

KIDS YOU PROBABLY NEED TO BE MOST WORRIED ABOUT.

FRONT OF THE ROOM

FIGURE 13-1. THIS ROOM IS SET UP DEEP; THE BACK ROW IS AS FAR AWAY FROM THE SPEAKER AS POSSIBLE; YOU MAY AS WELL MAIL THOSE STUDENTS YOUR TALK.

It's tough to change that fact without making it a big deal and maybe putting some of those very students on the defensive. And a room set up deep only accentuates the problem. So rather than trying to move those students away from the back of the room, move the back of the room closer to the front of the room. That can be done in a number of ways:

Turning the room around and making it wide instead of deep (Figure 13-2):

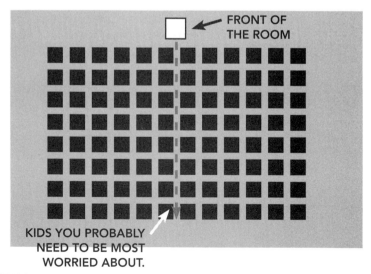

FRONT OF THE ROOM

KIDS YOU PROBABLY NEED TO BE MOST WORRIED ABOUT.

FIGURE 13-2

Using artificial walls (Figure 13-3):

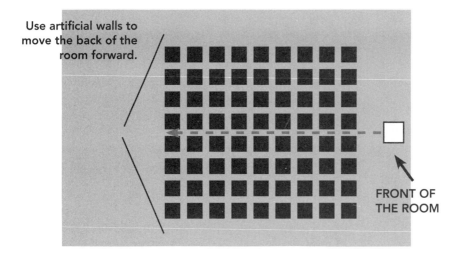

Use artificial walls to move the back of the room forward.

FRONT OF THE ROOM

FIGURE 13-3 ARTIFICIAL WALLS WERE USED TO MAKE THE ROOM FEEL SMALLER.

Moving the front of the room toward the back of the room (Figure 13-4):

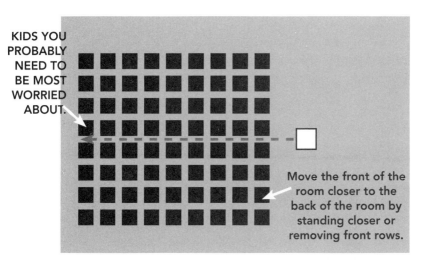

KIDS YOU PROBABLY NEED TO BE MOST WORRIED ABOUT.

Move the front of the room closer to the back of the room by standing closer or removing front rows.

FIGURE 13-4 MOVE THE FRONT OF THE ROOM TOWARD THE BACK WALL TO MAKE THE ROOM FEEL SMALLER.

Backing the room into a corner (Figure 13-5):

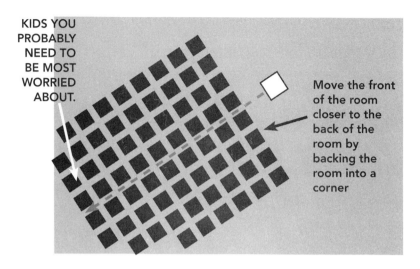

KIDS YOU PROBABLY NEED TO BE MOST WORRIED ABOUT.

Move the front of the room closer to the back of the room by backing the room into a corner

FIGURE 13-5 YOU CAN MAKE A ROOM SMALLER BY BACKING IT INTO A CORNER.

In many settings you'll be able to control the arrangement of the room. But there will be times when you're invited to speak somewhere, and when you walk into the room, you'll know it was set up by someone who's never spoken before. At that point you're faced with a decision: *Do I risk hurting someone's feelings and ask if I can help rearrange the room? Or do I leave it how it is and risk an average environment?* That's a tough question with an easy answer—change the environment. Someone might have their feelings hurt, but if you ask with a gentle, humble, and "I'll make it happen" attitude, you might be able to prevent a speaking disaster. The environment is a big deal when you're speaking to teenagers.

Also, whenever possible try to keep the main entrance at the back of the room. That way you avoid distractions every time someone walks in late or walks out to go to the bathroom.

Using Media: Let Them See What You Say

When the Gannett Company first began publishing *USA Today* in 1982, they started by asking a basic question about the way news is delivered: *What would happen if there was a daily newspaper that not only offered news, but offered news in a format that was visually exciting? If color photos and charts replaced grainy black-and-white images, would people be more inclined to pay attention to daily headlines?* Now, several decades later and with a daily circulation in the millions, it's beginning to look like they may have been on to something.

Seeing may not be believing, but clearly it's more convincing and more memorable than just hearing. Research has confirmed that teenagers are likely to learn considerably more when ideas appeal to both the eye and the ear than when they appeal to the ear alone.[93] And when presented with visual aids (an object, sketch, poster, chart, graph, digital imagery, etc.), students are likely to remember the information over longer periods of time[94] (Figure 13-6).[95]

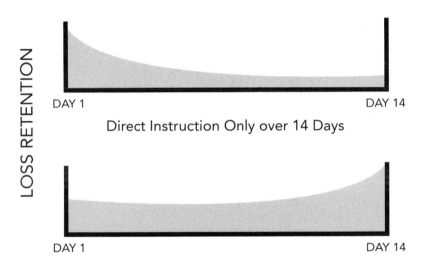

LOSS RETENTION

DAY 1   DAY 14

Direct Instruction Only over 14 Days

DAY 1   DAY 14

Direct Instruction Combined with Visual Aids over 14 Days

FIGURE 13-6. EFFECTS OF VISUAL AIDS ON STUDENT RECALL.

Most of us in youth ministry don't need to be convinced that visual media can be a powerful tool for communicating the good news of Jesus Christ. The marketplace is flooded with tools and resources to help youth workers use visual imagery more effectively. We've come a long way from filmstrips, flannel graphs, and cave drawings.

At this point, most of us are sold on the effectiveness of media. The question is—How do we use media strategically? The only thing worse than a gimmicky dog and pony show is a gimmicky dog and pony PowerPoint show with audio cues of dogs barking. Our goal isn't visual excitement; our goal is to use images that visually invite and incite our students to hear God's good news.[96] What are some guidelines for using media effectively?

Here are some questions to ask yourself:

1. *What are the most important ideas in my message?* What is it that the students must come away with to make this message work? Obviously, that should be the primary focus of your visual presentation.

2. *Are there any concepts or ideas that the students might find confusing?* With these concepts, would it be more effective to show them or tell them or both?

3. *How many visual aids should I use?* Remember, sometimes less is more. If you already have an object lesson, a drama sketch, a worship song, a video clip, a dancing mime, and a sparkler in the shape of a cross, maybe your puppets can wait until next week. Don't use visual media just because you can.

4. *What is the size of my audience?* Some visual aids that might work well for a group of 20 would be less effective for a larger group. Make sure to take group size into consideration when making media decisions. A coin trick that no one can see isn't memorable or magical. Instead, it's self-amusement, since you're the only one close enough to see it.

5. *If I make the message media-dependent, can I be sure we'll have dependable media equipment and someone who knows how to work it?*

6. *Will the time I spend developing this media presentation rob me of time I should invest in studying the Bible and developing good content?* There's no virtue in saying nothing, even if nothing gets said in a really creative, eye-catching way.

Using Colorful Language

There are five essential elements that allow the human eye to process meaning from its field of vision: contrast, tilt, curvature, line ends, size, and color. And, to steal a line from the apostle Paul, "The greatest of these is color."[97] So when you're using visual aids of any kind, give careful consideration to color.[98]

We know, for example, that yellow is the first color distinguished by the eye,[99] so it's an excellent color to use for highlighting, and a particularly good font color when used with a dark background. At the other end of the spectrum, purple is one of the most difficult colors for the eye to discern. If the desire were to draw attention to a text, purple would be an especially bad choice...even if it's your favorite color. There aren't any hard-and-fast rules about which color to use where because the interpretation of a color depends on culture, profession, personal preference, and context. Blue, for example, is typically considered to be a color of serenity and tranquility. But in the world of K-Mart, it usually means excitement, as in, "Oh, wow, a 'blue light special'—a chance to save some money." And in the world of law-enforcement, it usually means indictment, as in, "Oh, dude, flashing blue lights!"

It's all about context. In general, red, orange, and yellow are "exciting" colors, and purple, blue, and green are "calming" colors. The bottom line with color is—use it strategically.

- Use colors to show differences and similarities between ideas.

- Use black or dark blue for text coloring on whiteboards and flip charts.

- Bright colors (orange, red, yellow) work well for highlighting important information.

- If using a yellow or orange font color, be sure to outline the letters with a darker color so the words can be read from a distance.

- It's usually a good idea to use the same background for each visual. It helps your audience to focus only on what you intend. Resist the temptation to use all of your cool backgrounds in one presentation. Stay away from any dark background that will diminish contrast.

- Use no more than four basic colors in a presentation; better yet, use just two or three.

- Don't crowd the screen. Let the background color offer some space between lettering and images.

For examples and free samples of these types of slides, visit www.speakingtoteenagers.com.

Warning: Giving a Talk Is Not the Same as Talking

There are two common mistakes speakers make where visual media is involved. The first is *overuse*. When I first started using presentation software like PowerPoint and MediaShout, I was so enamored with what *could* be done that I lost some of my focus on what I *should* be doing. I had a slide for every sentence; each syllable demanded a change of slide that would obnoxiously come on the screen as a dissolve, spiral, left-to-right, or drop in. I began to notice I wasn't developing rapport with students like I normally did. They were engaged, but they were mesmerized by my media and not listening to me.

That's when I realized that every time the students looked at the screen, they were looking away from me (which was good for their stomachs, but bad for me). I was basically competing with myself for their attention.

Of course, having students look at me wasn't the point. When teenagers look too long at a middle-aged man with my body type and no hair, that can have its own negative consequences. But it was vital for me to build rapport with the students. It was important for them to bond with me and trust me because I was going to be asking them to make some very serious decisions. And they were more likely to respond to those decisions if they had a good relationship with the person making the appeal. We don't develop that kind of rapport by forcing students to engage with a screen. So I began to cut way back on the number of slides I used, and I showed just enough to help me make the point. Then I began to feel as though I'd found a better balance and more of their attention.

The second mistake that speakers make with visual media—youth workers in particular, regardless of what kind of media it is—is *focusing too much on the show and not enough on the tell*. Wanting to make sure the object lesson works or the video plays or the PowerPoint animation looks just right, we end up *giving* a talk instead of *talking* to our teenagers. One is presentation; the other is communication.

When it's done right, attention should never be focused on the media; the media should help focus our students' attention on our main points. Ideally the audience should sort of "forget" you're using media because it's a supplement and not the main meal. So the key is to make sure you don't let your media presentation interrupt the listeners' thoughts—after all, it's supposed to help keep their focus. Otherwise it might sound like this:

> *Guys, I want to talk to you tonight about God's love.*

> Okay, he's talking about God's love...now he's showing us this big painting...I wish we could see it over here...

> *God's love is big and unconditional.*

> Oh wait, it looks like he's trying to show a video.

> *God's love is...*

> Oh, wow, I've never seen a projector do something like that...he looks nervous!

> *...even when it feels like God has forgotten us...*

> Dude, did he just kick that projector?

We don't want the students to watch us give a talk; we want them to listen to one. Anything that draws attention away from the message is negative. Of course, one possible way to alleviate this potential problem is to have someone else control the media for you. And if there's someone you trust, someone who knows your message and knows your timing (very important), then that may be a good solution.

On the other hand, if someone is doing the media and they don't know your talk or they don't know your timing, it can be very distracting—like one of those bad international news feeds where the reporter's mouth is about three seconds ahead of his audible speech.

Without question, visual media can be a powerful tool. If it's important to set the stage for a talk, then visual media provides us the lights, props, and backdrops on that stage. It frames the message so your students' attention will be drawn to the big picture. But beware the frame that overshadows the big picture. When that happens, the story just gets lost.

The Basic Guidelines

If you do decide that visual media will enhance your message, here are some basic rules of thumb:[100]

DO...	DON'T...
• Simplify visual materials as much as possible.	• Don't stand between your audience and the visual aid.
• Print in big, block letters.	• Don't write longhand on a visual aid; it's too hard to read.
• Use the simplest words you can.	• Don't assume that the necessary equipment always will be in good working order.
• Use as few words as you can.	
• Use negative space. Blank areas on a slide or poster force the eye to look at other points in the picture. Use those negative spaces to get your audience to focus on the part of the slide you intend.	• Don't use a visual aid unless it will be visible for the whole room.
	• Don't use a visual aid that is so vivid, so arresting, such a show-stopper that it distracts your audience from the point you want to make.
• Use as few media images as possible, but don't use fewer than you need. Seeing will enhance hearing.	• Don't design a slide to tell the whole story; design it with only enough information to help you tell the whole story by using the slide.
• Follow this sequence when using a visual aid: Introduce it, display it, comment on it, and then get rid of it.	• Don't compete with yourself for the audience's attention.
	• Don't fall in love with presentation software. Yes, text animation in PowerPoint is wonderful, cool, and hypnotic. But presentation software is designed to help you create an open window through which your audience can get a better view of the truth you want to communicate. Windows that draw attention to themselves and distract from the view are poorly designed windows.

When the stage is finally set, that's when you're ready to deliver your lines. And in the next chapter, we'll discover how to do that clearly and convincingly.

CHAPTER FOURTEEN

The Wonder of Delivery: Speaking to Birth New Life

Neither of us has ever given birth to a child. I can only speak for myself, of course, but I'm fairly certain that neither of us has ever been pregnant. (Actually, I think Doug had a scare about two years ago, but it turned out to be that stale pizza.) And yet both of us know something about the wonder of birthing new life.

Anyone who speaks on a regular basis, whether to a small group, a large group, or something in between, knows something about that birthing process—conception, preparation, and delivery. And what we all understand is that delivery is always the high point of the drama. All of the planning and prep work, all of the Bible study, all of the brainstorming—what it all comes down to is the moment of delivery. The exciting part is not just thinking about and crafting the message; it's about bringing that baby to life.

Conception, study, and preparation—those are necessary labor pains of speaking. But sooner or later it all comes down to delivery—not what goes into the talk, but what comes out *when* you talk.

They Don't Call It *Labor* for Nothing

Most of us know well Paul's charge: "Preach the word; be prepared in season and out of season" (2 Timothy 4:2).

We also know this task can be tough work.

Some say it can't be done or that it shouldn't be—that teenagers today don't respond to spoken messages the way they used to. Some very creative and articulate youth ministry thinkers believe we should be moving away from "the talk" as we've thought about it in the past. They believe our communication needs to be more visual in delivery, more active in approach, and less linear in form. Paul may have said, "Preach the word...in season and out of season," but perhaps it's time to declare open season on the spoken message as a form of effective communication to teenagers. As we suggested in chapter 5 (Listening to the Audience), these are legitimate and thoughtful questions.

Research, for example, tells us the vocabulary of North American ninth graders has dropped from 25,000 words in 1940 to 10,000 words in 1990.[101] This is an audience that spends hours a day in a virtual environment in which people watch on average only 21.8 seconds of a 30-second online video ad (Figure 14-1).[102] The average segment of attention without a break in television programming is a grand total of seven minutes.[103] That reality begs for a realistic question: *Is it really wise and strategic to speak to a teenage audience for 10, 20, or 30 minutes using the spoken word?*

Category of Online Site	Avg. Viewing Time for 30-Second Online Video
Home Video	22.5
Technology	22.2
Music	22.1
Theatrical	21.4
Travel	21.2
Consumer	21.2
Automotive	21.0
Gaming	20.5
Television	20.0
Financial	19.0

FIGURE 14-1. OURS IS NOT A CULTURE THAT ENCOURAGES LONG, FOCUSED THOUGHT. THERE ISN'T MUCH TIME TO MAKE THE POINT.

We believe strongly that it is.[104] But we also believe that to do it effectively is difficult work—often *very* difficult. No wonder Paul followed up his charge in 2 Timothy 4:2 with these words:

> Correct, rebuke and encourage—*with great patience and careful instruction.* For the time will come when people will not put up with sound doctrine. Instead, to suit their own desires, they will gather around them a great number of teachers to say what their itching ears want to hear. They will turn their ears away from the truth and turn aside to myths. But you, keep your head in all situations, endure hardship, do the work of an evangelist, discharge all the duties of your ministry. (2 Timothy 4:2-5, emphasis added)

Like every other skill, good speaking requires intention and execution. And like every other impossible mission, it requires the power of God. The power of God, of course, comes mostly by prayer; but good execution comes mostly by practice. In this chapter and the next, we'll review some of the essential practices of good speaking.

Let Them Hear Your Body Talk

If you've ever watched a foreign film with subtitles, then you know the director attempts to bring you the story in at least three different ways—simultaneously. The director understands that the language may be unfamiliar to us, and he doesn't want us to miss the power of the story. So first we're offered words of dialogue. They come to us through the subtitles written across the bottom of the screen. But then there's the acting (the second form), which includes gestures, movements, and the actors' facial expressions. And finally there's the soundtrack, soaring in moments of intense action and fading as the action slows.

Good speaking requires that we tell God's story with the same intention and intensity. Of course, we understand the words are important. We want to give careful thought to what we say. And, as we discussed in the previous chapter, we may even want to underline the speaking part with some kind of visual or audio media. (These can serve as the soundtrack and subtitles of your talk.) But as much as possible, we also need to make use of posture, gestures, eye contact, and facial expressions because our bodies can be amazing tools for telling stories in a more engaging way.

As a matter of fact, research psychologist Albert Mehrabian found that we communicate more through nonverbal cues than through all the elements of verbal speech combined (Figure 14-2).[105]

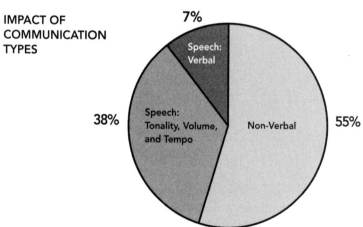

IMPACT OF COMMUNICATION TYPES

7% Speech: Verbal

38% Speech: Tonality, Volume, and Tempo

Non-Verbal 55%

FIGURE 14-2. RESEARCH DEMONSTRATES THAT OUR ACTIONS REALLY DO SPEAK LOUDER THAN OUR WORDS.

Communication theorists have identified at least five ways that we communicate nonverbally.[106] Three of them are especially strategic in the way we communicate God's great grace drama to teenagers.

First of all, *body motions can take the place of a word or phrase.* If you can recall the last time you cut off someone in traffic, then perhaps you've observed this. He wasn't fully able to engage you verbally; but by making good use of a certain universal gesture, he was able to amply communicate his true feelings toward you. Good communicators understand the power of a strong gesture.

Obviously most gestures vary from culture to culture and audience to audience (*pathos*).[107] For instance, that little gesture we make when we form a circle by connecting the thumb and forefinger is the *okay* sign in the United States. But in France it means *zero* or *worthless*; in Japan it's a symbol for *money*; and in Germany and Brazil it's considered a gesture of flagrant *vulgarity.* (Remember this if you're ever invited to speak at the United Nations. Otherwise, the American delegation will think you're a nice guy, the Japanese will think you're offering them a bribe, the French will think you're insulting them, and the Germans will think they've cut you off in traffic.)

Second, *body motions amplify what a speaker is saying.* There are those moments, for example, when Germans, Brazilians, and Americans on occasion, will combine what they consider to be vulgar gestures *with* vulgar comments. When they do this, combine the verbal and nonverbal, the body motions actually serve to underline the spoken word and offer a clear demonstration that the right gesture can both interpret and amplify the verbal message.

Third, *body motions nonverbally express feelings.* These are the more reflexive nonverbals: the wringing hands of nervousness or despair, the head hung low in disappointment, or the hand to the mouth at a moment of astonishment or confusion (as when the American tourist asks, "Why would that German curse at me while giving me the okay sign?").

One easy way to think about body language is to think of it in terms of two modes of expression: (1) the head (eye contact, facial expressions, head position, etc.), and (2) the body from the neck down (gestures, posture, stance, etc.). Let's give some thought to each mode of body talk.

The Eyes Have It

It was Ralph Waldo Emerson who said, "The eyes of men converse as much as their tongues, with the advantage that the ocular dialect needs no dictionary, but is understood the world over." That sounds so true; unfortunately, we *do* need a dictionary to be sure what *ocular* means. But there's no question that eye contact is one of our most powerful tools in the delivery arsenal of nonverbal communication.

What's key for speakers to understand is that communication research confirms the importance of a speaker making eye contact with the audience. This is especially true in the United States where studies have shown that eye contact is perceived as a sign of sincerity.[108]

Indeed, in one study, with the eye-catching title "Communicative Effects of Gaze Behavior," the authors demonstrate that speakers who fail to make ample eye contact with their audience are perceived to be ill at ease and often insincere and dishonest.[109]

What does it all mean for those who speak to teenagers?

- *Make sure you're always maintaining eye contact with your students.* The smaller your group, the more noticeable and important it is.

- *Don't allow anything to obstruct your students' view of your eyes.* This may sound silly, but lots of youth workers stand up to speak every week wearing a baseball hat. If there's any overhead lighting, the hat's bill casts a perfect shadow over the eyes. The only thing worse would be placing a catcher's mask over the entire face.

- *It takes less than a second to make eye contact with a student in your audience.* And that's usually plenty. This isn't *Children of the Damned* where we stare at them until they explode or turn into stone. Nor should we be Tammy Typewriter where our eyes methodically scan back and forth, left to right across the crowd as if the audience were an ear of corn to be consumed. Most public speaking texts suggest starting with a Z pattern, which gives good attention to the people in the back of the group (we remember that crowd from the last chapter), and offers an opportunity to work across the middle and up to the front.

Of course, if there are teenagers who are talking during a message, or who look as if they need to be reeled in a bit, I'll usually engage them with a bit longer look—more like I would if I were involved with them in conversation. It's not a glare that says, "Hey, I'm *looking at* you." It's an intentional engagement of the eyes that says, "Hello, I'm *talking* to you, and I really care about you, and I want you to get this." If they continue to talk or become disruptive, then I do actually stare at them until they explode or turn into stone.

Notes or Not

One of the questions relevant to eye contact is whether or not it's good to use notes for your talk. It's an important question, and it deserves some attention. Objective studies have tested listener reactions to a speaker reading from a manuscript (the entire message written out word for word) versus speaking extemporaneously (with few or no notes). In terms of listener response, it really is a slam dunk. Listeners retain approximately 38 percent more content when the message is delivered using extemporaneous speech.[110] Further testing found that audiences tend to be more sympathetic and more attentive when speakers use extemporaneous delivery rather than preaching from a manuscript.

I know very few youth workers who ever speak from a word-for-word manuscript, although I do it occasionally (depending on the setting and how prepared I am). I like the way a manuscript forces me to write out exactly what I want to say, which in turn forces me to think more precisely about which words I'll use and how I'll transition between points. When I write my manuscript, I write out everything, even jokes, stories, and other material that, to the audience, probably sounds like an ad lib, an aside, or a throwaway line. I manuscript the whole thing.

Having said that, I never speak from a manuscript unless I've read it through at least eight times, which, for me, is enough to pretty much commit it to memory. That allows me to have the manuscript, but to maintain steady eye contact.

There are those who are dead set against using notes, as well as those who feel that speaking without notes is like driving without a map. In fact, there are very effective communicators in both camps. Although his sermons don't read like it, John Calvin almost always preached without notes. And, supposedly, John Wesley often preached with his eyes closed. That doesn't say much about his ability to make eye contact, but it certainly proves he wasn't too dependent on notes.

The best benefit of preaching without a lot of notes is its naturalness. Students are less likely to hear our words as authentic if we have to read them too carefully.

If You Choose to Use Notes...

- *Don't be too dependent on them.* They should be more like a surfboard and less like a life preserver. One helps you stay on your feet as you ride the wave; the other is something you cling to in order to keep your head above water. One makes the audience want to ride with you; the other makes the audience want to rescue you (or drown you).

- *Practice your talk several times.* You don't want to be so intent on giving the talk that you're unable to talk to your students. As you practice, make sure you practice with different voice inflections (more on this in chapter 15).

- *Memorize the opening and conclusion of your talk.* That's when eye contact is most important. When you have to search through your notes to find out what it was that you "really believe from the bottom of [your] heart," uh, that's not very persuasive. A genuine opening and closing can make up for a few mistakes in the middle.

- *Let the length of your talk determine the format of your notes.* Notes for a short talk can perhaps be written on a note card that's paper-clipped to a page in your Bible. If it's a longer message, you may need to use 8 ½-by-11-inch paper (or a really, really big paper clip and Bible).

- *Write your notes on only one side of the page.* That way you can easily slide the notes aside as you move through the talk without flipping the paper over. I [Doug] put an arrow on each page that serves as a guide for when to slide my notes to the other side of the music stand. The arrow is usually placed at a point in my notes where I know I might read something, and then while I'm reading it, I subtly slide the page. It's barely noticeable.

- *Use a colored highlighter* to emphasize transition lines, main points, and so on.

- *Always number your pages.* If you've ever dropped your note cards during your talk, you know how exciting it is to practice your multitasking skills—being passionate, expressive, and inspiring while trying to arrange the cards back into sequence without soaking your shirt in sweat. And it's even more exciting when you don't get them back in order accurately and don't realize it: "In conclusion...(new page)...my first point is...."

- *Use the smallest stand possible to hold your notes.* Massive pulpits are intimidating, especially to teenagers, and they often hide parts of your body with which you need to communicate. A good, tight music stand (not one that wobbles back and forth or doesn't stay up) works great. Make sure it has a lip that will keep your notes on the stand.

- *Place the stand at a comfortable height.* I [Duffy] always raise it as high as I can—around chest high (for me, that's about three feet). I want it to be high enough so that when I'm looking *down* at my notes, it looks like I'm still looking *out* at my audience. It shouldn't be high enough to block my face, but neither should it be so low that I have to look toward the floor to see what I'm going to say next.

I [Doug] have a similar style with the music stand, but I'm probably a little more note-dependent than Duffy because unlike Duffy—who travels and speaks to lots of different audiences—I'm speaking to the same audience every week, and that means every week I'm giving a new message for the very first time. I have a hard time memorizing my message, so I have fairly detailed notes. I've learned a trick that allows me to use my notes without making me look as note-dependent as I feel: I stand several feet back from the music stand. By doing this, my head doesn't dip down to my notes. I can make eye contact with the students and still look at my notes when necessary. There have been times when I've felt as though I looked at my notes a lot. But then I'll ask my own children (who are teenagers) or some of my volunteers, and they'll usually say, "I never saw you look at your notes." I attribute that to an adjustable music stand and a large font (and pastors' kids who know how to work for their allowance).

- *Make sure your notes are written in oral style.* The danger of writing out your message is that you'll be tempted to write it in a way that you wouldn't naturally speak it. As a result, it will sound artificial to your audience. Oral communication is marked by (1) short words, (2) contractions, (3) a moderate to high level of repetition, and (4) use of concrete terms.[111] In short, oral communication is normal conversation (see Figure 14-3).[112]

MARKS OF ORAL STYLE	EXAMPLES OF WRITTEN STYLE	EXAMPLES OF ORAL STYLE
Conversational	"As was mentioned earlier..."	"It's like we said a few minutes ago..."
Sounds the way you normally speak	"One cannot avoid people with this characteristic..."	"It's really tough to avoid people like that.."
More personal	"A hypothetical case in point might be a situation where government..."	"Imagine this. Let's say Uncle Sam..."
Uses mostly contractions except for emphasis	"It is not..."	"It isn't..."
Descriptive language is awesome, but it has to sound like you, and not Jane Austen	"The azure hues of a wondrous sky bedecked with the jewel of a golden orb..."	"A beautiful, blue sky, with a blazing sun.."
Keep the dialogue in second person (I-You) instead of third person.	"People who say such things are often accused of heresy..."	"Now, I know some of you kids think that last statement smacks of Sabellianism..."

FIGURE 14-3. WRITE OUT YOUR TALK THE WAY YOU'D SPEAK IT; DON'T SPEAK YOUR TALK THE WAY YOU MIGHT WRITE IT.

If You Choose Not to Use Notes...

- *Don't get lazy and sloppy.* Make sure you take adequate time to prepare and craft your message. Charles Spurgeon said it well:

> Beware of letting your tongue outrun your brain. Guard against a feeble fluency, a garrulous prosiness, a facility of saying nothing, my brethren. It is a hideous gift to possess, to be able to say nothing at extreme length...Elongated nonsense...[is] the scandal and shame of extemporizing. Even when the sentiments of no value are beautifully expressed and neatly worded, what is the use of them? Out of nothing comes nothing. Extemporaneous speech without study is like a cloud without rain, a well without water, a fatal gift, injurious equally to its possessor and his/her flock.[113]

Speaking Face to Face

Here's an assignment: Go stand in front of a mirror and—using only your face—express the following phrases:

1. "Doctor, are you sure it's triplets?"

2. "What does it mean when my screen goes blank and smoke appears from the back of the computer?"

3. "What do you mean there's another husband I don't know about? I don't care if he *is* a great guy!"

4. "I don't believe this: The church board just voted to double my pay, give me a new car, pay off our mortgage, and tutor the children in Greek!"

5. "Dieser lächelnde Amerikaner gab mir eine vulgäre Geste gerade, als ich ihm Richtungen gab!" *(German-to-English translation: "That smiling American just gave me a vulgar gesture when I gave him directions!")*

Facial expressions are typically the most important means of communicating basic emotions—sadness, happiness, anger, fear, surprise, and disgust. What's remarkable is how these six facial expressions have the same meaning throughout the world,[114] even slight gestures like raising the eyebrow to communicate recognition or wriggling one's nose with a contorted facial expression to communicate repulsion.[115]

And it all happens by our manipulation of three basic facial features: "(1) the brow and forehead; (2) the eyes, eyelids, and root of the nose; and (3) the cheeks, mouth, remainder of the nose, and chin."[116]

When we're speaking to a group of teenagers, we want to be "unconsciously aware" of these facial features at all times. That probably sounds like an oxymoron of sorts, but it's not. On the one hand, we want this to become an *unconscious* behavior because if we try too hard to make ourselves look angry, serious, compassionate, or worshipful, we'll usually come off looking phony or constipated (very similar facial expressions). On the other hand, we need to be *aware* of our facial features because we want them to affirm and amplify our words at all times. Research demonstrates that listeners are very good at reading emotions by looking at the face.[117] The wrong expression can dim or deny the power of our words.

Here are three ways our face can overrule our mouth.

Lack of Expression

Some people are naturally expressive and their faces are open books. But there are others whose range of facial expressions is more limited. Their faces are also open books, but the words appear only about every third page. Both types of people can be effective communicators, but the latter group will have to be more intentional.

It's like two people playing a guitar when one instrument has six strings and the other has three. Both musicians can play the same song, but the person with the three-stringed guitar has to focus a lot more effort on the melody. So don't fret (couldn't resist the pun); even if you're not a demonstrative person, you can still be an effective communicator. But it will require focused awareness.

The very best suggestion for improvement is to practice in front of a mirror. Just as an experiment, practice expressing some of the phrases in your talk without using any words. Just mime it with your face. (Warning: This exercise may cause you to feel slightly stupid. You'll feel very stupid if someone walks in on you. And you'll feel really, really stupid if you're practicing in front of the bathroom mirror at church while someone, unbeknownst to you, is in the stall.)

Incongruent Expression

I remember being assigned to preach a sermon on the Ascension of Jesus when I was in seminary. I was nervous and, frankly, a little underprepared. I didn't know my talk the way I wanted to, but it was my turn to go. About five minutes into the sermon, I spoke the words, "Jesus went up," but, unfortunately, I was simultaneously looking down at my notes to see what happened when he got up there. And, of course, that's the precise moment when the

Recently I've tried something that I've never really done before, and I'm surprised at the response I've been getting. I've started over-exaggerating some of my nonverbal reactions. For example, if I'm showing surprise, I'll ratchet it up from what was normally a 5 to a 9 (on a scale of 1 to 10). If you and I were having a conversation, my "surprise look" might naturally be a 2. But when I'm speaking, the over-exaggeration receives a much bigger response than when I didn't exaggerate my expressions. — Doug

preaching professor froze the videotape of my talk so he could ask me, in front of the class, "Mr. Robbins, did Jesus go up, as your mouth is telling us, or did he go down, as your head is telling us?" It was a valid point. My head and face didn't match my words. That's incongruent expression.

Pained Expression

Speaking is hard work, but it shouldn't *look* like hard work. That means a good communicator is constantly aware of trying to maintain a pleasant and comfortable facial expression. It's like the ice skater who, despite the difficulty, does her flips and jumps with a smile on her face even though there's likely bruises under her skating attire.

Of course, that doesn't mean you should keep a perpetual grin on your face while you're speaking—i.e., "Bozo's Happy Visit to the Corinthians." There are times when a smile is incongruent and inappropriate. But students have a preconceived idea that teachers are there to scold and to scare them. Don't allow your face to confirm that expectation. Let your default facial expression be one of friendliness, warmth, and genuine concern, not, *I hope I can get through this routine without taking a fall.* If you're comfortable and have fun while you're speaking, then your audience will sense it and your message will be received with more value.

You've Got the Whole Word in Your Hands

We've all met people who can't talk without using their hands. These people are called "speakers." Giving a talk without using gestures is like going into battle unarmed. (I couldn't resist that one either.) Yet developing good gestures is another skill that requires practice. Let's look at how *not* to gesture first.

Distracting gestures and body movements fall into two categories:

1. *Those you do all the time*—pushing your glasses up the bridge of your nose, tucking your hair behind your ear, stroking your beard, twiddling the ends of your moustache (especially distracting when done by women), cracking your knuckles, jerking your head quickly to throw your hair up out of your eyes.

2. *Those you do only when you're speaking*—clearing your throat, tapping your pencil on the lectern, flapping your note cards like a

fan, rocking back and forth on your feet, sweating profusely, taking a puff on your pipe (seminary students only), cracking your note cards down on the lectern to continually square the stack.[118]

None of these physical gestures is bad the first time. But when they're consistently repeated, they become a distraction. Teenagers begin keeping records of various gestures, and entertain themselves by scoring specific habitual body movements: Pushed glasses equal five points, hair tucks and head jerks are three points, and clearing the throat is two points. Like any other habit, we often don't even notice we're doing it until someone points it out to us.

Sometimes it isn't the mannerism that detracts from our message; it's the whole body posture. What follows are some of the default postures that disarm us and diminish the power of communication that happens through body movement. Why don't you try them with your own body while you're reading through the list and see if any of them feel familiar?

- *The Bear Hug.* Arms across the chest, with each hand reaching to the opposite side of the body.

- *Reporting for Duty.* Body is straight, arms are stiff, and wrists are nailed firmly to the side.

- *The Flesh Wound.* One arm hangs uselessly at the side, while the other arm reaches over and serves as a tourniquet above or below the elbow.

- *Vienna Boys Choir.* Hands clasped at waist level with fingers intertwined.

- *The Firing Squad.* Legs slightly spread, hands clasped tightly behind the back.

- *The Monk.* Same as the *Vienna Boys Choir*, but hands are clasped at chest level.

- *The Fig Leaf.* Legs open slightly. Hands cupped together in front of the body and placed strategically. Often referred to as *The Penalty Kick.*

- *Lady Macbeth.* Hands wrung nervously as if continuously attempting to wash away the stain of a bad talk.

- *Mr. Happy Pockets.* Keeping hands in the pockets where they can jingle keys, coins, good luck charms, and the laser pen you confiscated from the seventh-grade boy.[119]

These postures lock us into positions that stifle good, nonverbal expression.

If those are some of the common mistakes, what are some guidelines for doing it right? How can we make the best use of our body movements?

• *When not gesturing, park your hands someplace that isn't distracting* (your pockets, the sides of the lectern—whatever feels most comfortable and natural for you), but then don't get locked into that posture.

• *Keep your gestures high up on your body frame.* You don't want the audience to have to choose between looking at you (your eyes and your face) or looking at your gesture. It depends, of course, on the gesture; but I usually stage my gestures about six to eight inches in front of my chin. So to look at my gestures, you have to look at my face. If the audience is looking at my face, then they'll have to see my gestures. This is especially important for female speakers who tend to keep their hands closer to their bodies. A hand that is gesturing emphatically at the end of an arm that's hanging straight down is like a police car with flashing lights—tied to the front hubcap. No matter how much it flashes, it draws little attention. Keep the gestures up where they'll be seen.

• *Match the breadth of your gestures to the size of your audience.* A larger audience might mean more exaggerated gestures; a smaller audience allows for more conversational gestures.

• *Time the gesture so it best serves your point.* When a preacher pounds the pulpit 10 seconds after he's made his point, it leaves the audience either confused about the preacher's intent or concerned about his reflexes. Neither response enhances the message.

• *Again, it depends on the gesture, but give your gestures a firm end point.* Imagine that a gesture leaves a mark in the air (i.e., a vapor

---

One way that I like to break up my body movement is to occasionally walk into my audience and stand near a group of students or one of my volunteers. That breaks the "invisible plane" of the stage and the crowd. Anything that moves me away from my music stand is another way that I use my body to send a conversational message.

It's amazing how simple it is. There are times when I'll put a leg up on the floor speaker and lean against my leg like I'd do if I were speaking to someone sitting down (more at their eye level). I'll always have a stool nearby that I can grab and sit down while I read or tell a story. Anything that breaks up my natural desire to either pace or stand still. I'll even go so far as adding the word *sit* into the margin of my notes at a place where I think a change in body language might communicate, "Okay, this is a more tender, heartfelt part of my message, and I want it to feel like it's just you and me having a normal conversation." — *Doug* trail). There should be an obvious beginning point and an obvious end point. That helps define the gesture, and it aids the audience in interpreting its meaning.

- *Don't overlook the power of stance.* Moving closer to the group, stepping over to one side, the way feet are positioned—all of these help to communicate focus, boldness, intensity, and importance.

Be attentive to how your whole body communicates. Remember, the Word became flesh! Let them hear your body talk.

CHAPTER FIFTEEN

The Wonder of Delivery: Announcing New Life

> Speech consists of more than words and sentences. The voice conveys ideas and feelings apart from words. We make judgments about a speaker's physical and emotional state—whether he is frightened, angry, fatigued, sick, happy, confident—based on the tremor of his voice, its loudness, rate and pitch.
>
> — HADDON ROBINSON, *BIBLICAL PREACHING* [120]

Remember when you were a child, and you were playing that game with your little brother where you'd hang him by his feet from the window of the tree house? And then your mom looked out the back door at just that moment, saw her baby dangling by a belt, screaming what you later tried to describe as a prayer of confession? Remember how she yelled across the backyard? I do!

I can still hear it: "DAVID WILLIAM ROBBINS, WHAT DO YOU THINK YOU'RE DOING? YOU HOIST YOUR BABY BROTHER BACK UP THERE RIGHT THIS MINUTE AND MARCH YOURSELF INTO THIS HOUSE BEFORE I COUNT TO 10! YOU ARE IN BIG TROUBLE, MISTER!"

Obviously, she didn't understand that I was trying to teach him about faith and trust and the importance of giving considerable thought to eternity.

But my point is that even if she'd spoken those same words in a foreign language, her message would have been crystal clear: *Mom is not pleased with your evangelistic methods. And it is you who will soon be in prayer since you are about to face judgment.*

Such is the wonder of the human voice. Like a musical instrument capable of playing sad, happy, loud, quiet, beautiful, or raw, our voices offer us an amazing range of ways to move students. And studies have shown that we humans are remarkably astute at hearing and interpreting these nuances in the human voice. Two-thirds of the time listeners can accurately detect anger in the voice, even if they don't understand the language. "More than half the time the sound of your voice can accurately communicate nervousness, and almost half of the time it accurately expresses sadness."[121]

Vocal Characteristics

All of this amazing variety of expression, and it comes through our use of four basic vocal characteristics:

1. *Volume*—the loudness or softness of the voice, tonal quality

2. *Pitch*—the highness or lowness of the tone of voice

3. *Rate*—the speed at which the words come out

4. *Quality*—the timbre or character of the voice[122]

To get a feel for how these four elements interplay, practice saying the following phrase in a way that communicates what the instructions suggest: *Luke the Force is with you* (notice how we've eliminated all punctuation because punctuation helps determine how you speak the sentence).

- Phrase Style #1: Say this as if you're Obi-Wan, shouting out a final word of encouragement to Luke as he flies off into the sunset to save the universe.

- Phrase Style #2: Say this as if you're a young superhero who calls himself "Luke the Force," and you've just walked through the door at Starbucks.

- Phrase Style #3: Say this as if you were Darth Vader, frankly a little surprised at how well Luke is doing in battle against you.

- Phrase Style #4: Say this is as if you're the host of the popular TV show *American Jedi*, and you're announcing that Luke has won the honor of having the Force with him.

Now, admittedly, one reason for doing a little exercise like this is purely for fun. But it also serves as a demonstration of how these four elements— volume, pitch, rate, and quality—can combine to offer an amazing range of expression.

Let's talk about how each element can help you be a better communicator.

Volume

Consider the different volumes you'd use while saying each of the following expressions:

- "Don't raise your voice to me, young man..."

- "Whisper to me sweet nothings, my love..."

- "I heard you the first time; you don't have to yell..."

- "Speak up; you sound like you're trying to hide something..."

- "I respected Doug and Duffy until I read this book..."

All of these everyday statements remind us of the communication power of volume because we immediately recognize the volume control connected to the statement—they are like hand in glove.

When giving a talk, volume helps us communicate everything from anger, to joy, to solemnity, to authority, to conviction, to intensity, to excitement, to enthusiasm, to panic, to fear. Knowing how to control and use your volume is a powerful tool. Little wonder that in the field of public speaking, volume is often referred to as *dynamics*. But the power of volume comes through contrast. For example, if the entire talk is given at a high volume, a low volume, or the same volume, it really bleaches out the impact. A good communicator will explore and express several different volumes within a message.

One of the easiest ways to dramatically alter volume is with the help of a microphone. Granted, you won't always need a microphone, but for those times when you do, it's good to know how to maneuver one. If the group size requires that you be miked, consider what type of microphone will work best for you and what makes you the most comfortable. There are two common variables: wireless or wired, and handheld or hands-free. You'll develop your own preferences, of course.

Wireless versus wired. The obvious primary advantage to a wireless mic is that it offers you mobility as you're speaking but without playing jump rope and getting tangled up in the microphone cord. A speaker can actually go into the audience and move freely around the front of the room.

The disadvantage is that wireless mics typically run on batteries, and batteries typically run out when someone is using them. Unless someone is very disciplined about replacing the batteries frequently—*before* they need to be replaced—a wireless mic becomes a booby trap that will detonate in the middle of your message when all volume drops out.

The other disadvantage of a wireless mic is the speaker has to remember to turn on the unit before she begins speaking and turn it off again when it's not in use. Many speakers have spoken their first words, only to realize their microphone isn't turned on. And when those first dramatic words have to be repeated, they don't sound quite as spontaneous and dramatic anymore: "I couldn't believe it! I...er...uh...oh...is it on back there? Can you hear me now? Oh...okay...all right, let's try again...I couldn't believe it!"

Handheld versus hands-free (lavaliere or headset). Most speakers really like having their hands free, and that's an obvious advantage of the lavaliere or headset microphone. As much as we've said about gestures, it just makes sense that you'd want to move your hands and arms freely—and all the more if you're a speaker who likes to have a Bible in your hand while you're teaching. Holding a mic and a Bible while getting a quick sip of water or holding up some prop is just one flaming torch short of juggling. It makes that headset feel like a pretty good idea.

On the other hand, when a speaker uses a lavaliere or a headset mic, all volume control is in the hands of the person working the soundboard. When you have the option of moving the mic closer to your mouth or farther away, it allows you some measure of control over the volume. You don't have that with a lavaliere or headset mic. The mic remains the exact same distance from the mouth during the entire talk. And that is a distinct disadvantage. Not being able to move the microphone very close to your mouth or hold it far away surrenders a significant tool for controlling the dynamics of the talk. That is why some speakers choose the handheld mike even though it requires some ingenuity with gestures.

Over the years I've accidentally deposited two microphone battery packs into the toilet. Not one, but two. If it were only one incident, it wouldn't be worth talking about. But I did it twice.

I often get very nervous before I speak, and it's not uncommon for me to use the bathroom several times just before giving my message. The microphone's battery pack clips to the back of my pants, and, well, the battery pack landed in the toilet.

The first time I just dried it off and pretended nothing happened. But when I got up front, it didn't work. Of course I blamed the sound guy, and they rushed me a new mic. Then after the meeting, the sound guy said, "Uh, do you have any idea how this got wet on the inside?" Well, not only did I know, but I was convinced he wouldn't want to know the truth. So I said, "I guess I sweat a lot!" (Actually, I told him the truth, apologized, and promised him that it was the *first* thing that dropped into the toilet.)

The second time it happened... well, I can't divulge. All I can say is be careful when you're going to the bathroom while wearing a microphone system. Please! Learn from my mistakes.

— *Doug*

As one of these types of speakers, I [Duffy] have developed the habit that whenever I need to use both hands (usually for reading the Bible), I use my right underarm as a mic stand. I simply tuck the mic under my arm while I'm reading the text. The mic is pointed up, so it still amplifies my voice—and then, when I've finished reading, I pull the mic out again. (And you don't even want to know where I keep my note cards.)

I [Doug], on the other hand, don't particularly like using a handheld mic because I feel it limits my motions and feels too showy (i.e., "Hey, kids, look at me! I'm the public speaker with a microphone!"). And I don't like the lavaliere mic because I find the sound drops a little when I turn my head. The lavaliere mic will still pick up my voice, but when I'm not facing forward (and speaking into it), the volume drops down when I don't intend it to be changed.

Since I haven't mastered the Duffy Robbins armpit maneuver, I prefer to use the headset microphone. With this mic, the mouthpiece rests so close to my mouth that it's very easy for me to adjust the volume, and it will pick up my voice no matter how animated I am or how much I turn my head. Basically, to each his own.

(After hearing Doug's bathroom story, from now on my mic preference whenever Doug and I speak together will be to use whatever mic Doug *doesn't* use.)

Pitch

In a *Reader's Digest* article some years ago, Michael Anania wrote "An Insider's Guide to Teen-Speak." I've read the following portion to parents who tend to find it especially accurate:

> The words teenagers use with one another have a variety of meanings. The keys to understanding them are tone, duration, and pitch—a little like Chinese.
>
> Most parents encounter the tonal dimension of teen language when dealing with the phrase, "All right." In response to an ordinary request like "Take out the garbage," "All right" can mean: (a) Don't bother me; (b) Did somebody cut off your legs; (c) I deeply resent the authority you have over me, but I acknowledge it and will take out your stupid garbage; (d) Out of affection for you and respect for your age, I'll take out the garbage; (e) Okay.
>
> Depending on tone, a harmless response such as "Great" can mean (a) Great; (b) Not that again; or (c) You've ruined my life. The answer "Sure" never indicates simple agreement, as in regular English. Depending on duration, "Sure" means: (a) That's just what I'd expect from an old person; (b) You don't know what you're talking about; or (c) You've ruined my life. "Yeah" has the same range of meanings, but in this case the briefest version has the most devastating intent.

As exit lines, "Great," "Sure," and "Yeah" require punctuation. For example, "Great (slam)," "Sure (stomp)," and "Yeah (abruptly turned head)." When punctuated this way, all three expressions mean, "You've ruined my life." But before you're overcome with guilt, you should know that "my life" only refers to the next 45 minutes (or until I need cash).[123]

It really is amazing how the same statement can have remarkably different meanings based solely on the speaker's pitch or inflection. In speaking to teenagers, this is a tool we'll want to use well. That means avoiding some of these common traps:

- *Monotone.* The most common mistake is a lack of inflection, speaking every sentence with the same drained emotion, whether it's, "It was a bad day; they killed my idea for the mission project." Or "It was a bad day; they killed my puppy." Or "It was a bad day, they tried to kill me." In a world without question marks, exclamation points, and periods, all ideas run together, and all phrases sound the same.

- *Story Time.* This is the opposite of monotone. It's adding so much inflection that your delivery sounds artificial—like a kindergarten teacher reading a story after lunch: "Hi, boys and girls! Today we're going to talk about fornication! And a king who did some *reeaally* bad things. Can you say *adultery*?!"

- *Upspeak.* This is a speech pattern that we hear so often, we don't even notice it. Every sentence ends with a raise in pitch, as if every statement were a question. "Okay, we're gonna talk tonight about Jesus? He was—like—really good? And really powerful?"

- *"May I?"* This is akin to upspeak in that it overuses raised pitch, but it's usually a little slower and more tentative—the question marks appear every few words. "Tonight?...we're going to listen?...and hopefully?...God will speak to us?" This sort of delivery makes it sound as though the speaker is asking permission to utter each new word or phrase. A variation on this type of error would be when the speaker actually replaces the question mark with a word or phrase such as, "Y'know?" I once heard an entire Easter sermon in which the preacher ended every phrase with the word "Okay?" as if he were walking on very thin ice and wasn't sure he'd find support for his next step. It completely undercut any sense of authority his words might have had otherwise.

- *Pastoral Pulpit Pattern.* This is a little tougher to describe, but we've all heard it often enough. It's that stereotypical preaching delivery that begins the sentence high on a note of passion, and ends it low on a note of gravitas. Again, there is nothing wrong with any inflection pattern in and of itself. But, repeated over and over, it's the oral equivalent of being exiled to life on a seesaw.

As you practice the talk, be conscious of your inflection, especially if you have fallen into any of the above habits. It may take awhile before it feels comfortable, but simply giving your talk out loud, *as you intend to speak it,* is the best way to improve. Don't just read it silently. You need to hear yourself and how you sound. If you need help with a specific pitch that isn't natural to you, practice saying it as if one of your friends were saying it. We all know people who do a better job at inflection than we do, and if you listen to others long enough, you can learn from them. Again, this is an issue of conscious unawareness, and it will require practice to change.

Rate

Let's begin with the math. The average American speaks at a rate of 125 words a minute in ordinary conversation. For a speaker in front of an audience, the rate slows down to about 100 words a minute. Here's the problem: The average listener *thinks* at a rate of about 400 to 500 words a minute.[124] To put it in numerical terms, every single minute we speak, our teenagers have the mental space to add about 300 to 400 words to those that you're speaking. Needless to say, that can be a problem because there's no guarantee the additional words they contribute will have anything to do with the words you're communicating.

That doesn't mean we should go into auctioneer mode or the fast-talking radio ad disclaimer for pharmaceutical products. (You know, the one that says, "This could cause acne, balding, genital warts, constipation, death, body pains, severe death, inflammation, ulcers, painful death, tremors, and itchy feet," but it's uttered so fast it sounds like, "This could be really helpful.") But picking up the pace a little does mean that we should be aware of three guidelines.

1. We need to speak faster than 100 words a minute. In the world of college debate, where the object is to present as much data as possible in an assigned time limit, competitors become verbal speed demons, routinely speaking up to 200 and even 300 words a minute.[125] That's not our task! Sometimes saying less is more. But the kind of slow, deliberate delivery that might work for adults who are willing to patiently wait for the payoff of another period and a new sentence won't work with teenagers. I speak much more quickly when I'm speaking to students than I do in normal conversation.

Having said that, this is a good place to talk about the power of a pause. Sometimes the power of silence between words can be as arresting as anything in the words themselves. It's scary at first because we're thinking, *Oh my gosh, I'm going to stop talking for a moment, and they're going to grab a few hundred words and write a mental novel!* Don't worry; we're not talking about a lengthy stop. This is not a coffee break; it's a pause. And the moment has to be right. You can't leave them hanging if you haven't hooked them first. But a good long pause (after a drop in volume) can provide a great contrast to a rapid-fire delivery. Give it a try and watch your students' drooping heads suddenly perk up because you paused. Teenagers might be thinking one of the following: (a) *Did something get caught in his throat?* (b) *Is he crying? Why isn't he saying anything?* (c) *Did he die and he just hasn't fallen over yet? If so, that was a short message...cool!*

2. We need to make those words count. Speech theorists talk about words that are *interferences*—words that interrupt the flow of fluent speech. If we fall into the habit of using them too often, words and phrases such as *er, uh, okay, you know,* and *like* give teenagers an opportunity to detour on a mental tangent. The best prevention of *interferences* is preparation—knowing what you intend to say and being able to recall it in mid-delivery. Obviously, that has to do with memory, learning how to make best use of your notes, and mental discipline (i.e., don't allow yourself to get distracted by the kid in the corner who just set his shoe on fire and is now crawling toward you). But again, the best way to use words that count is to write out your talk beforehand. Know in advance how each illustration will be explained for maximum impact, how each transition will be made from one point to the next, and how you'll segue from the introduction to the main body. Knowing these turns before you get to the intersection will keep your students from passing you on a side road.

3. Know when to stop. It sounds simple, but one of the easiest ways to make sure you don't run out of words before you run out of time is to know your finish line and stop when you get there. William Sangster, one of the great preachers of the last century, put it this way:

> Having come to the end, stop. Do not cruise around looking for a spot to land, like some weary swimmer coming in from the sea and splashing about until he can find a shelving beach up which to walk. Come right in and land at once. Finish what you have to say and end at the same time. If the last phrase can have some quality of crisp memorableness, all the better, but do not grope even for that. Let your sermon have the quality that Charles Wesley coveted for his whole life: let the work and the course end together.[126]

Here are some simple suggestions that may be helpful:

- *Avoid false endings.* Words and phrases like "finally," or "to wrap this up," or "so what's the bottom line for all of this?" signal to the audience that we are coming to an end point. If we continue talking, not only does it irritate them, it confuses them about what is the final big idea they should take away from the talk. When you mention anything related to finishing, you've created great expectations and enthusiasm for your teenage audience. They want you to bring it in for a landing.

- *Don't introduce a new idea in the conclusion.*

- *When you finish, stop talking.* Don't minimize the impact of your closing words by saying, "And I guess that's all I have to say" or "I think that's it" or "I wish I had more time because there's a lot more I could talk about that I didn't have time to say."

- *Remember that what you say in the last minute or so of your message will be what your students are most likely to remember.* That's what they'll walk away with.

Quality

Raspy, smoky, squeaky, throaty, deep—these are all terms we use to describe vocal quality. The main point is—your voice has a unique timbre. You don't need to try to sound like anyone else. However, what we do need to do is make sure we're using the maximum range and variety in our voices. Sometimes a comic line will be funnier if it's spoken with a nasal tone. Sometimes a statement will sound more intense and earnest if it's said with a raspy, breathy sound (think Clint Eastwood). Or you might use a certain timbre in your voice to articulate a question that might be on the mind of your audience. All of these are samples of vocal quality.

As with any other instrument, the way to develop the full range of repertoire is to practice, practice, practice. Before you go to the next paragraph, re-read this section (Quality) again, using three distinctly different voice qualities as a way of practicing.

It could be that, as you read through this chapter, you're thinking, *Wow, I thought I could just share my heart and that would be enough to communicate the gospel.* The bad news is that's not exactly true, at least it's not any more true than you calling someone on your cell phone, sharing your heart, and expecting that to make an impact, even though (a) the person hasn't answered the phone, (b) the person isn't listening to you speak on the phone, (c) the person has a bad sound connection on her end of the phone, or (d) the person doesn't speak the language you're speaking into your end of the phone. It would be great if speaking to teenagers were that simple (although it might diminish our sales of this book), but it's not. Good speaking requires that we incite teenagers to listen, that we somehow connect with them, and that they understand what we're trying to communicate. That's a tough assignment. But when it works, by the power of God, we get to witness the splendor of new life coming to be. And that makes the effort most worthwhile.

God Doesn't Need Flawless Communicators... Just Faithful Ones

Perhaps as you've read through this book, you've had thoughts like the following. (Check the ones that hit close to home):

- [ ] "I can't do that..."

- [ ] "I'm afraid to try that..."

- [ ] "I don't have time to do that..."

- [ ] "I don't know if I can pull that off..."

- [ ] "Wow! Doug and Duffy are a couple of sick puppies..."

- [ ] "Great! Now I know all the things I'm doing wrong..."

Whatever you're feeling right now about your ability to speak to teenagers—whether it's eager enthusiasm or some combination of dry heaves and hacking cough—we want you to know that good speaking has never been about flawless performance. Moses led the people of Israel out of bondage, and from all we can tell, he was a fairly mediocre communicator (Exodus 4:10). When Isaiah received his call from God, his first response was, "Woe is me, for I am a man of unclean lips!" (Isaiah 6:5) And about half the time Jesus spoke people didn't have a clue what he was talking about (Matthew 13:53-57). And the Apostle Paul could hardly speak in public without starting a riot or getting arrested (Acts 17:2-5).

The good news is God isn't waiting for your perfect youth talk to do a mighty work through you. For centuries men and women of God have been announcing the good news of new life through Jesus Christ—and many of these people were untrained, uneducated, and probably unskilled (Acts 4:13). That's why the most important element of speaking always comes back to prayer: "God, breathe on the dry bones of this message, and make it come to life."

Remember these words from the apostle Paul,

When I came to you, I did not come with eloquence or human wisdom as I proclaimed to you the testimony about God. For I resolved to know nothing while I was with you except Jesus Christ and him crucified. I came to you in weakness with great fear and trembling. My message and my preaching were not with wise and persuasive words, but with a demonstration of the Spirit's power, so that your faith might not rest on human wisdom, but on God's power. (1 CORINTHIANS 2:1-5)

If we were to offer you one critical suggestion about where to start your journey to more effective communication, it would be this: Start where you are. Maybe you feel there's much in this book you're not ready for, don't have time for, or don't feel you have the gifts for. That's fine. Don't worry about all the stuff in this book that you feel you can't do. Start with the one idea you believe you can do. Pick out one skill to work on—one of the S.T.I.C.K. elements that you can develop, one preparation step to which you can give more attention. Start there. Just because you can't do everything doesn't mean you can't do anything. And as you gain some confidence, start to work on another skill, and then another. The best way to become a better speaker is to speak.

And while you're working on this stuff, thinking about your audience (*pathos*), trying to develop a construct pattern that fits, clipping out newspaper articles for your illustration file, and standing in front of the mirror giving your talk to yourself, watching your gestures and facial expressions, we want you to know this: We are so very honored to stand with you as coworkers in youth ministry. And we believe that God will make good use of your effort. Thanks so much for allowing us to share with you this high and holy adventure!

"THEREFORE, MY DEAR BROTHERS, STAND FIRM. LET NOTHING MOVE YOU. ALWAYS GIVE YOURSELF FULLY TO THE WORK OF THE LORD, BECAUSE YOU KNOW THAT YOUR LABOR IN THE LORD IS NOT IN VAIN."
(1 CORINTHIANS 15:58)

End Notes

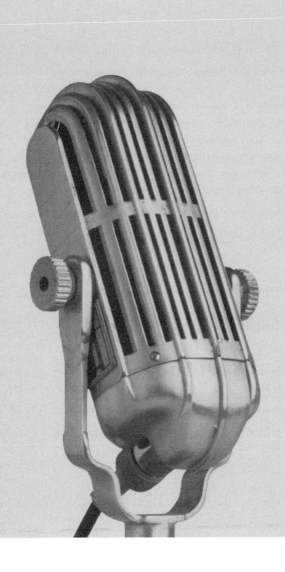

Chapter 1. "The Stakes Have Never Been Higher"

[1] Frederick Buechner, *Telling the Truth: The Gospel as Tragedy, Comedy, and Fairy Tale* (New York: Harper Collins, 1977), 22–23.

[2] Thomas J. Crawford, "Sermons on Racial Tolerance and the Parish Neighborhood Context," *Journal of Applied Social Psychology* 4 (1974): 1–23. In James Engel's landmark assessment of the success of evangelistic outreach [*Contemporary Christian Communications: Its Theory and Practice* (Nashville: Thomas Nelson, 1975), 22] he offered this sobering note: "[We have] conducted over 1,000 interviews in churches in the greater Chicago area asking basically one question: 'What was the main point of the sermon this morning?' A minimum of five people from each church are interviewed immediately after termination of the service. Over half of those interviewed cannot accurately state the main point of what they have heard, and two key factors always are evident. First, there may have been no main point because of a barrage of material presented; hence, the ability to recall is substantially hindered. Second, the essential content is missed because it does not touch practical, everyday living. Thus a lecture is heard, comprehended only in part, and lives remain untouched." Do we really think, several decades later, that our communication attempts are any more effective?

[3] James F. Engel, *What's Gone Wrong With the Harvest?* (Grand Rapids, Mich.: Zondervan, 1975).

[4] One respected market researcher (Engel) offers this example as a picture of the challenge we face as Christian communicators: "On the average...out of every one hundred people who are actually exposed to a television commercial (they do not leave the room or divert their attention elsewhere), thirty actually attend to its content; i.e., they know what is being said; fifteen understand the content (one half of those who attended to it initially); and only five retain its content in active memory twenty-four hours later. This is a graphic illustration of how the human perceptual filter selectively screens incoming information." From Bolt and Myers, *The Human Connection* (Downer's Grove, Ill.: InterVarsity Press, 1984), chapter 6.

[5] Not really! We just thought it would be a funny subtitle. But the main title is legit.

[6] James W. Gibson and Michael S. Hanna, *Public Speaking for Personal Success* (Dubuque, Iowa: Wm. C. Brown, 1989), 11.

[7] Ibid., 316.

Chapter 2. Building Bridges That Connect

[8] Ken Olson, *Can You Wait Till Friday?* (Prescott, Ariz.: O'Sullivan Woodside, 1976).

[9] For those who are intrigued by construction debacles and misappropriation of public funds, you may read the whole story at http://www.michiganhighways.org/indepth/zilwaukee.html.

[10] Charles H. Kraft, *Communication Theory for Christian Witness* (Maryknoll, N.Y.: Orbis, 2002), 3.

[11] James W. Gibson and Michael S. Hanna, *Public Speaking for Personal Success* (Dubuque, Iowa: Wm. C. Brown, 1989), 14–15.

[12] Engel, ob. cit., 1975, 21

[13] Ibid., 21-22.

[14] Ibid., 22.

[15] Charles H. Kraft, *Communication Theory for Christian Witness* (Maryknoll, N.Y.: Orbis, 2002), 2. This chart is adapted from Kraft.

Chapter 3. God: The Bridge-Builder

[16] Charles H. Kraft, *Communication Theory for Christian Witness* (Maryknoll, N.Y.: Orbis, 2002), 15ff. These four principles are an expansion of three principles set forth by Kraft.

[17] See *burning bush* (Exodus 3:2); *talking donkey* (Numbers 22:21–35); *illustration with mustard seed* (Matthew 13:31); *potter working his wheel* (Jeremiah 18:2–3); *withered fig tree* (Matthew 21:18–22); *distant star* (Matthew 2:1–2); *a man and his pet lamb* (2 Samuel 12:1–14); *strange graffiti on the banquet room wall* (Daniel 5:5); *swarms of frogs and locusts* (Exodus 8:1–15; 10:1–20); *countless dreams and visions* (cf. Genesis 37:5; 1 Samuel 3; Isaiah 1:1; Revelation 9:17); *stunning miracles* (Matthew, Mark, Luke, John); *prophet commanded to marry a whore named Gomer* (Hosea 1:2–3); *Word become flesh* (John 1:14).

[18] Marshall McLuhan, *Understanding Media: The Extensions of Man* (Cambridge, Mass.: The MIT Press, 1994), 7.

[19] For a pretty thoughtful and provocative study of some of these issues in much deeper detail, see Shane Hipps, *The Hidden Power of Electronic Culture* (Grand Rapids, Mich.: Zondervan, 2005).

[20] Select extracts from "Friends' Religious and Moral Almanac" (Philadelphia: No. 304 Arch Street, 1893).

[21] James W. Gibson and Michael S. Hanna, *Public Speaking for Personal Success* (Dubuque, Iowa: Wm. C. Brown, 1989), 84. For further exploration of this notion, Hanna and Gibson suggest Stephen W. Littlejohn, *Theories of Human Communication*, 2nd ed. (Belmont, Calif.: Wadsworth Publishing, 1983).

[22] Charles H. Kraft, *Communication Theory for Christian Witness* (Maryknoll, N.Y.: Orbis, 2002), 35.

[23] Em Griffin, *The Mind Changers: The Art of Christian Persuasion* (Wheaton, Ill.: Tyndale, 1976), 14–16.

[24] Ibid., 14.

[25] C. S. Lewis, *The Magician's Nephew* (New York: Collier Books, 1955), 125–126.

[26] Ibid., 125.

[27] Em Griffin, *The Mind Changers: The Art of Christian Persuasion* (Wheaton, Ill.: Tyndale, 1976), 4–9.

[28] Charles H. Kraft, *Communication Theory for Christian Witness* (Maryknoll, N.Y.: Orbis, 2002), 47–50.

[29] Earlier in the book, we defined these words in objective terms: *Ethos* refers to the speaker, *pathos* refers to the audience, and *logos* refers to the message. Here we look at the words through the more subjective lens of the audience members: What do they think of the speaker (*ethos*), how do they think the speaker feels about them as listeners (*pathos*), and what do they think about the message (*logos*)?

Chapter 4. Who You Are Speaks Louder Than What You Say

[30] This sentence was brought to you by Hallmark. Stop reading right now and go call someone you love.

[31] Em Griffin, *The Mind Changers: The Art of Christian Persuasion* (Wheaton, Ill.: Tyndale, 1976), 30. Plato uses this imagery in his *Phaedrus*, and Soren Kierkegaard makes use of this same analogy in *Philosophical Fragments*.

[32] Ibid., 32–40. Griffin identifies two other personas in addition to the ones discussed here.

[33] Apart from the work of the Spirit, of course.

[34] We prefer these three terms to get to the heart of the credibility question. The same basic ideas are represented in communication literature with different terminology. For example, Michael Winkler and Stanely Krippner ("Persuasion," *The Encyclopedia of Human Behavior*, V.S. Rachmachandran ed. [N.Y.: Academic Press, 1994, 482-483.]) suggest these four criteria: credibility, liking, similarity, and attractiveness. Griffin (*The Mind Changers*, 118-131) identifies authoritativeness, character, and dynamism. And Rudolph F. Verderber and Kathleen S. Verderber (*Communicate*, Belmont, Calif.: Thomson Wadsworth, 2005, 289.) cite the three criteria as knowledgeable, trustworthy, and personable.

[35] Cited in Ralph Lewis and Greg Lewis, *Inductive Preaching: Helping People Listen* (Westchester, Ill.: Crossway Books, 1983), 24.

[36] James V. O'Connor, FAQ's #1 Cuss Control Academy [Online] (2000). Also available: http://cusscontrol.com/faqs.html.

[37] Michael Winkler and Stanely Krippner ("Persuasion," *The Encyclopedia of Human Behavior*, 482) explain that the research indicates it's a little more complicated than, "Like them and they will listen." "Although the effects of liking tend to be weaker than those of credibility factors, they still play a dominant role in persuasibility." See their article for a more nuanced explanation.

[38] Actually, I went to UNC-Charlotte, and while we're usually competitive in basketball, honestly, there have been some seasons when we couldn't out-dunk your doughnut. Go Forty-Niners!

[39] Griffin (*The Mind Changers*, 127–128) cites an unpublished study (Paul Krieger and Dan Veltman) demonstrating that people were willing to make judgments about other people purely on the basis of the kind of dog they own! In a fascinating study of workers in various fields of employment (computer science, construction, doctors, airline pilots), researchers showed that "in eleven out of twelve cases, the perceived status of the workers shifted in the direction of the dog he owned." For instance, a construction worker who was judged to have a relatively low-status job came up in the world when seen with a Saint Bernard. The reverse was also true. "A common fox terrier hurt the image of the computer technician."

[40] Verderber and Verderber, *Communicate*, 377. Cf. Mark Snyder, Elizabeth D. Tanke, and Ellen Berscheid, "Social Perception and Interpersonal Behavior: On the Self Fulfilling Nature of Social Stereotypes," *Journal of Personality and Social Psychology* 35 (1977): 656-66. Their study was not primarily focused on this point, but it implicitly proves this point.

[41] Peter Watson, "What People Usually Fear," *The Sunday Times* (London), October 7, 1973, © Times Newspapers Ltd, 1973, cited in Duane Litfin, *Public Speaking: A Handbook for Christians* (Grand Rapids, Mich.: Baker Books, 2001), 329.

[42] Michael J. Beatty and Gregory S. Andriate, "Communication Apprehension and General Anxiety in the Prediction of Public Speaking Anxiety," *Communication Quarterly* 33 (Summer 1985): 175.

[43] C. S. Lewis, *The Weight of Glory* (Grand Rapids: Wm B. Eerdmans, 1973), 14–15.

[44] John Wolfe, cited in Carol Kent, *Speak Up With Confidence* (Kansas City, Mo.: Thomas Nelson, 1987), 15.

[45] For a more thorough and insightful look at satanic strategy, see C. S. Lewis, *The Screwtape Letters* (New York: MacMillan, 1959).

[46] Ralph R. Behnke, Chris R. Sawyer, and Paul E. King, "The Communication of Public Speaking Anxiety," *Communication Education* 36 (April 1987): 138–141; Michael J. Beatty, "Situational and Predispositional Corelates of Public Speaking Anxiety," *Communication Education* 37, (January 1988): 28–29.

[47] Think of a dry Slip 'n Slide.

Chapter 5. Listening to the Audience

[48] Jay Leno, *More Headlines* (New York: Warner Books, 1990), 8, 32, 33, 55, 59, 61, 94, 95.

[49] Gary Larson, *The PreHistory of The Far Side* (New York: Andrews and McMeel, Universal Press Syndicate, 1989), 230.

[50] Chap Clark, in his article "The Changing Face of Adolescence: A Theological View of Human Development" (*Starting Right*, ed. Kenda C. Dean, Chap Clark, and Dave Rahn [Grand Rapids, Mich.: Zondervan, 2001]) voices precisely this concern: "It is rare when a youth minister stops to ask some fundamental questions like, 'Just what is a *youth*? What kind of person am I trying to minister to? What are the distinctive elements between the students I work with in junior high and high school and the fifth graders who will be joining us?...Anyone who cares about children and adolescents has no choice but to take a new and careful look at how a postmodern, technological, and urbanized context affects the adolescent journey."

[51] Calvin Miller, *The Empowered Communicator* (Nashville, Tenn.: Broadman and Holman, 1994), 142–143.

[52] Adapted from Kraft, *Communication Theory for Christian Witness*, 68–78.

[53] This is not the same thing as saying, as George Barna does in *Marketing the Church* (Colorado Springs, Colo.: Navpress, 1988), that "the audience, *not the message*, is sovereign" (emphasis added). It's simply saying we can't *communicate* the message to an audience who is unwilling to hear it. For more on this, see Marva J. Dawn, *Reaching Out Without Dumbing Down* (Grand Rapids, Mich.: Eerdmans, 1995), or Philip D. Kenneson and James L. Street, *Selling Out the Church: The Dangers of Church Marketing* (Nashville, Tenn.: Abingdon Press, 1997).

[54] "[Anthropologists] have dwelt on the differences between peoples while saying too little about the similarities...At the same time, anthropologists have exaggerated the importance of social and cultural conditioning, and have, in effect, projected an image of humanity marked by little more than empty but programmable minds. These are distortions that not only affect the way we look at and treat the rest of the world's peoples, but also profoundly affect our thoughts about ourselves and the conduct of our own affairs." Cited in Charles Kraft, *Anthropology for Christian Witness* (Maryknoll, N.Y.: Orbis Books, 1996), 118.

[55] In his book *The Wounded Healer* ((New York: Bantam Doubleday, 1979), 34), Henri Nouwen writes: "Many young people are convinced that there is something terribly wrong with the world in which they live and that cooperation with existing models of living would constitute betrayal of themselves...They know that what is shouldn't be the way it is, but they see no workable alternative. Thus, they are saddled with frustration, which often expresses itself in undirected violence which destroys without clear purpose, or in suicidal withdrawal from the world, both of which are signs more of protest than the results of a new-found ideal."

[56] Cited in Brent Curtis and John Eldridge, *The Sacred Romance* (Nashville, Tenn.: Thomas Nelson, 1997), 30.

[57] Ibid., 35.

[58] St. Augustine of Hippo, *Confessions*, Book 1, Section 1, R.S. Pine-Coffin trans. and ed. (New York: Penguin Books, 1961), 21.

[59] Pastor and author Calvin Miller, in his book *Marketplace Preaching: How to Return the Sermon to Where It Belongs* (Grand Rapids, Mich.: Baker, 1995), 137, suggests something very similar when he writes that every time he preaches, he tries to bear in mind that there are six questions posed by every generation: "(1) What is the purpose of life? (2) What am I doing here? (3) How did I come to be? (4) Where will I end up? (5) How can I be happy, or happier, at least? (6) What does it mean to be human?"

[60] Ibid., 15.

[61] You can watch the commercial by using the link at www.speakingtoteenagers.com.

[62] See chapter 3—God: The Bridge-Builder.

[63] Stage One—Awareness, Stage Two—Interest, Stage Three—Evaluation, Stage Four—Choice, Stage Five—Implementation, Stage Six—Readjustment, Stage Seven—Reassessment. See Kraft, *Communication Theory for Christian Witness*, 78-79. Also, James F. Engel, *Contemporary Christian Communications: Its Theory and Practice* (Nashville, Tenn.: Thomas Nelson, 1979) and Everett M. Rogers, *Diffusion of Innovations*, 3rd ed. (New York: Free Press, 1983).

[64] Kraft, *Communication Theory for Christian Witness*, 79.

[65] Kraft, in *Communication Theory for Christian Witness*, cites research by Viggo B. Sogaard, "Applying Christian Communication: Book I—Media in Mission," unpublished manuscript, (Pasadena, Calif.: School of World Mission, Fuller Theological Seminary).

[66] Winkler and Krippner, "Persuasion," *The Encyclopedia of Human Behavior*, 484.

[67] Adapted from a working strategy used when I was on Student Staff with Young Life in Charlotte, North Carolina.

[68] As missiologist Richard Peace rightly observes in *Pilgrimage: A Handbook on Christian Growth* (Grand Rapids, Mich.: Baker Books, 1976), 65, "There are various levels of Christian commitment." Doug has taken some time to identify five levels of commitment in his book *Purpose Driven Youth Ministry* (Grand Rapids, Mich.: Zondervan, 1998)—Community, Crowd, Congregation, Committed, and Core.

[69] Ibid., 69ff.

[70] Graham Johnston, *Preaching in a Postmodern World* (Grand Rapids, Mich.: Baker, 2001), 94.

[71] Griffin, *The Mind Changers*, 58.

[72] Daniel A. McRoberts and Cindy Larsen-Casselton, "Humor in Public Address, Health Care and the Workplace: Summarizing Humor's Use Using Meta-Analysis," *North Dakota Speech and Hearing Journal*, (2006): 26ff. Just as an aside, the data also suggests that "humor induces positive psychological effects that are at least comparable if not superior to the effects of exercise." Isn't that great? My new exercise routine is watching old Monty Python sketches.

[73] Elizabeth Achtemier, cited in Graham Johnston, *Preaching in a Postmodern World*, 92.

Chapter 6. A Good Message Starts with Thoughtful Planning and Careful Preparation

[74] Gary Pomerantz, *Nine Minutes and Twenty Seconds: The Tragedy and Triumph of Flight 529* (New York: Simon and Schuster Audio, 2001), Disc 6, Track 2, 1:30.

[75] Ibid., Disc 6, Track 1. It's an interesting side note that between the time of the crash and the time of the final NTSB hearings, Chris Bender recommitted his life to Christ. He left Hamilton Standard on November 6, 1996, and moved to Tyler, Texas, where he trained for the mission field at the Youth With a Mission Training Center.

[76] Ibid., Disc 6, Track 2, 3:15 "I was told if you had a rejected blade, and there was no damage or pitting, but if you had ridges, you could blend...That was told to me by a multiple...by a multitude of people."

[77] This curriculum originally appeared in Duffy Robbins, *The Ministry of Nurture* (Grand Rapids, Mich.: Zondervan, 1990), 85.

Chapter 8. Study: Improve Your Content and Increase Your Confidence

[78] David Neff, "Don't Read the Bible 'Alone': An Interview with Christopher Hall," *Christianity Today*, November 1, 2003.

Chapter 10. Illustrate: Add a Little Color to Your Messages

[79] Ralph Lewis and Greg Lewis, *Inductive Preaching: Helping People Listen* (Westchester, Ill.: Crossway Books, 1983), 144.

[80] Roger Dobson, "Broadcast of star's colonoscopy puts up screening by 20%" *BMJ* 324, (May 2002): 1118, http://www.bmj.com/cgi/content/full/324/7346/1118/c.

[81] Duffy Robbins, *This Way to Youth Ministry* (Grand Rapids, Mich.: Zondervan, 2003), 109–111. This is an adaptation of a much fuller treatment of these questions.

[82] Cited in Eric Jensen, *Brain-Based Learning* (San Diego, Calif.: The Brain Store, 2000), 126.

[83] William Safire, *What's the Good Word?* (New York: New York Times Company, 1980), cited in Verderber and Verderber, *Communicate*, 281.

[84] Adapted from Lewis and Lewis, *Inductive Preaching*, 142.

Chapter 11. Construct: Organize and Pull It All Together

[85] Adapted from Ralph Lewis and Gregg Lewis, *Inductive Preaching*, 70.

[86] Andy Stanley and Ronald Lane Jones, *Communicating for a Change* (Sisters, Ore.: Multnomah Publishers, 2006), 105.

[87] Ibid., 119–130. Basically I've tried to summarize his chapter titled "Create a Map." I've told Andy that I've probably butchered his original intent by using my summary instead of his exact words, but I didn't think it was ethical to quote an entire chapter. If his construct resonates with you, I'd highly encourage you to pick up his book. Again, it's an excellent resource, and it's very easy to understand. The guy knows communication—he's been doing it every week for decades. He's one of the best communicators I've ever heard.

[88] Ibid., 127.

Chapter 12. Keep Focused: Crafting for Clarity

[89] Graham Johnston, *Preaching in a Postmodern World*, 171.

[90] Rick Warren, *The Purpose Driven Church* (Grand Rapids, Mich.: Zondervan, 1995).

Chapter 13. Prep for Delivery: Making the Space Work for You

[91] Robert Ornstein, *The Amazing Brain* (Boston: Houghton and Mifflin, 1984), cited in Eric Jensen, *Brain-Based Learning* (San Diego, Calif.: The Brain Store, 2000), 81. See also, Michael Gazzaninga, *Nature's Mind* (New York: Basic Books, 1992), cited in Jensen, *Brain-Based Learning*, 81. Also, Gordon Bower and T. Mann, "Improving Recall by Recoding Interfering Material at the Time of Retrieval" *Journal of Experimental Psychology* 18, no. 6, (November 1992): 1310–1320.

[92] For a great resource full of such ideas, see Rick Bundschuh, *On Site: 40 On-Location Youth Programs* (Grands Rapids, Mich.: Zondervan/Youth Specialties, 1989). The book is out of print, but you might be able to pick up a used copy online.

[93] Barbara Tversky, *Memory for Pictures, Maps, Environments and Graphs in Intersections in Basic and Applied Memory Research*, D.G. Payne and F.G. Conrad, eds. (Mahwah, N.J.: Erlbaum, 1997), 257–277.

[94] M.E. Patterson, D.F. Danscreau, and D. Newburn, "Effects of Communication Aid on Cooperative Teaching," *Journal of Educational Psychology* 84, (1992): 453–461.

[95] From J. O'Keefe and L. Nadle, The Hippocampus as a Cognitive Map (Oxford, England: Clarendon Press, 1978), cited in Eric Jensen, *Brain-Based Learning* (San Diego, Calif.: The Brain Store, 2000), 59. There have been other studies which have agreed that visual images improve speaker credibility and increase the persuasiveness of the message, but have questioned whether visual imagery actually improves retention (see William Seiler, *The Effect of Visual Materials on Attitudes, Credibility and Retention* at Education Resources Information Center Web site, www.eric.ed.gov). Experience and common sense suggest that it probably depends a lot on the imagery.

[96] This is a very important point that we aren't able to develop in this book. But there are some important questions that underlie the whole discussion of media. We alluded to one of them in chapter 3 where we spoke about Marshall McLuhan's famous dictum, "the medium is the message."

How do we change the gospel when we reduce it to electronic images? At what point do we make the gospel so exciting and amusing that we cease to be faithful to our mission? Are youth workers getting to the point where we're too focused on how to communicate and not focused enough on what we communicate? For more thinking about these and other issues related to media and communication, consider these two books: *Amusing Ourselves to Death* (Penguin, 20th anniversary edition, 2005) by Neil Postman, and *The Hidden Power of Electronic Culture: How Media Shapes the Faith, the Gospel, and the Church* (Youth Specialties/Zondervan, 2006) by Shane Hipps.

[97] Eric Jensen, *Brain-Based Learning* (San Diego, Calif.: The Brain Store, 2000), 55.

[98] In his book, *The Power of Color*, Morton Walker cites the groundbreaking work of UCLA psychologist Robert Gerard who, along with two other researchers, Max Lüscher and S. V. Krakov, attempted to demonstrate that different colors actually promote different moods and behaviors in people. (e.g., yellow is associated with happiness; red increases athletic performance; blue is a calming color; bright colors like orange, red, and yellow spark energy and enthusiasm). Some accept these findings as valid. Some call it junk science. See, for example, Edward B. Nuhfer, "Some Aspects of an Ideal Classroom: Color, Carpet, Light and Furniture," in a paper prepared for the Idaho State University Council for Teaching and Learning, 2005 (http://www.isu.edu/ctl/nutshells/IdealClass_files/IdealClass.html). There certainly seems to be evidence that different colors affect us in different ways, and graphic artists widely agree that this is the case. Web designers know, for example, that while black and white have the highest color contrast, white banners on a web page have the lowest click-through ratio (CTR) of any banner color.

[99] Eric Jensen, *Brain-Based Learning* (San Diego, Calif.: The Brain Store, 2000), 57.

[100] Many of these suggestions relate solely to digital media, but some of them are relevant for other types of media as well—object lessons, sketches, art, lettered posters, charts, graphs, etc. To really get expert advice about the use of electronic media, an excellent resource is *Just Shoot Me* by Jay Delp and Joel Lusz (Grand Rapids, Mich.: Youth Specialties/Zondervan, 2002).

Chapter 14. The Wonder of Delivery: Speaking to Birth New Life

[101] Todd Gitlin, "The Death of Eloquence," *The San Francisco Chronicle*, (November 25, 2002) cited in Frederick Isaacson, "Framing Artful Speech: Focusing Persuasive Discourse with Fine Arts Imagery," *The Journal of Visual Literacy* 23, no. 1 (Spring 2003): 31–40.

[102] Research done by Klipmart Corp., a provider of online video delivery. Reported by Kris Oser, *Advertising Age* 76, no. 41 (October 10, 2005): 31–39.

[103] William R. Chaney, "Top of Hour Break Renews Attention Span," *The Teaching Professor* 19, no. 6 (June–July 2005).

[104] We don't believe this is an either-or proposition. We agree that how we craft spoken messages must be shaped by the audience factors we've discussed in this book. That's critically important. And we strongly encourage youth workers to use lots of different types of communication. We've written books such as *Spontaneous Melodramas*, *Memory Makers*, and *Everyday Object Lessons* because we understand that our youth groups are filled with students who learn in lots of different ways. We totally endorse visual delivery, active learning, and narrative forms of teaching. We're just not ready to say, "Speaking is passé," and we're not ready to do that for the most basic of reasons: We've seen the impact of the spoken word in the lives of teenagers.

[105] Carol Kent, *Speak With Confidence*, (Nashville: Thomas Nelson, 1987), 89.

[106] P. Ekman and W. V. Friesen, "The Repertoire of Non-Verbal Behavior: Categories, Origins, Usage and Coding," *Semiotica* I, (1969): 48–49. The two types of nonverbal communication that we don't refer to in the text are (4) *Body motions can regulate the flow in a conversation*—a nodding of the head might *Communicate*, "Okay, I get the point; now move on, or at least let me talk." And (5) *Body motions can relieve tension*—a person shifts weight to one leg or the other.

[107] R. E. Axtell, *Gestures: The Do's and Taboos of Body Language Around the World* (New York: Wiley, 1999), cited in Verderber and Verderber, *Communicate*, 76.

[108] Again, there are cultural variations with eye contact. In the United States and most western European countries, people expect you to "look them in the eye." But in Japan, where it's considered impolite to make direct eye contact, people direct their gaze to the neck and the Adam's apple. Chinese, Indonesians, and rural Mexicans consider direct eye contact bad manners. When in conversation, they lower their gaze as a sign of deference and respect. Arabs are just the opposite. They look intently into the eyes of the person with whom they are talking. L. A. Samovar and R. E. Porter, *communication Between Cultures* (Belmont, Calif.: Wadsworth, 2001), 178, 159.

[109] J. K. Burgoon, D. A. Coker, and R. A. Coker, "Communicative Effects of Gaze Behavior: A Test of Two Contrasting Explanations," *Human Communication* Research 12, (1986): 495–524.

[110] Ralph Lewis and Greg Lewis, *Inductive Preaching: Helping People Listen* (Westchester, Ill.: Crossways Books, 1983), 149.

[111] James W. Gibson and Michael S. Hanna, *Public Speaking for Personal Success* (Dubuque, Iowa: Wm. C. Brown, 1989), 174.

[112] Adapted from *The Speaker's Handbook* (2nd ed), Sprague, Jo and Stuart, Douglas (New York: Harcourt Brace Jovanovich, Publishers, 1988) 217.

[113] Charles Spurgeon, cited in Lewis and Lewis, *Inductive Preaching*, 152.

[114] Samovar and Porter, *Communication Between Cultures*, 177.

[115] J. N. Martin and T. K. Nakayama, *Intercultural Communication in Contexts*, 2nd ed. (Mountain View, Calif.: Mayfield, 2000), 183–184.

[116] Verderber and Verderber, *Communicate*, 73.

[117] J. Burgoon and T. Saine, *The Unspoken Dialogue* (Boston: Houghton Mifflin Company, 1978), 208.

[118] Adapted from Sprague and Stuart, op. cit., 262.

[119] Adapted from material in Sprague and Stuart, Ibid., 264-265.

Chapter 15. The Wonder of Delivery: Announcing New Life

[120] Haddon Robinson, *Biblical Preaching* (Grand Rapids, Mich.: Baker, 1980), 160.

[121] James W. Gibson and Michael S. Hanna, *Public Speaking for Personal Success* (Dubuque, Iowa: Wm. C. Brown, 1989), 189.

[122] Verderber and Verderber, *Communicate*, 77.

[123] Michael Anania, "An Insider's Guide to Teen-Speak," *Reader's Digest*, (April 1992) condensed from *In Plain Sight*, reprint ed. (Kingston, R.I.: Moyer Bell, 1993).

[124]Ralph G. Nichols, *The Supervisor's Notebook* (Chicago: Scott, Foresman & Co.) 22, no. 1, (Spring 1960), http://www.dartmouth.edu/~acskills/docs/10_bad_listening_habits.doc.

[125] Kent R. Colbert, "A Quantitative Analysis of CEDA Speaking Rates," *The National Forensic Journal VI* (Fall 1988): 113–120. CEDA stands for Cross Examination Debate Association.

[126] Cited in Haddon Robinson, *Biblical Preaching* (Grand Rapids, Mich.: Baker, 1980), 172.

SpeakingtoTeenagers.com

A SPEAKING WEBSITE FOR YOU...
WITH HELP FROM YOU

Doug FIELDS + **Duffy** ROBBINS

- **FAQs**
- **Message Boards**
- **Illustrations**
- **Free PowerPoint Backgrounds**
- **Video Examples**
- **Additional Training**
- **Fun, colonoscopy facts**
- **Links**
- **Seminar Requests**

Visit us online to see where Doug & Duffy are doing a Speaking toTeenagers Conference near you or get info on how to bring them to your city or denominational training.

Add your endorsement to potentially be included in the next printing.

www.speakingtoteenagers.com

"Purpose-Driven Youth Ministry *is packed with learnable concepts that do more than educate—they stimulate. It wins us over to a way of doing youth ministry the way it ought to be.*"
—Mike Yaconelli, Youth Specialties

"Doug Fields has not just written a book about youth ministry phi-losophy, he has provided a thorough and workable handbook for any youth ministry program, big or small. I believe Purpose-Driven Youth Ministry will be the standard by which all youth ministry programs are judged for years to come."
—Chap Clark, Ph.D., Director, Youth and Family Ministries Program,
   Fuller Theological Seminary

"The focus of a purpose-driven church has had a wonderful impact on our church. The same principles have reshaped our youth program. Doug offers hands-on practical insights for igniting young people!"
—Max Lucado

Purpose Driven Youth Ministry
9 Essential Foundations for Healthy Growth
Doug Fields
RETAIL $17.99
ISBN 0-310-XXXXX-X

visit www.youthspecialties.com/store
or your local Christian bookstore

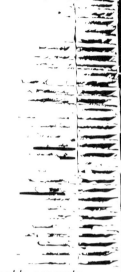

youth
specialties

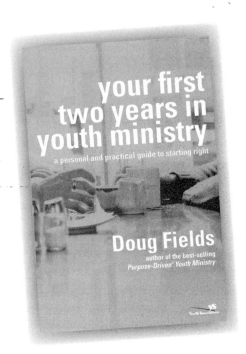
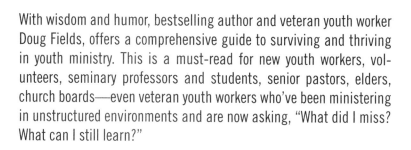

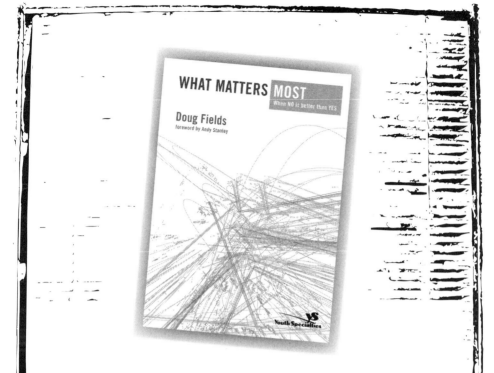

It's not that you don't want to read the Bible; maybe you just don't know there's more than one way to read it.

Enjoy the Silence's 30 Guided exercises plug you into the ancient discipline of Lectio Divina. Each lesson provides a selection of scripture, prompts for meditation, a chance to listen to God, and a way to respond to what you've read.

You know that being a student leader is no small task—nor is it something to lose sleep over. If you have student leaders—or at least students who are willing to lead—use this book to pair their willingness with tools and techniques to create effective leaders who lighten your load.

Help! I'm a Student Leader!
Practical Ideas and Guidance on Leadership
Doug Fields
RETAIL $9.99
ISBN 0-310-25961-4

Think back to a time God taught you about His love, about His grace. Memories help us recall our spiritual journey. Without pivotal events and moments seared in our consciousness, it would be nearly impossible to enjoy knowing how much God has done for us. The 50 ideas in this book will help you turn events into memories that your students will take with them for the rest of their lives.

Memory Makers
50 Moments Your Kids Will Never Forget
Doug Fields
RETAIL $9.99
ISBN 0-310-21013-5

youth
specialties